Gifted
MIND

The Dr. Raymond Damadian Story,
Inventor of the MRI

JEFF KINLEY
WITH DR. RAYMOND DAMADIAN

First printing: September 2015

ISBN: 978-0-89051-803-8
Library of Congress Number: 2015910750

Unless otherwise noted, Scripture quotations are from the King James Version (KJV) of the Bible.

Please consider requesting that a copy of this volume be purchased by your local library system.

Printed in the United States of America

Please visit our website for other great titles:
www.masterbooks.com

For information regarding author interviews,
please contact the publicity department at (870) 438-5288

Master
Books®
A Division of New Leaf Publishing Group
www.masterbooks.com

Contents

Dedication

The Apostle Paul discloses "in whom [God, the Father, and Christ[are hid all the treasures of wisdom and knowledge" (Colossians 2:3). And so it was in the advent of the MRI, the Lord's revelation of a new TRUTH for the betterment of His creation and toward His objective of eliminating the "vain babblings" (1 Timothy 6:20) of a "science falsely so called" (1 Timothy 6:20), i.e., evolution, and toward His ultimate objective of rescuing His Creation, mankind, from the ravages of this false theory.

Promoted by its proponents, without evidence, as the "scientific" basis of origins, its consequences are dire. This "science falsely so called," by denying our direct origination from the Lord (Genesis 1:26), is then asserted as an exemption from God's Laws by asserting its creation science claims as "religion" in order to falsely claim the origins debate as a debate of "science versus religion," when in fact it is in actuality a debate of genuine science vs. science fiction. While providing an exemption from God's Laws for the purpose of indulging individual lusts, its social consequences are catastrophic, currently ravaging our society and our civilization exponentially.

Our miraculous nation of democracy, founded on the unbounded power of the TRUTH is now *programming* our school children and our young university students with the Lie of Evolution together with its exemption from God's Laws, thereby voiding their chance to be protected from this fiction and its ravaging consequences. Tantamount to insisting that the earth is FLAT while excluding the evidence that refutes it, they refuse to let them hear the total absence of scientific evidence to support this lie and the dire consequences of not knowing God and His devotion to HIS creation.

While Jesus provides forgiveness for sincere repentance, God's Laws cannot be broken without consequence (Leviticus).

"Behold, thou desirest truth in the inward [innermost] parts and in the hidden part thou shalt make me to know wisdom" (Psalm 51:6).

While the most intangible of all, wisdom constitutes the ultimate vehicle for achieving perfection while the sure pathway to it is commonly uncertain. David's Psalm (51:6) provides the pathway, the course that led us through the convoluted pathways to MRI.

INTRODUCTION

Greatness is often measured in different ways. In business, it's usually calculated by the bottom line, or how much money is generated. In sports, it's determined by wins. In war, it's victory over the enemy. But how do we measure the greatness of a life? Or more specifically, what exactly is the "measure of a man"?

When I agreed to help Dr. Raymond Damadian write his story, I knew just enough about the man to pique my interest and curiosity. I was aware he was responsible for the concept and creation of what today is known as the MRI, an invention that forever changed the face of medicine. However, beyond this, I knew little else. Further in-depth research revealed much more about the man and the remarkable life and legacy that led to this crowning achievement in science and medicine. Even so, much of what I discovered was one-dimensional compared to meeting Damadian in person. Flying to New York, I soon found myself in his Long Island office. Books, papers, files, studies, and an assortment of documents were stacked in various places around the modest room. Armed with a recorder, and with pen and pad in hand, I took a seat on the couch and began listening. For nine straight hours Damadian told his story, and more than once I interrupted, asking him to clarify the meaning of a medical term or to have him explain a particular biological fact or medical process.

Working through lunch, and fueled only by the regular refill of coffee from his longtime assistant, I remember thinking to myself, "This man knows more about the human body and its function than any 25 doctors I've ever known!"

Intrigued and amazed, I knew I was in the presence of real genius. Men like Raymond Damadian are rare, and for that reason alone they are valuable to humanity. If someone thinks Damadian is a great man because of what he has accomplished in the field of science and medicine (much of which you'll discover in this book), then they would be correct. His contribution to medicine through the invention and application of the MRI is virtually immeasurable, as millions have benefited from its use. There are no definitive records of how many lives have been saved due to early MRI detection of cancer. Chances are you know someone who's alive today because of his invention.

But if that's all you knew of Dr. Damadian, you would miss the real heart of his story. For even beyond having a gifted mind, Raymond Damadian is also an authentic servant of Jesus Christ. And as such, he exudes an uncommon humility for a man of his accomplishments. He is always eager to recount the story of the MRI, but he's even quicker to make sure you know it was prayer and God's prompting that led him and his team to this historic discovery.

There are men who adorn themselves with a thin veneer of humility, but Damadian's desire for God to receive all the glory goes all the way to the heart of the man. That kind of genuine humility is not only real, it's also refreshing. And it's as much a part of the French-Armenian Doctor as his trademark mustache. Tell him he's great and he will quickly correct you. "No, I'm not great. But I serve a great God."

And he does.

It's because of this and many other admirable qualities, that I know you will enjoy Dr. Raymond Damadian's remarkable story. As you journey through this book, I trust you will also be enlightened and inspired, and drawn closer to the One who alone is truly "great."

— Jeff Kinley

CHAPTER

1

THE
TRUTH

From where I sit in my Long Island office, I am surrounded by vivid reminders of over 50 years of science and research. Volumes of books, papers, and research are stacked neatly (or sometimes not-so-neatly) on shelves or strategically placed on my desk — every one of them with a unique story to tell. Across the room, I can see a photograph of me and President Ronald Reagan in which he awarded me the National Medal of Technology. Behind me hangs an embroidery depicting the first-ever MRI scan of a human being. Looking to my right, I see an entire wall is devoted to pictures of my children and precious grandchildren. Each of these pictures forever captures a moment in time, some memorable snapshot of my life, family, and work.

But one of these photographs tells a particularly interesting story. It's a black and white photo of a mustached man seated inside an odd-looking contraption made of wood and canvas. The man is clothed in a thick wool sweater and an equally dense wool overcoat. Leather boots, laced and buckled up over his calves, add a touch of adventure to his outfit. Leather gloves protect his hands from cold weather. What looks like a herringbone tweed cap is tightly perched atop his head. And a nearly extinguished hand-rolled cigarette dangles from his mustached mouth.

The furrowed brow on the man's face appears to say, "Well, get on with it. Hurry and take the photo and get out of the way."

But there is an interesting back-story behind this particular picture, and one that affects every one of us today. The picture has its genesis in

Dayton, Ohio. It's the 1890s, and two local brothers have decided to start their own bicycle shop. With hard work and perseverance, before long they expanded their bicycle business to some five locations on the west side of Dayton. But with competition rapidly growing in the bicycle industry in those days, the brothers decided it wasn't enough just to sell other company's products. So they decided to invent their own brand of bicycle, which they eventually succeeded in doing. Their top-of-the-line model was called the "Van Cleve," which sold for $65, while the less expensive "St. Clair" could be bought for $42.50. Neither of these was considered "minor purchases" in a time when the average American income was just over $300 per year. Today, over a hundred years later, only five of the bicycles manufactured by the brothers' company are known to exist.

But even in the 1800s, cyclists felt the "need for speed," and a brisk bicycle ride was often compared to the exhilarating sensations a bird must feel when it flies. This concept sparked an insatiable curiosity in the two men, and soon they began setting their sights on creating the first-ever heavier-than-air flying machine. For some six years they tested and re-tested their ideas, and after many failures and trial runs, on December 17, 1903, their previously ridiculed idea finally became a reality. On that historic day, Wilbur and Orville Wright successfully made four short flights at Kitty Hawk, North Carolina. The age of flight was officially born.

One of those who worked closely with the Wright Brothers on their new invention was a man by the name of Marcel Pénot Jr., my grandmother's brother. That's Marcel (figure 1), my great-uncle pictured in the photograph on my wall. And that "contraption" he's seated in is an early version of the Wright Brother's airplane, the "Wright Flyer." Orville Wright once said, "If birds can glide for long periods of time, then why can't I?"[1] Marcel Pénot, my grandmother's father (figure 62), was a pioneer of France's internal combustion engine.

It is precisely this spirit of curiosity and inquisitiveness that has driven mankind throughout history — pushing the boundaries of discovery in exploration, medicine, science, and technology. What the Wright Brothers did was simply to dream and then experiment with those dreams. In time, and based on what they learned from their failures, they slowly began discovering and experiencing the previously unknown properties of flight — weight, drag, thrust, and lift — all physical science principles demonstrated all around us in creation. In

Figure 1. Marcel Pénot Jr., Dr. Damadian's grandmother's brother,
collaborator with the Wright Brothers Wright Flyer

inventing the world's first successful heavier-than-air flying machine, the Wright Brothers accomplished more than just birthing one of the greatest technologies in all of human history.

They uncovered God's truth.

As a Christian, this truth is everything to me. It is the foundation of knowledge and the basis of all understanding. Some may choose to leave this pursuit of truth to philosophers and theologians, but not me. While all truth ultimately originates in the person of God, for He Himself *is* the truth, I believe it also has a fundamental place in science as well (John 14:6). The goal of science is to explore, investigate, validate, understand, and explain knowledge of our human kind, the world, and the universe. We do this so we can take this knowledge and use it for the benefit for all humanity.

I believe God, as Creator, has embedded certain truths within everything He has made (Romans 1:18–20). As man discovers and acknowledges these realities, we understand that the universe and all it contains reveals the fingerprints of God — His invisible attributes, His eternal power, and divine nature. But that's not the end of the story. What is obvious about God on a macro level (the universe) is equally true on the micro level (the atom). The Creator has brilliantly designed creation in such a way that no matter where we look, we see the undeniable handiwork of amazing intelligence. We have but to open our eyes and minds, and what unfolds before us is the creative, imaginative, powerful, and awe-inspiring display of His greatness and glory. It's there, just waiting for us to discover it. Without a Creator, there is no universe or mankind. No God = No Humanity. Without God, there is no verifiable reality for us and thus no ultimate truth.

For me, therein lies the real reward of science. Discovery of God's truth bridges the gap between philosophy and science as well as showing us something greater than the two. Pursuit of the truth generates *new* knowledge — understanding that not only opens up new vistas about God, but also has proven to profoundly impact humanity for good as well. This quest is part of what drives me, propelling my research forward, because truth is critical to every aspect of human life. It can be ignored and denied, but it *cannot* be defeated. Truth, by its very nature, is invincible, and those who dishonor it ultimately dishonor themselves, impede discovery, and hurt humanity.

Over a century ago, our 20th president, James Garfield, proclaimed, "The truth shall make you free" (John 8:32). He then quickly added, "But first it will make you miserable." He was right. The truth has a way of being decidedly inconvenient at times.

Surprisingly, today it's not freedom from bondage or tyranny that most of us in the Western world seek. Rather, unfortunately we seek to break ties from the very God who graciously grants us our freedom to choose. Mankind's ultimate aspiration seems to manifest itself through becoming the final authority in all aspects of his own existence. In other words, we want to be in charge, replacing God as supreme authority. Ironically, it's *this* brand of "freedom" that eventually makes slaves of us all.

You've no doubt heard the saying, "Being free comes with a price," and that's true. We typically think of this freedom during holidays, recognizing those who have given their lives so that we in the United States of America could remain free. But it's a fair question to ask, "Can anyone be genuinely 'free' apart from the truth of Jesus Christ?" Can we know real freedom apart from the truth of God that exposes the lies of mankind? Jesus unashamedly claimed to be "the way, the TRUTH and the life; no man cometh to the Father, but by me" (John 14:6, emphasis added). That's a very bold and exclusive statement, and one not made by any other major religious leader in history.

Jesus' words, quoted by both presidents and Apostles, remind us that He is truth *personified*, as well as the exclusive expressway to it. When President George Washington rejected kingship following the American Revolution, choosing democracy instead, he intentionally transferred political power to the "power of the truth." This effectively replaced the British king's power with the unbounded power of the truth. I believe our subsequent advancements in science and technology are the fruits of such an empowerment. Seemingly miraculous discoveries in these fields have helped create the most extraordinary economic prosperity in human history, so much so that God's *truth* becomes the real "Founding Father" of Western civilization and ultimately, the United States of America.

As far back as A.D. 1455, Johannes Gutenberg's invention of the printing press helped spark this revolution of truth. And what was the first book to roll of his press? The Holy Bible. Before this time, the common man (those outside the privileged circle of priests and clergy) had virtually no access to Scripture and its fascinating truths, including scientific truths. But from the moment God's Word was revealed through Gutenberg's invention, reverence for the truth has been the foundation of Western civilization. I find it more than coincidence that the vast majority of mankind's major scientific discoveries were made *after* the Bible "went public" in Western civilization. It ignited the renaissance (rebirth) of God's Laws. Remarkably, the colossal industrial revolution and economic explosion in the West that followed access to the wisdom of God's Word in Gutenberg's Bible did not occur in Asia where there is no shortage of smart people. It is also interesting that those who made such discoveries either cited Scripture's truths or were inspired by them (figure 2)!

In granting us access to His *truth*, God has gifted us with the ability to make scientific discoveries that reveal things previously known only by Him. Inventions like the MRI simply liberate and unveil His truth for the benefit of mankind, just as it was with His revelation of electricity to Faraday, wireless transmission to Armstrong, electric lighting to Edison, and aerial transport to the Wright Brothers. We did not *create* these truths, but instead merely *discovered* ways to harness them for our benefit and progress.

Therefore, without robbing inventors of the credit due them, we should nevertheless recognize these phenomenal scientific advances for

Figure 2. Gutenberg and the other pioneers of modern science, Newton, Pasteur et al.	1455	1481	1492	1543	1596	1600
	Johannes Gutenberg	**Leonardo DaVinci**	**Christopher Columbus**	**Nicolaus Copernicus**	**Johannes Kepler**	**William Gilbert**
	First Printing of the Bible (1455 AD)	Experimental Science; dynamics, optics, anatomy, hydraulics

"Adoration of The Magi" (1481 AD)

"Last Supper" (1497 AD) | Discovery of the New World: Terrestial Sphericity

"fully accomplished were the words of Isaiah, 'He shall gather together the dispersed of Judah from the four corners of the earth.'" (Letter to Queen Isabella and King Ferdinand 1502 AD) | Heliocentric Planetary System

"I shall try with God without whom we can do nothing." (Revelations of Heavenly Spheres 1543 AD) Andreas Vesalius Father of Anatomy

"God , the supreme Architect in His wisdom formed...the foundation for the whole body." ("Fabric of the whole body." 1543 AD) | The Elliptical Orbits of Planets: Motions of the Planets

"I am devoting my effort for the Glory of God who wants to be recognized from the Book of Nature." (letter to astronomy teacher M. Matelin, U. Tubingen) | First Investigator of the Powers of the Magnet

The Earth's Magnetic Poles and Terrestrial Magnetism

"By the wonderful wisdom of the Creator, therefore, forces were implanted in the earth..." ("On the Lodestone" Magnetic Bodies and the Great Magnet Earth 1600 AD) |

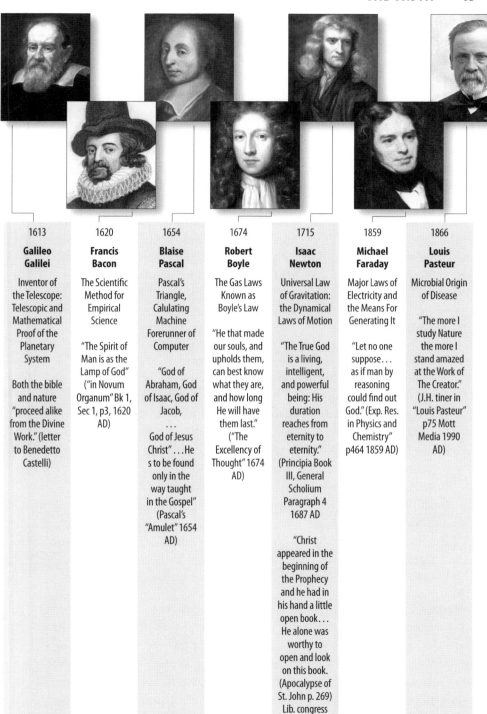

1613	1620	1654	1674	1715	1859	1866
Galileo Galilei	**Francis Bacon**	**Blaise Pascal**	**Robert Boyle**	**Isaac Newton**	**Michael Faraday**	**Louis Pasteur**
Inventor of the Telescope: Telescopic and Mathematical Proof of the Planetary System	The Scientific Method for Empirical Science	Pascal's Triangle, Calulating Machine Forerunner of Computer	The Gas Laws Known as Boyle's Law	Universal Law of Gravitation: the Dynamical Laws of Motion	Major Laws of Electricity and the Means For Generating It	Microbial Origin of Disease
Both the bible and nature "proceed alike from the Divine Work." (letter to Benedetto Castelli)	"The Spirit of Man is as the Lamp of God" ("in Novum Organum" Bk 1, Sec 1, p3, 1620 AD)	"God of Abraham, God of Isaac, God of Jacob, . . . God of Jesus Christ" . . . He s to be found only in the way taught in the Gospel" (Pascal's "Amulet" 1654 AD)	"He that made our souls, and upholds them, can best know what they are, and how long He will have them last." ("The Excellency of Thought" 1674 AD)	"The True God is a living, intelligent, and powerful being: His duration reaches from eternity to eternity." (Principia Book III, General Scholium Paragraph 4 1687 AD)	"Let no one suppose... as if man by reasoning could find out God." (Exp. Res. in Physics and Chemistry" p464 1859 AD)	"The more I study Nature the more I stand amazed at the Work of The Creator." (J.H. tiner in "Louis Pasteur" p75 Mott Media 1990 AD)
				"Christ appeared in the beginning of the Prophecy and he had in his hand a little open book... He alone was worthy to open and look on this book. (Apocalypse of St. John p. 269) Lib. congress 91-074116		

what they actually are: products of God's all-encompassing truth! In Colossians 2:3, Paul acknowledges, *"In [Christ] are hid all the treasures of wisdom and knowledge."* Thanks to Gutenberg, for the first time in history, all mankind was granted expanded access to God's Word, the Bible. It may surprise you to know that many of modern science's founding fathers cited God's Word as the origin of their discoveries, including Isaac Newton, Galileo, Copernicus, Kepler, and Faraday (figure 2).

Prior to the printing press, Leonardo DaVinci delved into experimental science, optics, anatomy, and hydraulics. But it wasn't until *after* Gutenberg's Bible that he brushstroked such masterpieces as "Adoration of the Magi" (1481) and the "Last Supper" (1497). A complicated and multi-faceted man, DaVinci's musings and experiments made pioneering contributions to the birth of present-day science. He would be followed by the likes of Christopher Columbus, who, upon discovering the new world, credited the truth of Scripture for his feat.[2] History records that many of mankind's great scientific pioneers were motivated by God and *His truth*, including:

Nicolaus Copernicus (1543) — Astronomy
Johannes Kepler (1596) — Astronomy
William Gilbert (1600) — Discovered earth's magnetic poles
Galileo Galilei (1613) — Astronomy, invented the telescope
Francis Bacon (1620) — The scientific method for empirical science
Blaise Pascal (1654) — Pascal's triangle, calculating machine, forerunner of the computer
Robert Boyle (1674) — The "Gas Laws," known as "Boyle's Law"
Isaac Newton (1715) — Universal laws of gravitation, the dynamic laws of motion
Michael Faraday (1859) — Major laws of electricity and means of generating it
Louis Pasteur (1866) — Microbial origin of disease

Similarly, I attribute the invention of the MRI entirely to the Lord's hand in revealing it to me. I credit His specific intervention to accomplish its reduction to practice.[3] Of course, one does not have to believe in God in order to discover the things He has made or to apply them to useful or medical purposes. *truth* is **truth**, no matter who discovers or stumbles upon it. However, the reason it is so important to understand the role of *God's truth* in scientific discovery is because without His truth as the foundation of all knowledge, we limit science to a closed system of natural law alone. In other words, man is all there is, and the physical laws of nature exist without any help from a Divine Being. But this atheistic approach implodes under its own weight due to both logical and scientific reasons. The universe cannot be infinite (as most honest scientists assert) because the laws of science and logic demand a *First Cause* for it. And our vast knowledge concerning man and the universe in which he lives has yet to adequately be explained solely through the inherent limitations of natural laws. Human reason requires the existence of an uncaused, Intelligent Being who caused man, the universe, and life to come into existence. Both logic and true science give evidence for this reality.

However, today we find ourselves at a unique juncture in history where the approach to science that yielded so many great advancements in the past is held back by a conventional, atheistic, and naturalistic approach. Further, I believe great damage has been done to our culture by removing God from life's equation. Imagine erasing Monet's signature off of one of his masterpieces, or stripping Van Gogh, Picasso, or Rembrandt of the glory due them? Or simply re-writing history, omitting Galileo or Da Vinci? Tragically, this is exactly what we have done to God by writing Him out of His own creation story.

I believe this is primarily why America is now in great peril. I worry that our phenomenal nation is fast losing her soul due to a radical departure from *the truths* on which she was founded some 240 years ago. Like the blood that slowly drains from a dying soldier on the battlefield, God's truth is systematically seeping from this great country, and she is growing steadily weaker because of it. And unless we do something, we could lose the battle.

Similarly, if we remove Jesus Christ from the thread of scientific discovery, we lose our foundational access to *His truth*, and along with it, its unbounded power. I've observed over my lifetime the tragic and painful transformation that occurs in men's and women's souls throughout Western civilization when they choose to ignore God. I have experienced this firsthand, as "open-minded" scientists who believe in a *closed system* (natural law only) look down on others (Christians who are scientists) viewing *them* as "closed-minded." They malign us who believe in an *open system* where God creates laws of nature but also sometimes overrides them.

Of course, all this began when man chose convenience over the Creator, pushing Him out of their new lives in the Garden. In doing so, Adam and Eve (and subsequent generations) exempted themselves from God's rule and His laws. Today, we do the same by blindly subscribing to a godless theory of human origins. The folly of evolution has officially replaced the Creator as the originator and developer of mankind.

But there is an unintended cause-and-effect consequence to this action. By rejecting His truth, we are not able to exempt ourselves from accountability to God or His Laws. *Truth*, like the law of gravity, is still in effect whether we recognize it or not. Even so, with the Creator's natural and supernatural laws eliminated from consideration, not only are we forced to invent an alternate theory of origins, but we also unleash a full range of human decadence and its devastations (i.e., adultery, fornication, homosexuality, drug and alcohol addiction, and all manner of degradations of human dignity).[4]

Without God as absolute lawgiver and source of morality (right and wrong), we are left with a sliding scale of morality. In other words, what is *good, fair, right,* or *wrong* now becomes a matter of one's own opinion or worldview. In the same way, without recognizing God as the *giver of truth*, we not only make up our own truths, but are also led to many wrong conclusions in life . . . and in science.

Nowhere is this reality more obvious than with the study of mankind's beginnings. Because men are often content to be what I refer to as "GSQs," or "Guardians of the Status Quo," they are either too afraid, too proud, or too unwilling to challenge the blindly accepted belief in evolution. As Darwin speculates:

> Therefore I should infer from analogy that *probably* all the organic beings which have ever lived on this earth *have descended from some one primordial form* into which life was first breathed[5] (emphasis added) (see figure 3).

This speculation, though widely and unquestionably accepted in the scientific and medical community, is founded, not upon science, but rather upon presupposition, intellectual bias, and the misunderstanding and misapplication of archeology and scientific knowledge. It begins with the presupposition that there is no God. This is the foundation upon which evolution is built. So if there is no God, He could not possibly have created the universe or man (because He doesn't exist to create them). Evolution also clings to a built-in bias (prejudice) against all matters of faith, presuming such to be the antithesis of science and the scientific method. But nothing could be further from the truth. You rarely hear of the gargantuan amount of faith required to convince oneself of evolution.

This then is the lens through which today's mainstream scientific community sees and interprets everything. Consequently, belief in creationism is in the category of "fairy tale" or "myth," while evolution is lovingly perched on the fireplace mantle like an idol, where it is regularly venerated and worshiped as unquestionable fact.

However, the "dirty little secret" of Darwinian evolution (the supposition that human existence is entirely the result of statistical chance

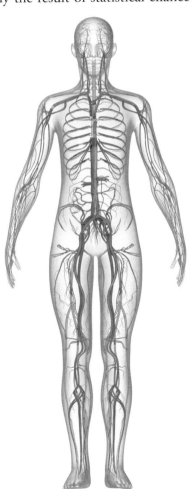

Slime Mold

Figure 3. Evolutionary Theory: Mankind's "Chance" Ascendance from the Slime Mold

Nervous System
Human Complexity
The nervous system is the body's major communication and control network. Data, in the form of electrical signals, is relayed constantly from the sense organs to and from the brain, through complex networks of neurons and on a timescale measured in milliseconds.

and random adaptation over billions of years) is that there is no *scientific evidence* to sustain such a postulate! The flimsy façade protecting this theory hides the fact that there's actually nothing to see behind the curtain. Evolution is merely the scientific community's "sideshow," with a few mythical freaks and some smoke and mirrors thrown in to divert the audience's attention. And like that circus sideshow, people feel cheated and deceived when they finally discover the real truth.

But all the modern-day scientific "carnival barking" cannot hide the fact that evolution is an empty box — a tragic hoax foisted upon mankind, distracting and dissuading them from the belief mankind (and science) held for thousands of years — that we are creations of a gracious God. I will deal more specifically with this in chapter 9, but suffice it to say that the acceptance of evolution as the official version of history and origins effectually marked the beginning of the end for Western civilization, and particularly the demise of the unique miracle that is America. As a consequence, the well-being of our very nation now hangs in the balance. The Christian worldview that brought centuries of blessing in all aspects of society is now pushed to the margins, deemed obsolete, and thrown into the trash bin. Belief in the Creator is currently under vicious attack, imperiled by selfishness and financial greed, underwritten and justified by the Darwinian deception of "survival of the fittest." In plain English, when the spiritual assets of a country are drained, its bank accounts go to a zero balance. I believe those accounts are being severely depleted, partially due to the removal of God from society.

An old maxim warns, "Those who ignore history are condemned to repeat it," and I fear that we are now standing on the threshold of repeating the error and chaos of Babel. Genesis 11:1–9 tells the story of a united human race in the generations following the Great Flood. In those days, Scripture records that humanity spoke a single language and soon began migrating from the east to the land of Shinar. Mankind had become skilled in engineering and construction, and had begun building a city whose tower, they said would "reach to heaven." By attempting to construct this ancient high rise, they asserted their man-centered pre-eminence over God along with their independence from Him.

That's when God paid their city a visit, and He was not pleased. This supposed *stairway to heaven* was only further leading mankind away from their Maker. Ironically, in building themselves up towards heaven, they were, in reality, digging a grave of their own demise. Instead of seeking truth from God, they desired to *become* gods themselves. Humanity's innate pride once again became its downfall (Proverbs 16:18).And so, according to Moses' account, God confused their language, causing them to speak multiple languages. As a result, they could no longer understand each other. This new language barrier halted construction of the tower and God scattered His creation throughout the earth. And we wonder why the world is so confused and chaotic today! All because of man's inherent pride and rejection of his Creator.

In short, we need God. We need Him for life. For salvation and for knowledge. We even need Him for science. Though many may disagree, I maintain that we cannot achieve profound goals in science without God. But progress toward achieving those goals is hindered due to the roadblocks of bigotry and bias. Young people today are not only denied access to genuine scientific truths regarding God, but are instead persuaded to believe in fabricated fairy tales masquerading as scientific fact.

The media also plays a role here. Thirty or 40 years ago, the sole determiner of public opinion was the media, with powerful entities such as *The New York Times* leading the way. Even back then, the media carried a built-in suspicion of anything religious. Some historians, both then and now, even believed Hitler's genocide had some religious roots. But the perpetrator of the crime, Adolph Hitler, was actually devoid of any valid religious beliefs. Instead of religion, Germany's diabolical dictator justified his heinous crimes through a belief in Darwinian evolution and it's "survival of the fittest" propaganda.[6] But you don't hear that taught today in high school history or science class, do you?

Some may think we are out of time, but I still believe there is hope. Though mankind's indifference remains consistent from generation to generation, history teaches us that God will always raise up those who are willing to shine the light of truth. We need more people like Henry Morris and Ken Ham, men who demonstrate that mankind can know the genuine truth about God's role in creation while at the same time exposing the falsity of Darwinian evolution.

But God's truth doesn't require that we have a charismatic leader or even a Billy Graham-like figure. Though prominent Christian leaders and spokesmen with large platforms of influence are important, it's *foot soldiers* just like you who will ultimately win the victory in this war for truth. The common Christian with an uncommon commitment to being equipped with God's Word is a far more powerful influence in helping to change our culture. We just need to do more in equipping believers with His glorious truth.

One day, while talking with one of my top scientific executives, Jay Dworkin, about our company, I suddenly realized that we were actually *selling each other* on our own products! This epiphany helped me understand that we are *all* in continuous sell mode — selling to each other, to non-believers, to evolutionists, to our spouses, to family members, etc. We're perpetually "promoting" — not ourselves, but Him! In everything we do, our principle activity is sales, not in the telemarketing or business sense, but rather in fighting the battle for the minds of this generation. For this to happen, the truth must be presented to them in a language and a format they can understand. Therefore, we have to be trained and adept at both demonstrating the *need* for truth as well as the *practical benefits* of it. In other words, when it comes to truth, we have to answer the question for them, "What's in it for me?" And there's nothing wrong with that. Ultimately, though, we want them to go beyond seeing their own benefit to understanding the glory of God in it all. In our efforts to help others know the "what" about God and truth, we have to reach people *where they are* . . . just like our Savior did.

In a world of competitive *counter-truths*, we must do our best to reveal why God's truth is credible, beneficial, and *better* than other ideas and speculations. This is the fundamental mission of Christian apologetics — to "give a defense" (i.e., a logical reason) for *why* we believe.

To effectively reach the secular world, we must utilize different methods from those we've used for the past few decades. It's obvious that secularism in all its forms has a stranglehold on the youth of this age; therefore it's imperative that we use both *creativity* as well as *credibility* in communicating to the secular world, particularly in our American culture. While I am certain that our great nation would never have arrived at this junction — medically, technologically, and scientifically — without the Lord and His *truth*, nevertheless knowing this is only half the battle. We have to advance, moving forward in helping others realize and embrace that same truth.

So if truth is really on our side, how do we tell others about it? I'm not sure I have all the answers, but I firmly believe it begins in America's pulpits. Believers must be trained and equipped in their churches as well as in their homes. But it can't end there. We must also penetrate the circles of the academic, legal, political, and scientific communities. We must inspire Christian young adults to pursue these fields. Only then will our influence be fully realized. That is precisely what I've tried to do in my own world.

For me, my greatest single discovery in life was not a machine or a physical principle. My highest purpose was realized when I discovered I could actually know God and serve His will, that I could live for something greater than science, medicine, or myself. When I found out that my life could bring joy to my Maker's heart, *that* began to greatly motivate my work as a scientist: exploring and applying the laws of nature and of nature's God for the benefit of mankind.

Yes, I sincerely believe there's hope. God still opens peoples' eyes to the truth and Jesus still grants us access to that truth we spoke of earlier. Our job is to make it available and clearly demonstrated in word *and* deed. In other words, our presentation has to go beyond talk, evidence, and scientific *facts*. It has to show up in the lifestyle and *faith* of those who claim to believe it.

However, despite my fierce commitment to this truth, I must confess that I haven't always held this belief. Faith has not always been the guiding light it is for me today. In reality, my journey towards a godly understanding is a long one, with a few dirt roads and detours along the way. Over my many years, I have come to realize that truth is not just something man discovers or accidently stumbles upon. Rather, I learned that *God* is the seeker and man is the object of His search. And to my surprise, I found out that this amazing God had been chasing me from an early age.

Endnotes

1. http://wrightbrothers.info/biography.php.
2. In a letter to Queen Isabella and King Ferdinand in 1502, Columbus wrote, "Fully accomplished were the words of Isaiah, 'He shall gather together the dispersed of Judah from the four corners of the earth.'"
3. *Creation Magazine*, 1994.
4. Romans 1:18–32 describes in detail the consequences of man's rejection of God as Creator and truth-giver.
5. Charles Darwin, *The Origin of Species* (New York: Barnes & Noble Classics, 2009), p. 380.
6. http://www.creationism.org/csshs/v08n3p24.htm.

CHAPTER

2

THE
BEGINNING

E ven as a young child, I was driven toward success. Unlike many children, discipline was never much of a problem for me. When my mother would send me to my room, usually for being mischievous, I'd crack open a book and read for hours. Back then there wasn't anything like the Internet, of course, and most homes didn't even have a television. We therefore primarily learned through reading books and magazines. In my spare time, I found myself working on mathematics problems or reading my science textbook. But apart from my schoolbooks, I also loved drawing and building things — like constructing and flying my own model airplanes. I can still recall playing with my Gilbert's Erector Set, fabricating tall buildings, Ferris wheels, and even parachute jumps. It seemed I had an insatiable appetite for learning. I simply wanted to *know*. Even now, in my late seventies, I still do.

I came into this world on March 16, 1936, as the second child of Vahan and Odette Damadian (figure 4). I later learned I had an older sibling who did not survive childbirth. Though we lived in Manhattan, soon after I was born my family moved to Elmhurst, Queens. There my parents celebrated my sister Claudette's birth a year and a half after mine (figures 5 and 6). Several months later, we moved from Elmhurst to Austin Street in the Forest Hills section of Queens. This is where I would spend the majority of my youth.

My dear mother was the product of French and Armenian ancestry. Her father, Haig, came to the United States from France in 1906.

Figure 4. Raymond Damadian's mother and father, Vahan K. Damadian and Odette

Figure 5. Left to right: Vahan K. Damadian (Raymond's father), Raymond, Claudette, Odette Damadian (Raymond's mother)

Settling in New York, he would later become the country's first distributor of Renault cars. After a brief stint as a race car driver, he opened a limousine service featuring the Renault brand. Both her parents lived with us until their deaths.

I've always been proud of my vibrant, Armenian heritage, through which I learned many important things. One of those was the value of respecting my elders, something that seems lost among many today. Another thing I inherited from my parents was a predisposition toward music (figure 7), which would prove significant during my formative years as a young boy. We Armenians are additionally known for our intellect and strong family ties. But we also have developed a fierce survival instinct, having endured a history that included foreign domination and even genocide.

My father (figures 8 and 9), also Armenian, was born in 1903 in the Turkish town of Kayseri, 100 miles north of Tarsus, the southern coastal city where the Apostle Paul was from. Kayseri is

Figure 6. Raymond Damadian, age 2½, with his sister Claudette, age 1

Figure 7. Jevan Damadian and Raymond Damadian practicing the violin on their farm in Vermont

Figure 8. Raymond Damadian at 3½ weeks in the arms of his father, Vahan K. Damadian

Figure 9. Raymond Damadian's father, Vahan K. Damadian

situated not far from where the Turkish peninsula joins the Saudi Peninsula. Prior to the Muslims arrival in A.D. 600, Kayseri was a dedicated Christian community, as the first Armenians were converted by the Apostles around A.D. 44. Armenia is also the region where Noah's ark landed after God sent the global Flood of Genesis 6–8 (see Genesis 8:4). In fact, Mount Ararat can be seen today from virtually any point in the old capital city of Armenia, Yerevan. This capital is one of the world's oldest continually inhabited cities, having been founded in 782 B.C. Early Christian Armenian tradition says that, upon leaving the ark, Noah exclaimed "Yerevet's" (meaning "it appeared!").[1]

When my father was 12, his uncle was forced from his home and shot by the Turks, who at this time were ruling that area of the world. Not long afterward, my father's family was also driven from their home village to Damascus. Their only possession was a Bible. They were permitted to hire only one donkey and a cart for their 40-day trek across the dessert. During this long and arduous journey, my father contracted typhus and nearly died. His brothers, who were living in America, somehow managed to contact Turkish soldiers, hiring them to search for them in the huge caravan. Eventually they located my father. In time, my family was able to obtain a special order from Turkey's Secretary of the Interior (made possible by the connections and influence of another uncle in Constantinople), which literally saved my father's remaining family. The rest of the refugees were marched to the deserts of Der Zoar, which proved to be the final and fatal destination of the Armenian genocide. My father's family was sent instead to Aleppo, Syria, where they remained until World War I ended three years later in 1918. Then, two years after this, with the help of the American Red Cross, my father's two brothers helped arrange passage for the family to travel from Syria all the way to Bridgeport, Connecticut.

Seven years later, my father moved to New York, and after being encouraged to pursue work in photo engraving, found work at the *New York World*, which later became the *World-Telegram*. He worked the midnight to 8:00 a.m. shift, which allowed him to be home with us during the day. As a young boy, that made me happy.

My parents had met at a supper dance soon after my father moved to New York. They married in 1932, and four years later I was born. My dad was a quiet man (figure 9), and yet he had a dynamic personality. He was incredible in so many ways, and left a positive and lasting impression on me. He was, and is, a beautiful soul. I think of him every day as a portrait of him is also prominently displayed in my office.

When I was five, my mother took me to Manhattan and signed me up for violin lessons. Like most children who take lessons, I loved to play my instrument, but I didn't particularly enjoy practicing. Three years into these lessons, I was progressing so well that my instructor encouraged my mother to schedule an audition for me at the prestigious Julliard School. Then, as today, Julliard is considered one of the world's premier music schools.

The day of my audition arrived and, true to form, I hadn't practiced at all. Further complicating the matter, as I was preparing for my audition, we discovered that the pegs on my violin were "frozen" from disuse. After considerable effort, we finally got the violin pegs unstuck and the violin in tune. However, unfortunately by that point, I had grown way too terrified to actually finish the audition! I left midway through, convinced my violin career was over and that I would never hear from the school again. Surprisingly though, about two weeks later I received a call asking me to come back to finish my audition. In spite of my previous inability to perform, I was accepted to Julliard and assigned to a teacher named Andrew McKinley (figure 10), under whose instruction I studied violin for the next seven years. Mr. McKinley saw potential in me that less-experienced teachers might have missed. He saw something worth nurturing. Ultimately, he would invest countless hours in me as a young musician. Under his tutelage, it didn't take me long to learn that classical music is a very *un*forgiving art form. It's demanding, as it requires you to "get it right," as in *every time*. Miss just one note, and everyone knows it. I believe some of my attention to detail and work ethic today stems from those long hours of preparation and practice, and of course from Andrew McKinley's brilliant instruction.

During that time, in the early 1950s, I entered Forest Hills High School, an institution that had gained a reputation for its excellence in science education. Forest Hills had won numerous Westinghouse Science Talent Search awards (now known as the Intel Science Talent Search awards). A research-based competition for high school seniors, these awards have been called the nation's oldest and most prestigious science competition.

At Forest Hills, two teachers, Dr. Brandwine, (science) and Wally Manheim (trigonometry), had a great impact on my academic life,

Figure 10. Raymond Damadian with his Juilliard
violin teacher, Andrew McKinley

sparking in me a heightened interest in science and math. These two fields would later drive my entire life's research and work. Dr. Brandwine was particularly inspiring in his discussion of the profound impact new scientific discoveries were having on mankind. Wally Manheim showed me the sheer delight and satisfaction that came from solving mathematic problems. Both men partnered in planting a seed within me, a desire to know, to discover, and to bring clarity to confusion.

But though my studies didn't prove to be a huge academic challenge to me, I still wasn't the most prolific student at the school. I finished that year with a 93 average, not nearly high enough to be ranked first in my class. That bothered me, and inwardly offended both a predisposition for excellence as well as my competitive spirit.

Then, when I was 15, I competed along with 10,000 other students for an advanced placement scholarship offered by the Ford Foundation, the Ford Foundatiaon's "Pre-Induction Scholarship" for children less than 16 years of age (some inductees were 12) for advancement to collegiate education prior to high school graduation. I ended up being one of 200 finalists who was offered a full college scholarship to attend one of the four universities participating in the Ford Foundation "Pre-Induction Scholarship" program: Yale, Columbia, the University of Wisconsin, or the University of Chicago. Oddly, finalists weren't allowed to select their own university, but instead were chosen in a draft similar to what professional sports use today. I was *drafted* by the University of Wisconsin.

However, this wonderful offer presented me with a difficult choice. If I accepted the scholarship, I would have no financial obligations while in college. That, to any prospective student, is a tempting offer. But on the other hand it also meant I'd have to give up my aspirations of becoming a concert violinist. I enjoyed playing publicly and performing, and had continued to excel at it, even having played publically for my church. In my heart, I knew what I should do, and yet I still valued the input and counsel of my Julliard violin teacher Mr. McKinley. He had guided me so well thus far and I greatly anticipated his advice. I will never forget his words. "Raymond," he stated in a tone carrying a note of wisdom, "you can name on one hand the number of violinists who've 'made it' on the concert stage" (figure 10).

That simple statement was all I needed to hear. His advice resonated with me and, in an instant, my decision was made. A career as an orchestral musician would not be my life's aspiration.

Without the scholarship that had been awarded to me, I'm convinced I would never have gone away to college. Looking back, it is clear that the hand of God was on me for my good. His divine providence was guiding me on a path whose destination was yet unknown to me at the time. Two years after entering college at the University of Wisconsin, I decided to enroll in the pre-med program there. Majoring in mathematics with a minor in chemistry, I eventually received my Bachelor of Science in 1956. Having taken a number of biology and science courses, I now had the prerequisites I needed for medical school.

However, math and chemistry didn't consume *all* of my time. During summer breaks from the university and from medical school, I also kept myself busy honing my athletic skills, giving tennis lessons at Dune Deck Hotel in Westhampton Beach. This proved to be a rewarding move, as I was able to make $2,500 for the summer, quite a healthy income back then.

My doubles partner, and singles competitor, at the Forest Hills West Side Tennis Club, home of the Forest Hills tennis stadium where the U.S. National Tennis Championships and Davis Cup Championships were played each year, was a guy named Charlie Brukl. Charlie had taken the job as the tennis pro at the Westhampton Bath and Tennis Club, a nearby resort, following his victory in our West Side Tennis Club Junior Championship match. A six-foot-tall sandy-haired man with a competitive spirit to match mine, Brukl and I grew to be friendly adversaries on the tennis court and best friends off it.

On one of those summer breaks from college, Charlie and I played against one another for the West Side Tennis Club Junior Championship. To my great disappointment, I lost to him in five sets, enduring temperatures that reached 105 degrees that day. By the time the fifth set arrived, I thought I would finally prevail, when suddenly I developed violent cramps in my legs, collapsing to the ground. Hardly able to move, much less compete, I limped through the fifth set, going home dejected, disappointed, and, worst of all, defeated. But what also bothered me was that I couldn't understand why Charlie had not also succumbed to the same cramps.

Later that evening, however, my question was answered. The phone rang and it was Charlie's mother, urgently requesting me to come over to their house right away. She informed me that Charlie had suddenly collapsed under the dinner table and was contorted in pain with muscle cramps. "He's completely unable to move, Raymond!" she frantically reported.

Charlie's cramps hit him just as they had hit me; only they had come three hours too late! I immediately raced over to his house and, upon arrival, found Charlie still under the table and in agony. Earlier in the day on the tennis court, Charlie had been my adversary, and I wanted nothing more than to soundly beat him. But when I got to his house that evening, all I could see was my friend, huddled under a table in excruciating pain. And I wanted nothing more than to help him.

Charlie and I remain life-long friends to this day.

While sweating in the summer heat that day, I had no idea that, in the stands watching our championship match was a man who was looking for a head tennis pro for the Westhampton Bath and Tennis Club. Since Charlie had won the match, he was naturally asked to be the pro, which he gladly accepted.

However, about a week later, Charlie called me to say that Westhampton's Dune Deck Hotel was also looking for a pro. He asked if I would be interested.

"Of course," I quickly replied.

Following Charlie's recommendation, I interviewed with the owner and was promptly hired.

Since we were both now making a bit of money, about this time Charlie and I decided the two of us should invest in a more permanent form of transportation. Pooling our funds, we bought a 1947 Studebaker, paying $40 apiece for it! Our agreement was that we would equally share the car, 50/50. Our first night following our purchase, Charlie asked if he could take the car out.

"Sure," I naturally responded.

Then the second night he asked again. And the third night too, and every night for a week thereafter! Finally my curiosity got the best of me and I probed, "Charlie, where are you going every night? I'd like to have use of that car too sometime. It's half mine, you know."

Charlie finally confessed he had been making regular trips to a corner drugstore called "Speed's Pharmacy." Speed's was one of those old-fashioned drugstores where you could also get ice cream, sodas, and candy. They had booths, benches, and barstools for customers to sit at while they ate. After some probing and prodding, I was able to pry the truth out of my friend. Charlie wasn't going to Speed's just for the ice cream, but rather for another "dish" altogether, actually an attractive young "soda jerk" girl. Charlie revealed that he would go to Speed's each night and just sit in a corner booth, waiting for a random opportunity to catch a few minutes of conversation with a particularly attractive girl. He'd just sit there and wait . . . *hoping*. Then, promptly at 9:00 p.m. each night when the drugstore closed, the girl's *boyfriend* would come and pick her up!

"Ah," I thought, "now it's all starting to make sense."

All of a sudden, my confusion and frustration toward Charlie about the car turned to a mild form of pity as I thought of him sitting in that corner booth each night waiting to talk to a girl who already had a steady boyfriend.

"Poor Charlie," I thought.

I found out that soda-jerk girl's name was Donna, and obviously Charlie had taken quite a liking to her. Soon he began looking for opportunities to see Donna . . . in situations that *didn't* involve sitting in a drugstore booth. About that time, the National Grass Court Championships at Forest Hills were taking place. I assumed that Charlie naturally would want to attend and take Donna . . . *and* the car, of course! But then he surprised me by suggesting that we make it a double date. I couldn't believe Charlie was actually going to let me use *my* car, so I quickly agreed. The only unanswered question was who I would take as my date, since I had no real prospects at the time. Fortunately for me, Donna had a friend who happened to need a partner, so it all worked out and everybody was happy. I decided to bring along my guitar and ended up playing just about the entire time we were in the car. Everyone seemed to have a great time singing . . . everyone evidently except Charlie. Upon returning to our hotel room that night, Charlie informed me that if he heard one more note out of that guitar, he would break it over my head! I guess he'd had enough of my guitar playing for a while.

Earlier that day at the Forest Hills Championship, I was able to introduce my father to Charlie and Donna. Not long after this, my father, being the straightforward man he was, bluntly asked, "Raymond, why can't *you* get a girl like that?"

Caught off guard and somewhat speechless, I didn't really have an answer for him. However, unbeknownst to me at the time, God was once again working behind the scenes on my behalf.

This became evident to me a few days later when Charlie shocked me by suggesting, "Raymond, I think Donna is more interested in you than me."

It had become clear to Charlie by this time that his nightly trips to Speed's had apparently gotten him nowhere. In effect, he was conceding the match and calling it a day as far as Donna was concerned.

Charlie further encouraged me, suggesting that I go ahead and ask her out. Surprised by his unexpected proposition, I initially hesitated, as I certainly didn't want to ruin, or even damage, the close friendship we shared. I had to confirm several times with Charlie if he was really okay with me asking Donna out on a date. Friendships have been strained and even broken over such activity. But it became clear to both of us that ours was a bond strong enough for such a thing.

Around this time, Donna told me about an event being held at Madison Square Garden in New York City. The event featured a fiery young evangelist named Billy Graham. Donna asked if Charlie and I had any interest in going. Though I'd been brought up in the church and had parents who provided great examples of Christian love, at this particular point in my spiritual journey the idea of salvation was still somehow a foreign concept to me. In fact, I don't really recall it being talked about that much at my church. It seemed the emphasis was placed on living a good moral life and abstaining from certain sins of the world. But salvation? That wasn't even remotely on my radar. I suppose had you asked me at the time about whether I was a Christian, I would have responded in the affirmative. Though I wasn't a "bad" person by anyone's standards, I later came to the realization that sometimes its not a person's "badness" that keeps them from Christ, but rather their "goodness." When compared to other people, it's easy to find someone more deserving of judgment than yourself. But when compared to God's righteous standard, we all fall short and find ourselves in desperate need of a Savior (Romans 3:23).

However, my foggy understanding of salvation wouldn't last for very long. That night Mr. Graham explained Jesus, my sin, the Cross, and faith in terms I had never heard before. And something supernatural happened as I listened to his words. I understood the gospel and became convinced that I needed salvation.

An energetic young evangelist, Mr. Graham concluded his presentation with his classic impassioned invitation to "come forward" for salvation. Thousands from the massive Madison Square Garden audience came streaming to the altar. And on this particular evening, I was one of them. Through faith in Jesus alone, my soul was gloriously rescued by God. My "Tennis Pro" life and values were immediately transformed, as they now took second place to a new, higher priority. As an inventor, I might be tempted to say I "discovered" God that night. But, in reality, it was He who discovered me (John 6:44). I was lost like a stray sheep, and needed to be found by the Good Shepherd. As Graham spoke, I had sensed a change in my spirit — a conviction that hadn't been there before. It marked the beginning of a long adventure of faith for me. I experienced a big change in my heart at Madison Square Garden that evening in 1957. And though my faith would later be severely challenged through experiencing doubts about God and His existence, I still mark that moment as the beginning of a new kind of life for me.

Figure 11. (top row) Sherry Terry, Tom Terry, Donna, David Terry, (bottom row) Amy Terry, Raymond, Ellis Donald Terry, Constance Terry

Following that experience, I began attending Sunday services with Donna's family at the East Quogue Methodist Church. I came to know the church's pastor, "Ollie Dongell," fairly well. Throughout the summer of 1957, Donna and I were faithfully ministered to by this impassioned servant of the Lord. For both of us, our relationship with the Lord surged forward, and we became closer to one another as we both grew closer to Him.

Our initial relationship really began that night at New York's Madison Square Garden in 1957. Donna Terry, the "duck farmer's daughter," was the child of evangelical Christians, Amy and "Bo" Donald Terry (figure 11), who held weekly prayer meetings in their home. Their ancestors, the Terry's and the Hallock's, were Puritans who arrived from Connecticut in 1640 to Southold, Long Island, aboard the *Abigail*. The Puritan community to which they belonged eventually became known as the "East Enders." Coming from such a strong spiritual heritage, Donna's faith had always been a fundamental source of strength for her. Charlie and I both figured that out when we dated her (well, I dated her and he "tried to"). She attended a Wesleyan Methodist school called Houghton College, in western New York, about an hour's drive from Buffalo. Then, after two years, she transferred to Columbia University in New York

City, where she eventually received her degree in nursing. An extraordinary woman of faith, Donna was, and continues to be, a real prayer warrior. But at that time, I was only beginning to know and appreciate this petite feminine gift from God in my life. Over time, our relationship grew socially, romantically, and spiritually. Soon, Donna even expressed an interest in learning tennis, so naturally I invited her for lessons. This of course meant we would get to spend even more time together. And that was something I was more than willing to do!

After completing my four-year studies at the University of Wisconsin, I longed to return to New York in order to be closer to home and family. And this is exactly what I did, applying to medical school at Albert Einstein College of Medicine at Yeshiva University, located in the Bronx. Named after history's most renowned theoretical physicist, the distinguished professor had agreed to become the namesake for the very first medical school built in New York City since 1897. Entering the school, I was one of only a handful of non-Jewish medical students enrolled there.

Throughout medical school, Donna became well acquainted with my classmates. I assembled together several members of the student body, forming the "Lymph Notes," a vocal octet singing group. This eight-man chorus group would entertain at medical school events, providing some welcome relief from the constant, multi-faceted pressures of medical education. On one occasion, the "Lymph Notes" traveled from the Bronx to Donna's dormitory, Maxwell Hall, at Columbia Presbyterian Medical Center in Manhattan. We had previously arranged for some of her classmates to take Donna onto the outdoor porch of their dormitory, about eight stories up, overlooking the Hudson River. The "Lymph Notes" octet located themselves on an adjacent porch overlooking the Hudson so they could serenade Donna directly across the space between the two porches. We crooned Rodgers & Hammerstein's "If I Loved You" followed by the spiritual, "Joshua Fit the Battle of Jericho." I'm wondering now if we were one of the original "Boy Bands."

Following my graduation from medical school and subsequent military obligation, I joined the faculty at the State University of New York (SUNY) Downstate Medical Center in Brooklyn as an assistant professor in medicine and biophysics. It was during this time that something unexpected happened to me. Over time, I gradually became persuaded that *science*, not God and truth, was the foundation of everything true and reliable. As a faculty member constantly exposed to scientific naturalism (and evolution), I became virally infected with such thinking, eventually reaching the conclusion that there *was* no God, and thus no longer any practical need for Him in my life. I have since observed that this experience is repeated by tens of thousands of churched young people today after a few semesters at college or graduate school.

Looking back, it's now easy to see how I was dissuaded away from faith to embrace the "rock solid conclusions" of science. This pressure to cast off all vestiges of faith was greatest in my life when I became a faculty member at Downstate. The unspoken focus at such schools is on "intellectual aptitude," to achieve status, recognition, respect, and most of all, tenure. The guarantee of lifetime employment was, and is, a goal every faculty member desires. And the undercurrent powering this world of academia was, as you might guess, atheistic Darwinian evolution. As such, there was exactly zero room for a "Supreme Being" in the equation. And so, wading into the river, I was carried downstream with the current.

One day, I shared my new conclusion about God's non-existence with my tech, who immediately became incredulous, replying that she couldn't believe I had said such a thing.

"You know it's a fact," I confidently asserted, unaware that I had become yet another victim of evolutionary fiction.

In that state of mind, I had effectively reversed my life course, turning my back, and mind, on my spiritual heritage. I abandoned my upbringing, as well as the decision for Christ I had made that night in Madison Square Garden. Having grown up in a strong Christian community, I had been an active and dedicated churchgoer throughout my youth, even to the point of being selected vice president of the Pilgrim Fellowship of my church. And the salvation decision I made had deeply impacted me. However, during my time in medical school, strong atheistic currents of the scientific community caused me to drift far from the shore of God's reality and truth.

Despite all my previous spiritual experiences while in college, medical school had subjected me to a heavy dose of fiction, disguised as science. Evolution was taught as though it were unequivocal scientific *fact*. There was no credible, scientific alternative available at the time. No Henry Morris or Ken Ham. No societies of scientists who were Christian in their thinking. And no strong biblical influence of any kind in

Figure 12. Donna and Raymond with their children,
left to right, Timothy, Jevan, and Keira

the medical community where I worked. Medical school programmed me to center my reasoning on naturalistic science alone. There was no room (or tolerance) for alternate explanations, especially as it related to origins of man and the universe. So I swallowed the bait — hook, line, and sinker. I even developed a certain "reverence" for evolution, accepting it as reality, believing that both science and math supported it. Eventually, this thinking eroded the foundations of my biblical upbringing. As a result, my house of faith all but collapsed.

As a child, I had been deeply influenced by faith. And yet, medical school was a long way from the Congregational Church of Forest Hills. I was now drawn toward the "higher truth" of science. Faith seemed so intangible. So *invisible*. So ethereal. Science, on the other hand, was something I could see, understand, and participate in. It was physical, concrete, and *real*. I could sink my teeth into it. It was also popularly accepted by not only my immediate peers and professors but also by the

Figure 13. Left to right: Calton Chan (Raymond's nephew), Raymond, Odette Damadian, Keira (Raymond's daughter), Jevan (Raymond's son), Vahan Damadian, Claudette, Timothy (Raymond's son)

greater medical community itself. Science was safe and sure. Faith was suspect and risky. So I would play it safe and stick with science for the foreseeable future. It certainly seemed to trump the truth and values I had been taught at church. However, I later discovered that though I had given up on God, He had refused to give up on me. I didn't know it at the time, but this chapter of my life would not be the end of my faith story. The Lord had planted a seed in me and though it lay dormant, it was not dead.

But apart from a strong faith influence, another thing had profoundly impacted me as a child. Growing up, my maternal grandparents, Haig and Jeanne Pénot Yazedjian, lived with us in the house on Austin Street. My grandmother (figure 14) and I had a special relationship, and I loved her very much. A strict disciplinarian, she also retained her French heritage in both language and style. I remember sitting in her lap for hours trying to learn to read, which wasn't easy because English wasn't her first language. She would often grow impatient with me when I didn't get it right. Even so, we were very close as she also took care of me while my mother was at work.

However, in 1946, when I was just ten years old, my dear grandmother was diagnosed with cancer in her left breast. This dreadful diagnosis was shocking news, especially in a day when not much could be done for her, medically

Figure 14. Raymond's French grandmother, Jeanne Victoria Pénot Yazedjian

speaking. Grandmother Jeanne Victoria was in constant pain, and her last few months were particularly agonizing. Hers was a terrible form of cancer. Her breast had become swollen and red, and exuded a foul odor. For months she lay in her second floor bed, moaning. In the days leading up to her passing, she frequently screamed out in pain, despite heavy medication. During her final days, we had a full-time nurse taking care of her. Having previously pleaded not to be put in a hospital, my grandmother eventually suffered a slow and agonizing death at home.

For a long time, it didn't really register with me that she was going to die. One day I asked the nurse when my grandmother was going to get well. She looked at me, explaining that my grandmother was never going to get well. Imagine the effect of such news to an innocent ten-year-old boy. Needless to say, I was devastated. Her suffering had a deep and lasting impact on me. This firsthand experience caused me to be exposed to the ravages of cancer at an early age. I saw up close what that horrid disease does to people. For months following her death, I could still hear the echo of her moaning in my mind.

My precious grandmother's death cut me deep inside, leaving a lasting emotional scar. While not the sole reason I pursued medicine, I believe her death was one factor that drove me into research, fueling my passionate quest to find a cure for cancer. Later, God would awaken that passion within me, driving me toward His truth, leading to a revolutionary medical discovery.

Endnotes

1. *Soviet Armenian Encyclopedia*, Vol. iii (Yerevan, Armenian SSR: Armenian Academy of Sciences, 1977), p. 548–564.

CHAPTER

3

SCIENCE AND THE SINGLE IDEA

Sometimes a single thought can make all the difference in the world. One idea. One concept. And like a light bulb being switched on, in an instant, everything changes. That best describes how the idea to create a machine to scan the human body came about. And though a number of events led up to that moment, the idea itself came to me in an instant. That one thought eventually birthed the creation of a device that is now instrumental in helping save lives all over the world.

Today, tens of millions in developed countries have benefited from this technological marvel of modern medicine. Millions more know someone who has been helped by MRI, whether it's a friend or a family member. Sometimes when I'm out with my wife for dinner, we hear people talking about their MRI scanning experience. Donna is often tempted to lean over and say, "Hey, this guy right here," pointing to me, "he *invented* the MRI."

When I first started out, I never originally intended to invent a device that would radically change the medical world. I only wanted to possibly come up with something that could alter or overcome the tragic consequences of the cancer disease. But that would require years and a lot of work and research. For the time being, I had to concentrate on surviving medical school.

During my time there, not only did my faith take a back seat to science, but I also wasn't the most prolific student at Albert Einstein Medical School. I wasn't used to the type of studying required to achieve high honors. Though I have a very analytical mind, medical school demanded that I devour and digest voluminous quantities of information in a short amount of time, and then later recall them in great detail during exams. Even so, I still kept studying and seeking to improve.

Near the end of my third year in medical school I came to the conclusion that internal medicine would be the best medical specialty for me. Looking back, I believe what led me to this area of concentration was because internal medicine deals with the *entirety* of medicine. But it also seemed to best fit my personality and background. Internal medicine is the most analytical of medical specialties, and that was consistent with my mathematical background and passion for problem solving.

This concentrated field of study would allow me to accomplish two things: (1) apply the chemistry from my undergraduate studies, and (2) use my analytical inclinations to solve problems. By the time I graduated, I could hardly wait to throw myself into research. Each person in the medical world has an important role to fulfill: nurses, surgeons, doctors, everyone. But by going into research, I believed I could exponentially help more lives than I could as a *practitioner* of medicine. I reasoned that a practitioner would impact thousands in their career, while a researcher could impact *millions*. I was as intent then, as I am now, on helping as many people as I possibly could.

A week after graduating from Albert Einstein Medical School in 1960, Donna and I were married. We subsequently moved into a three-room apartment in Upper Manhattan. Our new home was conveniently located near Columbia University where Donna was a nursing student. We paid $65 a month for rent, a paltry amount by today's standards.

My internship and residency were done in Internal Medicine at the Downstate Medical Center of the State University of New York, in central Brooklyn. Downstate is comprised of the College of Medicine, Colleges of Nursing and Health Related Professions, Schools of Graduate Studies and Public Health, and the State University Hospital of Brooklyn. One of the major hospitals in the SUNY system was a 4,000-bed facility in Brooklyn called Kings County Hospital, adjacent to Downstate. With so many patients at my disposal, I had ample opportunity to see a lot of pathology. This only further fed my appetite for research. Interning in the Department of Internal Medicine, I was supervised by Department Chairman Ludwig Eichna, a 6'4" Germanic man who immediately took a liking to me. It became apparent when making rounds in the hospital with Dr.

Eichna, that I had an aptitude at making accurate diagnoses on patients. My analytical and problem-solving skills were beginning to pay off.

Another influential mentor during that time was Dr. Paul Dreizen, who later became the Dean of the Graduate School under which my future assistants, Larry Minkoff and Mike Goldsmith, were granted their PhD's. Both Eichna and Dreizen recognized I had a knack for research, and together they encouraged this skill in me.

Of all the medical specialties, internal medicine quickly became my focus, primarily because I saw it as an opportunity to potentially identify the root causes of medical diseases. From the outset, I was fascinated by the kidney and its powers to regulate the electrically active ions of the body (like potassium [K+] and sodium [Na+]).[1] The kidney is an amazing organ whose job it is to balance out the pH of the body's fluids and the electrically active atoms of the body. This is a delicate role, central to the maintenance of the proper electrical state in the human body. I chose to focus on how the kidneys function, specifically how the kidney is always able to excrete the right amount of electrically active ions and water each day. Unknown to me, this research involving water would later prove vital in the thought that sparked the idea for the MRI.

After completing my residency at Downstate, Donna and I moved to St. Louis, Missouri. There I worked with Dr. Neal Bricker as a Post-doctoral Fellow in Nephrology. This work put me in the renal division of the Department of Internal Medicine, Washington University School of Medicine. Bricker had earned a respectable and somewhat famous reputation for his kidney research.

While there, a comment by Dr. Bricker set me on a peculiar path to find an elusive protein called the "sodium pump." A lot of research at that time centered around the balance between the sodium ion and the potassium ion in the body, which is critical for the maintenance of "tissue electricity," which is at the basis for life itself. At death, this electricity immediately ceases in our cells. No electricity = no life.

One day, while at a meeting of research fellows, I asked Dr. Bricker if anyone had ever successfully isolated (found and identified) the "sodium pump." He replied, "No, but the man who does that will win the Nobel Prize."

That comment got our attention.

In the late 1960s, Nuclear Magnetic Resonance (NMR) technology had been around for approximately 15 years. Basically, NMR and MRI

(Magnetic Resonance Imaging) are the same technology. But when we eventually came to introducing the NMR scanner to the medical community, the physicians wanted the letter "N" (for nuclear) removed since it implied *radioactivity*, which MRI did not use. On the other side, the radiology community wanted the "I" (for imaging) added to identify MR as an *imaging* technology. That's how the acrostic MRI developed.

Early in my research I became fascinated by the phenomenon that every human being is a walking electrical plant generating his (her) own electricity. This electricity enables the normal live-human physiologies of cerebration, muscle contraction, locomotion, etc. The *origin* of that life-originating electricity was a major curiosity to me. Two scientists in the United Kingdom, Hodgkin and Huxley, had shown that this electricity was originating from the asymmetric distribution of the charged (1+) potassium atom, (ion) across the cell's outer surface, the cell membrane. Internally, the potassium (K^{39}) ion concentration was 140 mmoles per liter. Externally, it was 4 mmoles per liter. If these values were inserted into the well-known electro-chemical equation for determining battery voltages, (known as the Nernst equation) you could calculate the same electric voltage for the living cell that you obtained when you inserted an electrode to measure the tissue's voltage *directly*. Doing this established that the cell's asymmetric potassium ion concentration across the cell's membrane was the source of that electric voltage.

Assuming that to be the correct answer to the origin of the "electricity of life," the immediate next question was "why potassium and not sodium?" The cell's sodium ion concentration, a 1+ charge atom equivalent to potassium, was exactly the *reverse*, a high sodium concentration (~140 mmoles per liter) *exterior* to the cell, with 4 mmoles per liter on the *interior*. Moreover, the atomic radius of sodium was less than potassium and would superficially appear to occupy less of the limited interior space of the living cell than potassium. So "why potassium and not sodium" as the cell's interior ion? Hodgkin and Huxley proposed the existence of a "sodium pump" on the cell's membrane that was "pumping" sodium out of the cell and potassium *into* the cell. But since no one had yet isolated the "sodium pump," I set as my own research goal to try and do so. When I expressed the desire to isolate and characterize the proposed "sodium pump" protein, my biophysics professor at Harvard, Dr. Arthur K. Solomon, said that his plan to accomplish that goal was already underway. His strategy was to isolate a mutant of the E. coli bacteria that could not accumulate potassium. Solomon and his post-doctoral research fellow, Dr. Stanley Schultz, had been experimenting with E. coli bacteria. The plan was to first isolate such a mutant of E. coli and then, by fractionating the proteins of both the parent strain and the mutant simultaneously, the parent strain protein that had no counterpart in the mutant would be the "sodium pump." With Dr. Solomon's encouragement, I committed to the research task of culturing E. coli with mutagenic agents to see if such a mutant could indeed be isolated. Gratefully, within six months I succeeded in isolating a mutant of E. coli that was deficient in its ability to accumulate potassium. It was unable to grow in potassium deficient culture media while the parent strain readily grew in the same media. With the mutant now isolated, I dedicated my remaining time at Harvard to fractionating the proteins of both the parent strain and mutant bacteria in search of the protein that was dissimilar between the two.

After six more months in Boston fractionating proteins, sadly I remained unsuccessful in my efforts to isolate a dissimilar protein pair from the parent and mutant bacteria. At this time I had moved to the School of Aerospace Medicine of the United States Air Force in San Antonio, Texas. The Vietnam War was in full swing at this time, and it was there that I would fulfill my military obligation.

This military service fell under the Government's "Berry Plan," or what could be described as a "Doctor's Draft." Basically, it meant that doctors could join the military branch of their choice (in my case, the Air Force) and receive full residency training in a chosen specialty. The tradeoff was that since the military wanted and needed more doctors with advanced specialty training, they would also receive the benefit of the doctor's training and education. Gratefully, my commanding officer, Colonel Lou Bitter, encouraged me to continue my research on the E. coli potassium transport mutant and the search for the "sodium pump." The tradeoff was that I was to include hydrazine in my research to simultaneously assess the cellular toxicity of this rocket fuel that the School of Aerospace was committed to investigate. Doing this benefited both myself and my country, which I was more than happy to do.

While doing research at Brooks Air Force Base, I came to the conclusion of the *ion exchange phenomena*. In other words, how does the cell build up such a large gradient of the same ion between the intracellular environment (inside the cell) and the extracellular environment (outside the cell)? By what mechanism was it able to distinguish between sodium and potassium on the outside of the cell and then opt for potassium? And what role did metabolism play in this phenomena? I still didn't have the answers I was searching for.

After being discharged from the Air Force in 1967, I weighed options from a number of universities before finally deciding to return to Downstate Medical Center in Brooklyn. There, I joined two departments: the Biophysics Department (chaired by Dr. Dreizen) and the Department of Internal Medicine (chaired by Dr. Eichna). At Downstate I would have plenty of opportunity to continue my research. I also taught biophysics in the graduate school where I was assigned 3 or 4 grad students. Apart from all these obligations, I wasn't very busy at all!

Dr. Eichna was the person most instrumental in getting me back to Downstate. He was the same man who had recommended me for my position at Harvard. Eichna firmly believed that one day researchers would play a strategic role in patient care. He also was a huge supporter of my research, which I quickly dove back into. It was nothing for me to work long hours with little or no break, as I was consumed by my work.

Not long after returning to Downstate, I ran an ad for a "tech." That's when I met and hired Mike Goldsmith, a big man with a brilliant mind. Mike topped the scales at over 300 lbs. He had a degree in chemistry and wanted to get his PhD under me. Then I added a student by the name of Larry Minkoff, another very gifted guy who had enrolled as a graduate student in physics. Larry still works with me today at FONAR Corporation as Senior Research Scientist. These men became the core of our MRI team. But the dynamic of our working relationship proved to be what you might call at times *interesting*. Mike and Larry didn't always see eye-to-eye, which resulted in them not always getting along. Both were extremely competitive men with conflicting personalities. Mike was the more scholarly of the two, while Larry, though also brilliantly gifted, was equally adept at building things. But despite their differences and disagreements, both became integral members of my team, working tirelessly with me to develop and build the first-ever MRI scanner.

But to my surprise, what we eventually discovered together in our research was that it was *intracellular* water that exercised the cell's control over the potassium/sodium exchange. The amount of water inside the cell and its structure were the dominant factors in controlling the cell's selectivity for the ions and its power to generate an electric voltage. This was important research at the time, and the results of our research were published in a paper titled, "Caloric Catastrophe."

Let's just say it "ruffled a lot of feathers." And here's why. Central to all of this research was the importance of the cell's water itself, which few researchers had considered at that time. Water is a dipole, and potassium and sodium are the dominant alkali metals regulating the cell's voltage generation. The bigger molecules with the largest surface area attract less water than the smaller ones, because the smaller ones have a greater charge density (volts per square centimeter) of charge. The smaller ions in a hydrated state end up with the greater number of water dipoles attached to them (their hydration atmosphere) because their higher concentration of electric charge (charge density) attracts more water dipoles. In terms of selectivity, if a cell has a limit as to how much water it can hold because of its anatomic size, then it will choose the ions that are smallest (i.e., the ions that have the smallest hydration atmosphere). Potassium is a larger molecule than sodium but has the same 1+ charge. As a larger atom than sodium, potassium has a larger surface area (mm^2). It however has the same 1+ charge the sodium has. Accordingly, potassium's charge per unit of surface area (e.g. volts per cm^2), its "charge density," is less than the sodium ion's charge density. If the two choices confronting a cell are sodium and potassium, the cell will choose potassium over sodium, since the fully hydrated potassium ion is smaller than the fully hydrated sodium. This is because potassium's lower charge density attracts fewer water electric dipoles to its surface than the sodium ion does. Accordingly, the potassium ion has a smaller hydration atmosphere than the sodium ion, with the result that the fully hydrated potassium ion is smaller than the fully hydrated sodium ion and accordingly takes up less space within the cell.

Also, when cells die, they relax and fill up with water. I reasoned that a controlling mechanism regulating the volume of water in a cell (the cell's tonus, known as cytotonus), would therefore also control the *volume* of the cell, and the loss of cytotonus following cell death would cause the cell to fill with water and swell.

All of this drove me in my effort to find the difference between healthy cells and cancerous cells.

More specifically, I was trying to successfully isolate the sodium/potassium "pump" from the parent and potassium transport mutant of

E. coli, which should have yielded such a pump protein.[2] But my three years of failed attempts to do this is what caused me to consider "pump free" alternate mechanisms for cellular potassium (ion) accumulation. My efforts in this chemical obsession drove me to spend a lot of time in the library. One day while browsing through the chemistry section there, I stumbled on a book titled *Ion Exchange* by Friedrich Helfferich, a German scientist at the University of California at Berkeley. Achieving the correct ion exchanges that enables the living cell to successfully generate the proper voltages is fundamental to the physiology of life itself. In ion exchange resins, as Helfferich details, the exchange of two electrolyte ions like the positively charged potassium and sodium ions is usually the exchange of an ion in aqueous (water) solution with an ion "complexed" to an oppositely charged (negatively charged) "fixed charge" that is part of the ion exchange resin's structure. The actual ion exchanges depend on the size of the ions, their charge, and their physical structure.

Though Helfferich's book had nothing to do with medicine, it did, however, have a profound impact on me. The book basically helped me to realize I should stop looking for the sodium pump. This conclusion was in direct contradiction to the "sodium pump" hypothesis proposed by Alan Lloyd Hodgkin, Andrew Huxley, and John Eccles, all of whom shared the 1963 Nobel Prize in Physiology or Medicine. In their hypothesis, Hodgkin and Huxley had proposed the existence of a molecule situated on the membrane of the cell that "pumped out" unwanted sodium and "pumped in" potassium.

But Helfferich's book, on the other hand, while not dealing with living matter, achieved the same ion exchanges in ion exchange resin beads (to a lesser degree than the living cell) *without* a "sodium pump." His book radically changed my thinking and approach toward my goal. The living cell could operate without a "sodium pump" and selectively accumulate ion in the same way an ion exchange resin bead selectively accumulates ions, i.e., by their attachment to oppositely charged molecules that were part of the cell's structure (e.g., protein carboxlates, nucleic acid phosphates). Without the new insight achieved from Helfferich's *Ion Exchange*, I might have looked for the sodium pump for years and never found it.

During my time in the library I discovered another key to the puzzle by Dr. Gilbert Ling, a distinguished Chinese-American professor of

Figure 15. Professor Gilbert Ning Ling, scientist /author of *A Physical Theory of the Living State: the Association-Induction Hypothesis* (London: Blaisdell Publishing Co., A Division of Random House, Inc., 1962,) in which Dr. Ling provided extensive theoretical and experimental evidence that cellular ion accumulation was occurring without an ion "pump" (i.e., the "sodium pump") but instead by "association" of the ions to counter-ions within the cell that were part of the cell's structure (i.e., negatively charged protein carboxylate ions).

physiology (figure 15). Dr. Ling had published in 1962 a comprehensive treatise on the ion exchanges of living systems, i.e., living cells and living tissue. In his book *A Physical Theory of the Living State*, he also provided evidence that cellular ions were accumulating within living cells by "associating" with fixed counter-ions within the cell without the participation of a sodium pump.

In April 1969 I attended a convention for the Federation of American Societies of Experimental Biology in Atlantic City, New Jersey. At this convention, I made some key connections, not the least of which was finally meeting Dr. Ling. One evening Dr. Ling and I dined at Zaberer's restaurant in Philadelphia. Joining us were Dr. Carlton Hazelwood and Dr. Freeman Cope, both devoted followers of Dr. Ling. I liked them both. The dinner conversation that evening was beyond stimulating. But I needed to go beyond conversation to solid research.

As graduate students at Downstate, Michael Goldsmith and Larry Minkoff had joined my research on different aspects of the physiology of the cellular *ion exchange* phenomenon as the subjects for their doctoral research. Their research effort constituted culturing large quantities of the bacteria, fractionating and carrying out electrophoresis of their bacterial proteins. It also involved measuring the metabolic energy expended by these bacteria during the process of selective ion accumulation and carrying out NMR analyses of these bacterial samples in small-bore field superconducting magnets, all in search of the "sodium pump" protein.

Unfortunately, all these efforts proved to be in vain.

Bottom line: no "sodium pump" protein was to be found! Our conclusion was that the living cell must have another means by which it achieves the intracellular selective ion accumulations with potassium as the dominant ion that is responsible for generating the "voltage of life." This led me to propose an alternative, which I called the "Cell Ion Exchanger Resin Theory." This theory was published along with our findings based on our mutant and parent chemical research. In this model, the concept of a membrane-bound "sodium pump" was totally abandoned. Instead, we attributed the cell's selective ion accumulation to an *ion exchange resin process*.[3]

While in the course of these studies, I received a phone call from Dr. Freeman Widener Cope of the Naval Air Development Center in Doylestown, Pennsylvania. Dr. Cope, a research scientist for the Navy, was an MD who had received his medical degree from Johns Hopkins and an undergraduate degree in math and physics from Harvard. He was calling to ask if I was interested in collaborating with him on a research project to determine if my hypothesis for the cellular accumulation of potassium could be experimentally verified. He himself had been experimenting with what he termed at the time "the new NMR technology," which he had used to measure sodium in whole tissue. He asked if I would be interested in testing my hypothesis that potassium ions were being accumulated within living cells by their attachment to the cell's "fixed" negative charges. Dr. Cope (figure 16) had gained access to a new NMR technology, "Pulse NMR," at a small company called "NMR Specialties" in New Kensington, Pennsylvania. This technology was capable of measuring the decay time ("relaxation time") of the nuclear resonance signal emitted by an atom. Cope maintained that the NMR decay time of a cellular potassium atom should be greatly shortened if it was indeed "complexed" to a "fixed" negative ion instead of being in free solution as I was hypothesizing in my "Ion Exchange Resin Theory."

Realizing that this new NMR technology might indeed contribute a valuable insight into the physiological properties of this cell voltage generating ion, I agreed. Cope then raised concerns regarding the feasibility of such direct experimental NMR measurements of the cell potassium

Figure 16. Raymond Damadian with his NMR collaborator and his teacher of NMR technology, Freeman Widener Cope, MD

ion. His first concern was that an NMR signal from an intracellular potassium atom might not be achievable because its magnetic moment was significantly lower than the magnetic moment of the customary hydrogen most commonly examined by NMR.

Additionally, the potassium concentration within the living cell was significantly reduced relative to the sample atom concentrations normally measured by test tube NMR. This further diminished the prospects of achieving a detectable K^{39} NMR signal from a "live" tissue sample.

I responded to Cope's concern, informing him that I might be able to provide a cellular sample that could help offset these deficiencies. I reported that I was aware of a bacteria from the Dead Sea, called Halobacter halobium, that possessed 20 times the normal intracellular potassium content. Cope's immediate inquiry was, "Damadian, can you obtain such a bacteria?" I indicated that it was possible I could, but that I would have to search the literature for a source, which I ultimately found.

When the samples arrived, Cope and I proceeded to New Kensington and NMR Specialties to see if we could successfully measure the

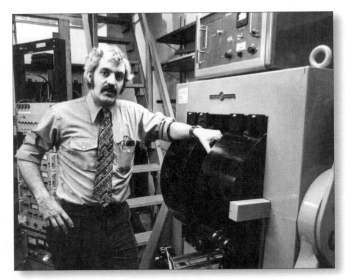

Figure 17. Raymond Damadian with the NMR Specialties magnet used with Dr. Cope

intracellular K^{39} NMR signal relaxation time of our Halobacter bacterium. We further hoped to verify that cell potassium was "complexed" to counter-ions within the cell, as opposed to being in "free-solution" as envisioned by the standard membrane "pump" theory.

Cope went to NMR Specialties to calibrate the NMR apparatus for our measurements. I continued on to the laboratory of my friend and colleague, Dr. Stanley Schultz, who was Professor of Physiology at the University of Pittsburgh at the time. Securing a large 30-liter culture vessel, I proceeded to grow up my Halobacter halobium in sufficient quantity to generate enough of a centrifuged test-tube pellet of Halobacter for the NMR measurement. This would allow a non-invasive NMR measurement of its cellular potassium content and its K^{39} NMR relaxation. Arriving at NMR Specialties, I presented my test-tube Halobacter sample to Dr. Cope so he could insert it into the NMR Specialties "pulse" NMR (figures 17 and 18) and measure its K^{39} NMR "relaxation" time.

The result was that it was dramatically shortened!

Indeed, K^{39} was "complexed" to "fixed" counter-ions within the cell and not in "free-solution," as presumed by the conventional sodium/potassium "pump" model.

Even more dramatically, though, I was astounded by what Dr. Cope had just achieved with my K^{39} bacteria.

Within seconds using NMR, he was *non-invasively* and accurately measuring the cell's potassium with an antenna wrapped around the

Figure 18. The 2¼" magnet gap technology available for test tube NMR samples at the time of Dr. Damadian's original experiments

outside of the test-tube. By doing this, he made a measurement that normally took me *days* by conventional wet chemistry and flame photometry.

"Freeman," I said, "I can't believe what you just did. In just a few seconds, you measured the potassium of my bacteria by this NMR technology with an antenna (figure 18) wrapped entirely around the *outside* of the sample. Without any invasion whatsoever of the sample itself, you measured the chemistry of a compound within the intact *interior* of a living cell entirely *non-invasively.*"

I continued, "Do you realize that if we could do such a thing on the human body with antennae external to the body we would be able to track down the live chemistry of any tissue within the body non-invasively? This would spark an unprecedented revolution in medicine."

In my mind, I pondered the prospect of Freeman collaborating with me in the venture. In front of us was our test tube, positioned within the 2¼" sample gap (figure 18) of our NMR magnet.

"A heroic prospect, Raymond," Cope replied. "But you would have to take this test tube magnet and build it big enough to put a human being into and then actually get it to generate an NMR signal from atoms deep within the anatomy." He added, "That would be a giant long shot."

Pausing, he said, "Furthermore, I can't imagine where you would even start. What experiment would you do first?"

I confidently confessed, "Freeman, I have an idea. What we should do for the first experiment is make NMR measurements on *cancer* tissue, because if they worked, nobody could outright arbitrarily reject our findings because of the *seriousness* of the disease. Moreover, if successful, it would be hard for the "GSQ's", the "Guardians of the Status Quo," to discredit the measurements because they will be easily reproducible by anyone who would question them."

I was hoping my passion, enthusiasm, and vision would persuade Dr. Cope to join me in the venture.

His curiosity aroused, he stated, "Raymond. What makes you think there would be any NMR difference between cancer and normal tissue in the first place?"

"There I think, Freeman, we've got a shot," I replied.

"I think if we are successful in demonstrating a difference in cancer tissue, we will have a potent response to the next objection they will be sure to generate, namely the absurdity of changing a 2¼-inch test-tube analyzer into an analyzer of the entire human body. With a demonstration that an NMR signal can be obtained from cancer tissue that is distinguishable from healthy tissue, the 'absurdity' contention regarding the construction of an NMR apparatus large enough to scan the live human body will be offset by the significance of the finding itself and its potential for contributing materially to the understanding of this disease! The financial risk of investing in the construction of an unachievable NMR scanner that is technologically beyond reach will be justified by the scanner's potential to dramatically enhance the successful outcome of patients afflicted with a disease that causes such agony."

Freeman wasn't yet convinced, and repeated his earlier question, "But what makes you think there will be any difference between the NMR signals from cancer tissue and normal tissue?"

I replied, "I think we have a reasonable prospect. I know from a lot of reading on the subject that the potassium and sodium content of cancer tissues is distinctly abnormal relative to normal tissue."

I continued presenting my case, arguing, "In my own tissue ion exchange experiments, I've never come across a situation where the ion composition of a sample is significantly altered and the 'water structure' as measured by the proton NMR relaxations of the sample is not *also* altered. Moreover, the water structure, such as determined from the water proton NMR relaxation of the cancer tissue can be readily measured by proton NMR. I expect it to be markedly altered relative to the water proton NMR relaxations of normal tissue."

Though I was confident and clear in my direction and hypothesis, I unfortunately could not induce Dr. Cope to collaborate with me in this venture. This prompted me in June 1970 to go directly to Paul Yajko, president and founder of the small NMR company, NMR Specialties Corp., where Freeman and I were carrying out our K^{39} NMR measurements. I asked him if I could return to Long Island, grow up some rats with cancers and return with them to New Kensington to measure the water proton NMR relaxations of their excised cancer tissues and normal tissues. Gratefully, Paul agreed, provided I would not require any assistance from members of his staff in the actual making of the NMR measurements.

A few weeks later I returned with rats bearing Walker sarcoma tumors. After calibrating my own reliability regarding the NMR measurements (since Freeman had performed all the NMR measurements on the Halobacter Halobium bacteria), I then placed the Walker sarcoma test tube samples excised from the rats into the magnet and held my breath. To my astonishment, notwithstanding my hypothesis that they should be different, cancers and normals were actually dramatically different in their NMR signals!

Moreover, (and happily unexpected), the normal tissues themselves *also* differed markedly in their NMR signals. Normal small intestine had a T_1 relaxation time, for example, of 257 milliseconds, while normal brain tissue had a T_1 relaxation of 595 milliseconds. The other normal tissue T_1 relaxations ranged in between. Ultimately, the pronounced differences in the NMR relaxations of the normal tissues became the origin of the exceptional soft tissue contrast that has revolutionized medical imaging.

For the first time in medical history, we would now have access to detailed visualization of the body's life-giving soft tissue vital organs (brain, heart, kidney, liver, spleen, pancreas, small intestine, etc.).

My research encouraged me, indicating that lives would be changed by this budding development. Even the world of medicine itself would never be the same. This could potentially be a breakthrough of hope for millions of suffering people.

All this from science and a single idea.

Endnotes

1. An ion is an electrically charged atom, e.g., the potassium ion (K+) that is the potassium atom carrying a 1+ charge.

2. A protein in the mutant when compared to the proteins of the parent strain that was either lacking altogether in the mutant or was degenerated, thereby accounting for the mutant's failure to pump potassium.

3. The 1+ positive potassium ion accumulated within the cell by attaching to the fixed negative charges within the cell. The negative charges on these macromolecules, namely the negative (1-) carboxyl and phosphate ions that were abundantly distributed on the cell's proteins (carboxyl) and nucleic acids (phosphates) respectively. The means by which these cellular ion exchanges achieved the cell's selection of the 1+ potassium ion over the 1+ sodium was presumed to be due to the smaller space-occupying diameter of the fully hydrated potassium ion over the fully hydrated diameter of the sodium ion.

CHAPTER

4

GRIT AND DETERMINATION

I t's been said that anything worth having is worth working for, and that anything worth doing is worth doing well. Over time, I have seen how those maxims have played themselves out in my life, leading many people to describe me as *Determined. Driven. Focused. Impatient. Intense.* Even *Obsessed.*

Guilty on all counts.

One reason people see me this way is because many years ago I developed a work ethic which fueled my full devotion to my work, sometimes translating into 24, 48, even 72 hours without sleep.

But this kind of dedication doesn't come without sacrifice. Unfortunately, those long hours in the laboratory often kept me away from home more than I would have preferred. The time and energy required in medical research can only be described as "brutal and relentless." Thankfully, I have been blessed with an understanding and supportive wife. By nature a nurturing woman, Donna nevertheless bore much of the burden in raising our children during my absences. Though parenting is a partnership, the value and contribution of a mother cannot be overstated. Their role inestimably impacts the lives of their children in ways a father cannot. And in many cases, such as those medically employed or militarily deployed, these remarkable women are forced to wear two hats, assuming the role of both mother and father for a time. I stand in awe of them, especially my own dear bride.

June 1970 was one of those times I was away for an extended period as I headed back to New Kensington to the same place where Freeman Cope and I had conducted our potassium tissue research. My goal was to see if the NMR signals emitted by the tumors excised from them differed from the NMR signals generated by excised healthy tissue. If they did, it would mean that such nuclear radio signals indicative of cancer would be generated when the anatomy was inside an NMR magnet and detected by placing the antenna externally on the body. In other words, we could see and detect cancer inside the human body without any type of surgery.

Cope and I used a *pulse NMR machine* that delivered the radiofrequency (rf) transmissions. These (rf) transmissions excited the sample atoms (nuclei) in pulses. This was in place of the uninterrupted steady stream of rf used to obtain the spectra of NMR *spectroscopy*. A pulsed NMR machine allows the researcher to watch the signals produced by the sample atoms (nuclei) over time. This enables measurements of the nuclear resonance signals *decay* time (or "relaxation time"). This pulsed radio frequency method gave us a direct accurate measure of the nuclear signal's "relaxation time" instead of indirectly *estimating* it from NMR spectra.[1] In the spectroscopy technology utilized by chemists to analyze the chemical composition of liquid test-tube samples, the vast majority of NMR determinations being made at the time measured the frequency responses of the molecules of the sample, *not* the time decay rates of the resonance signals.

On June 18, 1970 (figure 19), I took the next step. A *big* one. On that day, I attempted my first cancer measurement. This would be it, a make or break moment in my research. I was hoping to see a significant difference in the cancer tissue reading as compared to the normal tissue reading.

And to my excitement, it *was* different! *Wow!*

Even so, I had to be certain. Fearful that I had done something wrong, I repeated the test numerous times. Each time the reading was the same. The T_1 measurements obtained from cancers were genuinely higher than those obtained from normal tissue. Suddenly, the actual prospect of an NMR apparatus to scan the live human body and detect cancer signals from within it was breathing signs of reality! I spent one week of experiments verifying the reproducibility of the differences I was finding between the NMR signals emitted by cancer tissue and the NMR signals emitted by healthy tissue. Having successfully done this, I assured myself the T_1 differences I was measuring between the signals of

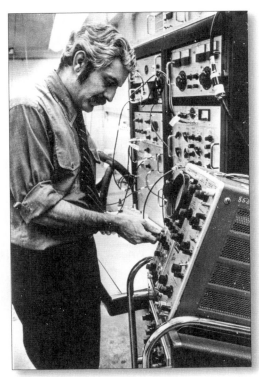

Figure 19 The NMR apparatus used by Raymond Damadian in his initial T_1 and T_2 measurements of cancer and normal tissues (chapter 8)

cancerous and normal tissues were genuine and not the result of any measurement errors in my determinations. That would have been disastrous if true. But it wasn't.

I left New Kensington elated about my results, which had led me to a confirmed discovery. The enhanced NMR relaxations (T_1/T_2) of cancer tissue I had observed indicated that my "far-out idea" to take this test tube analyzer and build it into an NMR apparatus for scanning the live human body to detect cancers was now a viable idea! Still, I needed confirmation on other types from more samples of different cancers. So I returned to Brooklyn and grew rats with the Novikoff hepatoma. In my mind, this would prove the trustworthiness of the NMR results. When those results came back positive, I finalized my paper, entitled "Tumor Detection by Nuclear Magnetic Resonance" for *Science* magazine. The article appeared in the March 19, 1971, issue[2] (figures 21 and 22).

In what was considered a groundbreaking article, I wrote that our findings had valuable applications in anti-cancer technology. Further, it indicated that our findings supported the concept of proceeding with the development of instrumentation (a machine apparatus) and probes that could be used to scan the human body externally to detect early signs of malignancy (cancer).

Up to this point, doctors only had x-rays to see inside the human body. An x-ray works by passing a beam *through* the body's tissues. In the same way, a CT (or CAT) scan x-rays the body from different angles,

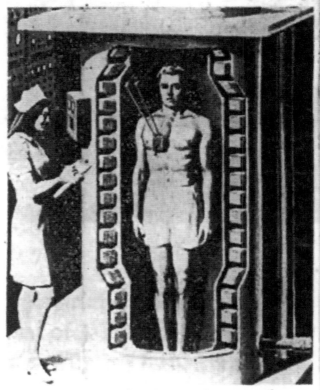

The New York Times

SATURDAY, FEBRUARY 9, 1974

Cancer Found Electronically

Distinct Signals Sent by Atoms From Cells

By STACY V. JONES
Special to The New York Times

WASHINGTON, Feb. 8 — A university scientist has discovered an electronic method of detecting cancer. Dr. Raymond V. Damadian, professor of biophysics at the State University's Downstate Medical Center in Brooklyn, was granted a patent this week for the apparatus and method. As Dr. Damadian explains, radio signals distinguish cancer tissue from normal tissue. Atoms from the cancer cells serve as transmitters, sending signals with distinct wavelengths.

According to Patent 3,789,-832, early detection of cancer is now hampered by the fact that many tumors are permeable to X-rays and are

Patents of the Week

Rendering shows patient in a nuclear magnetic reso-

Figure 20. *New York Times* report (above and on following page) of Dr. Damadian's discovery of the abnormal T_1 and T_2 values of cancer tissue measured by NMR

have pushed aside normal parts of the body. The new process employs nuclear magnetic resonance, not X-rays.

In one procedure, small samples of surgically removed tissue are tested for the presence of cancer cells; their quantity may indicate the degree of malignancy. Dr. Damadian has tested successfully 106 specimens obtained from the Sloan-Kettering Memorial Hospital.

A second method, also covered by the patent, is to flood the body with radiation and conduct tests without surgery. So far, this has succeeded with mice, but the apparatus for human examination is still under development.

Dr. Damadian says that, by studying the frequencies given off by different atoms, the complete chemistry of tissue can be determined.

The patented method is intended for use in clinical and diagnostic laboratories and in the operating room.

Besides his medical degree, the inventor has had advanced training at Harvard in physics, electronics and physical chemistry.

Dr. Raymond V. Damadian of State University's Downstate Medical Center in Brooklyn invented device.

producing more of a multi-dimensional image. But unfortunately, in both the simple x-ray and the x-ray CT scan, the patient is exposed to radiation, while an MRI uses *zero* radiation. An x-ray takes a few seconds compared to an x-ray CT scan which takes around five minutes, while a full MRI scan requires anywhere from ten minutes up to an hour or more. Additionally, x-rays and x-ray CT scans are best suited for looking at bones, lung, and chest imaging. However, the MRI can produce high resolution images of *soft tissue organs* — ligaments, tendons, spinal cord, brain, liver, kidneys, heart, pancreas, etc. — allowing us to identify diseased cells and tissue, such as cancer. And all this is done without even touching the patient. That's what we mean by "non-invasive."

With that as background, the problem that medical x-ray imaging had been impaired by, ever since Roentgen's 1895 invention, was that the difference between the passage of x-rays through the body's normal tissues and its passage through cancerous tissues was very small. In other words, when these x-ray and x-ray CT scans were visualized as images, the image contrast (visibility) between the tumors and surrounding normal tissues was poor. This meant tumors were virtually indistinguishable by x-ray from other soft tissues like the body's soft tissue vital organs. They were thus being unsatisfactorily visualized and detected by conventional x-ray technology. Bones and soft tissues, on the other hand, had very different x-ray penetration because of the tissue density difference between bone and soft tissue. X-ray images produced sharp contrast between bone and surrounding soft tissue because of the x-ray penetration differences of the two, thus providing excellent bone visualization by x-ray. Science needed to come up with a better idea. A more innovative technology. A better way.

Reprinted from
19 March 1971 Volume 171, pp. 1151-1153

SCIENCE

Tumor Detection by Nuclear Magnetic Resonance

Abstract. *Spin echo nuclear magnetic resonance measurements may be used as a method for discriminating between malignant tumors and normal tissue. Measurements of spin-lattice (T_1) and spin-spin (T_2) magnetic relaxation times were made in six normal tissues in the rat (muscle, kidney, stomach, intestine, brain, and liver) and in two malignant solid tumors, Walker sarcoma and Novikoff hepatoma. Relaxation times for the two malignant tumors were distinctly outside the range of values for the normal tissues studied, an indication that the malignant tissues were characterized by an increase in the motional freedom of tissue water molecules. The possibility of using magnetic relaxation methods for rapid discrimination between benign and malignant surgical specimens has also been considered. Spin-lattice relaxation times for two benign fibroadenomas were distinct from those for both malignant tissues and were the same as those of muscle.*

At present, early detection of internal neoplasms is hampered by the relatively high permeability of many tumors to x-rays. In principle, nuclear magnetic resonance (NMR) techniques combine many of the desirable features of an external probe for the detection of internal cancer. Magnetic resonance measurements cause no obvious deleterious effects on biologic tissue (*1*), the inci- plastic tissues could be recognized from their NMR signals, I studied the proton resonance emissions from cell water. Recent NMR work of Cope (*2*), Hazlewood *et al.* (*3*), and Bratton *et al.* (*4*) has provided fresh insight into the physical nature of cell water. These authors have independently concluded that the decreased NMR relaxation times observed for cell water relative

Figure 21. Dr. Damadian's 1971 publication in *Science* of his discovery of the abnormal T_1 and T_2 values of cancer tissue that originated the MRI and provided the NMR (MRI) signals to make the image (chapter 10)

Necessity has been called the "Mother of Invention," but in this case that necessity was made clearer by the inability of existing scientific technology. Our discovery of the pronounced T_1 and T_2 NMR relaxation differences between cancers and the body's normal soft tissues, and between the normal tissues themselves provided for the *first time* in the history of medical imaging the pixel contrast needed to visualize this distinguishing detail.[3] The marked variation of the NMR relaxations among healthy tissue as reported in our 1971 *Science* paper is the reason that NMR can now reveal such exceptional anatomic detail in the MRI images of these life-giving vital organs. As the source of the extraordinary contrast range made possible by the pronounced range of relaxation values observed for the first time among the body's healthy tissues, these diverse tissue relaxations enabled MRI to picture the anatomy of these soft tissue vital organs with far more detail than had ever before been possible in medical imaging.

For many, understandably this is pretty heady stuff, so let me try and simplify. T_1 and T_2 function as contrast agents allowing us (through MRI) to determine if a spot inside the body is a tumor or possibly a fluid (such as blood). All of this was important for us to discover and understand before moving forward.

The Discovery of the Abnormal Cancer (1971) MR Relaxation
Rodent T1 Relaxations* (Hydrogen) [seconds]

Tissue	Normal	Tumor
Brain	0.595	
Muscle	0.538	0.736
Kidney	0.480	
Liver	0.293	0.826
Stomach	0.270	
Intestine	0.257	

R. Damadian, M.D.
Science (1971) 171, 1151

[Experiments performed June–July 1970]

* Decay Time of the MR Signal

Figure 22. Dr. Damadian's publication in *Science* that reported the elevated T_1 NMR relaxation times of cancerous tissue as compared to normal, as well as the pronounced differences of the T_1 relaxation times among the normal tissues themselves

Another important aspect of achieving NMR scanning of the live human body was the need to be able to *identify* the volume elements (voxels) within the body that were generating the abnormal cancer signals so that the cancers could be removed. The NMR body scanner I envisioned would detect cancers using an antenna wrapped around the torso. However, because this antenna would detect ALL the NMR signals being generated by the body's atoms, it was necessary to be able to identify where those tissues generating the abnormal signals were located. This is referred to as "spatial localization." In order to achieve the spatial localization of the nuclear resonance signal needed to perform a scan, we needed to engineer some discrete location, a "focused spot," within the MRI magnet that would generate a spatially localized NMR signal. This was done by shaping the magnetic field within the magnet as well as the magnetic field of the radio frequency transmission itself. Doing this created the conditions necessary to generate a spatially localized *nuclear resonance signal*.[4] I knew we could make a machine big enough to put a human inside, and my paper was the first to suggest such an idea. I reasoned it should work for detecting cancer in the live human body if we moved the body stepwise across the spatially localized focused resonance location in the magnet. We knew even then that when dealing with a disease such as cancer, early detection was the key.

We just needed to figure out how to construct a body scanner to accomplish it.

The problem we faced is that the scientific community is unduly conservative when it comes to new ideas, especially bold ones like ours: converting a 2¼" test tube analyzer (figure 18) to a full-sized scanner of the human body. And understandably so. This concept engendered a lot of questions, and legitimate ones at that.

In writing the paper that appeared in *Science* (figures 21 and 22), I knew I had to express my concept of an NMR body scanner as conservatively as possible or else the reviewers of the article would reject it. In other words, I had to be careful in the way I "sold" the concept to the medical community. And yet, despite toning down my original article, the paper was nevertheless met with great resistance. The reaction ranged from "hare brained" to "simply impossible." That is except for Dr. Olson (Kenneth B. Olson, MD) (figure 23). Dr. Olson had just been appointed to head a new division of the National Cancer Institute (NCI) of the National Institutes of Health (NIH), the Cancer Diagnosis

Figure 23. Dr. Kenneth Olson, Chairman of the Cancer Diagnosis Division of the National Institutes of Health (NIH) that funded further investigation in human tumors of the abnormal T_1 and T_2 values in rat tumors discovered by Dr. Damadian

Division. The division was initiated by the National Cancer Institute to advance the technologies of cancer detection and cancer diagnosis to facilitate earlier diagnosis and detection and optimize the outcomes of treatment. Having read my publication in *Science*, Dr. Olson wanted the Cancer Diagnosis Division of the NCI to fund our new discovery of NMR's power to detect cancer in tissue and ultimately, if further and more detailed NMR research on cancer tissue was successful, to then further the program to fund construction of an NMR body scanner to detect cancers *in vivo*. At Dr. Olson's direction, three two-year grants were awarded, one to us at the SUNY Downstate Medical Center (Brooklyn, NY), one to a scientist at the Baylor College of Medicine (Houston, TX), and one to a scientist at the Johns Hopkins Medical Center (Baltimore, MD).

With the grants awarded, Dr. Olson organized an international symposium on cancer diagnosis in Bethesda, Maryland, a year later (1976), sponsored by the National Cancer Institute. Cancer scientists from all over the world attended. The conference addressed research in the full subject of cancer diagnosis, of which the NMR investigations were a part.

In the conference segment on NMR detection, I presented the first paper and we were grateful to be able to show the first image of a cancer in a live mouse. Dr. Carlton Hazelwood from Baylor presented his tissue NMR data confirming that he had obtained the same elevated NMR relaxation measurements of cancer tissue that we had.

The Johns Hopkins scientist then presented his findings to the conference. He reported that "his measurements of the NMR relaxations of cancer showed the same elevated relaxation times in cancer tissue as observed by Damadian, but that the measured NMR relaxation times of diseased tissues that were not cancerous were also elevated," whereupon he concluded with the statement *"Therefore any further discussion of scanning the human body by NMR is visionary nonsense."* What the Johns Hopkins scientist had overlooked was that *both* the cancerous tissues and the non-cancerous tissues had NMR relaxation times that were elevated relative to the NMR relaxations of normal tissue. Thus, when the elevated NMR signal relaxations and their resulting signal amplitude elevations were employed to set the brightness of the image pixels that make up the image, the pixels of both the cancerous tissue and the non-malignant *diseased* tissues would be brighter than the pixels of the surrounding normal tissues because of their elevated relaxation times, making them eminently more visible in the final image than the surrounding normal tissues and eminently detectable. Upon that comment and its *"visionary nonsense,"* three hands in the audience instantly shot up.

The first questioner stated, "Now Doctor, if you just tell us where to put the needle, we are way ahead of where we are today." What the questioner was stating was that with the poor soft tissue visualization provided by conventional x-ray technology because of the poor soft tissue contrast of x-ray images, diseased tissue of all kinds, cancerous as well as non-cancerous, were being missed by conventional medical imaging and that the NMR's potential for improved visualization of these diseased soft tissues could overcome this longstanding deficiency in medical imaging. Cancerous as well as non-cancerous diseased tissues would become eminently visible on MRI pictures and enable an examiner to spatially locate a lesion within the anatomy, e.g., within the abdomen, so a needle biopsy of the visualized lesion could be performed to establish malignancy, or lack of it, so that the visualized lesion could be effectively treated. Other Johns Hopkins scientists disagreed with the assertion of *"visionary nonsense,"* and articulated their disagreements at more than one MRI conference.

Interestingly, the same argument was asserted by GE in the 1995 FONAR v. GE trial on the infringement of my original 1974, '832 MRI patent. During trial, GE's attorneys made the argument that the elevated NMR relaxations of cancer tissue were not unique to cancerous tissues but were also elevated in diseased tissues that were not malignant. FONAR's attorneys responded by saying, *"Ladies and gentlemen of the jury, are you going to punish the guy because his patented discovery detects more diseased tissues than he originally envisioned?"* The jury agreed.

Additionally, at the time, NMR spectroscopes spun test tube samples (figure 18) at 10,000 rpm to achieve the necessary homogenization of the magnet's magnetic field to accomplish the frequency resolution needed for high resolution NMR molecular spectroscopy. This was an issue with some who read the paper. At one of the NMR conferences at which I was asked to present our findings, the chair of the conference at the conclusion of my presentation asked, *"Now, Doctor, how fast do you propose to spin the patient?"* Obviously, I had no intention of "spinning the patient." Rather, I believed we would achieve the necessary magnetic homogeneity for scanning by other technologies (e.g., "shim coils").

Unlike my esteemed colleagues in the scientific community, I was convinced we were on the verge of something huge, and I had just the team that could make it happen. All we needed was construction of the necessary equipment to scan the human body and, of course, the funds required to achieve it. I would soon find out that neither was easy to obtain.

Eleven days after I returned from my experiments with Dr. Cope in 1969, I wrote a letter to Dr. George Mirick of the Health Research Council of the City of New York, requesting $89,000 to purchase the pulsed NMR spectrometer needed to continue the NMR experiments in my laboratory at Downstate (figure 24).

I believed that in time the MRI would change the landscape of medicine, and I was right. After the initial ridicule, others soon began to realize the same thing. Before long, we had competitors for the funds we needed to proceed. Our 1971 publication in *Science* had generated worldwide interest. A host of scientific groups now wanted to pursue the research and wanted the funds to enable it. In one sense, it was a race not unlike the space race between the United States and the Soviet Union in the 1950s and 1960s. It was all about who would get there first, and subsequently claim "bragging rights." After my story appeared in *Science*, a few even took the information and started research of their own. Some credited me, some didn't. Either way, it has been conclusively proven over the years that we were the *first*. And that was key to achieving the further research needed to accomplish construction of the NMR body scanner we envisioned. It's also crucial for the acknowledgement of scientific priority, which greatly influences the future academic scientific careers of scientists continuing in research.

STATE UNIVERSITY OF NEW YORK

DOWNSTATE MEDICAL CENTER

BIOPHYSICAL LABORATORY
• DEPARTMENT OF MEDICINE

September 17, 1969

George S. Mirick, M.D.
Scientific Director
The Health Research Council
  of the City of New York
Department of Health
455 First Avenue
New York, New York 10016

Dear Dr. Mirick:

In accord with our telephone conversation of September 16, 1969, I am forwarding a letter describing the success of our "Pittsburgh Experiment" and the request for support it has inspired.

On August 21, 1969, Dr. Freeman Cope and I left for a small company (Nuclear Magnetic Resonance Specialties Corporation) on the outskirts of Pittsburgh with the remote hope that we could measure potassium by NMR spectroscopy and establish, once and for all, that cell potassium is not free in solution as usually supposed but organized in structured cell H_2O and complexed to fixed charges within the cell. Our hopes were remote since K+ of any kind, cellular or inorganic, had never been measured by NMR and most experts seemed to agree that our prospects were grim. Grim, because out of all the nuclei on the atomic table, its resonance point was among the lowest. Consequently, its signal was expected to be much weaker than could be detected by existing equipment.

We banked our hopes on a superconducting magnet* that Nuclear Magnetic Resonance Specialties Corporation had agreed to make available to us for a few days use. If we could generate large enough magnetic fields, we had a chance. The superconducting magnet was rated for 50,000 gauss (the best of the commercially available electromagnets generate 25,000 gauss), which would permit us to receive the signal at 10 megacycles instead of 2, thereby amplifying our sensitivity 25 times. Other modifications such as the use of a signal pre-amplifier and a time averaging computer when taken together were estimated to produce an additional 10 fold amplification of signal.

Superconducting magnets make use of the absence of electrical resistivity of certain alloys (e.g. niobium zirconium, niobium titanium, niobium tin, etc.) at cryogenic temperatures (e.g. 4.3° Kelvin - achieved by immersion of the solenoid in liquid helium). Zero electrical loss is the result and it is possible to produce magnetic fields with an efficiency that approaches 100%. Conventional electromagnets dissipate most of the energy supplied to the windings as heat. Consequently the fields that can be generated are limited by the heat tolerances of the windings.

Figure 24 (here and on the following two pages). Dr. Damadian's original 1969 letter to the Health Research Council of the City of New York seeking funding for the prospect of developing an NMR scanner of the live human body to detect cancer (chapter 10)

George S. Mirick, M.D.   -2-   September 17, 1969

We completed the final assembly of the spectrometer and superconducting magnet in the early evening of August 30. At 2:30 A.M., we attempted to find the potassium signal in a saturated solution of K_2CO_3. Needless to say, we were jubilant when our first scan produced, a resonance signal almost precisely where we expected to find it. The first NMR measurement of potassium of any kind had been made. (Attached below is a photograph of the K^+ resonance signal as it appeared on our oscilloscope - - an off-resonance beat pattern).

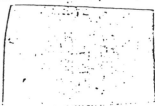

Additional measurements and some controls assured us that we had sufficient sensitivity to measure potassium in biological samples. Using Halobacterium Halobium, selected for its high intracellular potassium content, the first NMR measurements of biologic potassium were made the evening of September 6. Furthermore, the pulsed techniques in our spin-echo spectrometer provided direct evidence (T_2 relaxation measurements) that potassium was complexed to fixed charge groups, and or, solvated by highly structured cell H_2O as we had originally suspected. It is decidedly not in free solution as usually supposed.

Since the superconducting magnet was now needed for other measurements, and we had exhausted the time allotted us, it was at this point that the experiment terminated.

Since no spectrometer-superconducting magnet systems of the type we assembled are available commercially and since no one to the best of our knowledge and the knowledge of Nuclear Magnetic Resonance Specialties Corporation in the continental United States or abroad possesses such an instrument, neither we nor anyone else can pursue our findings. The experiment will remain suspended until someone can assemble the equipment we have described. (See attached manuscript).

Our findings usher in a major revolution in biology and we have only scratched the surface. To suspend our momentum at this point would be unfortunate indeed. Accordingly, I am writing to ask the Health Research Council for the support to equip my laboratory at the State University of New York, Downstate Medical Center, with a High Field Spin Echo Nuclear Magnetic Resonance Spectrometer, so that we can resume work as soon as the spectrometer is constructed. The quoted price for the finished instrumentation by Nuclear Magnetic Resonance Specialties Corporation is $89,000. Although they would prefer to receive the full sum on delivery of the instrument, they have agreed that, if necessary, they will accept a 3-year leasing agreement of $40,000 on delivery and $24,500 in the second and third year. A third alternative would be equally divided payments of $26,666 over a three-year period. Furthermore, if these terms are still too encumbering, I feel fairly

George S. Mirick, M.D.   -3-   September 17, 1969

certain Nuclear Magnetic Resonance Specialties can be persuaded to accept a
longer term lease-purchase agreement.

Hopeful that the Health Research Council can help us expand the exciting success
of a project it has sponsored from infancy, I remain,

Sincerely yours,

Raymond Damadian

Raymond Damadian
Assistant Professor
Department of Internal Medicine

RD:aj
Enc.

P.S. I am enclosing a first draft of the manuscript we are submitting to Science
for publication. I want to mention that our findings have powerful application
in anti-cancer technology. Malignant cells have marked alterations in the physical
structure of their protoplasm. To the best of my knowledge, it is generally true
that all malignant cells have been marked by elevated cell potassium values and
depressed Ca^{++} levels. I am very much interested in the potential of NMR spectroscopy for early non-destructive detection of internal malignancies. To the extent
that our primary research objectives will permit, I will make every effort myself
and through collaborators, to establish that all tumors can be recognized by their
potassium relaxation times or H_2O-proton spectra and proceed with the development
of instrumentation and probes that can be used to scan the human body externally
for early signs of malignancy. Detection of internal tumors during the earliest
stages of their genesis should bring us very close to the total eradication of
this disease.

[Next article in the field of MRI by another person not published until 1973
(P.C. Lauterbur, Nature 2042, 1973, 190-191)]

But moving forward, funding became a big issue, to put it mildly. Constructing a highly improbable NMR scanner that could be built to successfully scan the live human body instead of a 10mm test tube (figure 18) would not be cheap. The funding difficulties generated a lot of frustration among our team. It was compounded by the fact that most of our rivals seemed to get whatever money they needed.

In President Nixon's January 1971 State of the Union Address, he asked for $6 billion ($1 billion a year for six years), to fund research for his "War on Cancer." In December that year, he followed through on his promise and the National Cancer Act became law. This law effectively started the war against cancer in which more than $300 billion has since been committed. The extra money allotted was to increase research and the development of more effective cancer treatments. Even then, some today feel that not enough progress has been made.

Following Nixon's commitment to cancer research, I applied for grants from the Health Research Council of New York. I was told the imaging was meaningless. I then applied to the National Institutes of Health for three grants to study cancer through NMR: $18,784 for the first year, $20,520 for the second, and $13,256 for the third. Much to our dismay, our application to the National Cancer Institute of the National Institutes of Health for the research funds to follow up our cancer discovery published in *Science* was also rejected.

But these kinds of obstacles are what, to put it bluntly, separates the men from the boys. And its precisely where such frustration over the funding of a project we deemed of such paramount importance that our determination kicked in. Many people in life have noble and worthwhile dreams, goals, and pursuits. However, few ever achieve those goals or see their dreams become reality. This is partially due to the fact that they allow the inevitable obstacles and opposition to stop them. A great question to ask yourself when pursing a noble task or passionate life dream is, "What will it take to stop me?" In the words of a well-worn phrase, "It's *always* too soon to quit!"

Those who give up on their pursuits are the ones who spend the rest of their lives wondering about the "what if's." Those lives become filled with disappointment and regret. I had decided and determined that I would *not* be numbered with that group, namely because we were well aware of the worldwide impact such a machine could make in people's lives. So we resolved to soldier on and keep trying.

As we moved closer toward our goal in creating the first MRI machine, one of the things I did was to apply for patents. The first — Apparatus and Method for Detecting Cancer in Tissue — was filed on March 17, 1972, one day after my 36th birthday. All told, we have applied for more than 160 patents pertaining to the design and creation of MRI body scanners. Some of the patents have been ignored. Some were plagiarized. The patent for Apparatus and Method for Detecting Cancer in Tissue was issued February 5, 1974 (figure 25). It was given the patent number U.S. Patent 3,789,832 and it was the *first ever* patent for Magnetic Resonance Imaging (MRI). As of February 10, 2013, it was the first of 4,552 patents for MRI issued by the United States Patent Office (figure 26).

Because the request for Apparatus and Method for Detecting Cancer in Tissue was the first of its kind, the patent office created a new subclass of patents called General Surgery Class 128, "Magnetic Resonance Imaging or Spectroscopy," with the subclass number of 653.2. At one point, a patent examiner approached me at a conference I attended to report to me that I was the highlight of her career. My patent, because of its uniqueness, required the creation of a new patent class at the USPTO to accommodate it and she had had the unusual distinction of being one of the few patent examiners that ever had the honor of creating an entirely new patent class.

This patent, which was contested and stolen numerous times over the years, established both the priority of my claim to the idea of the NMR whole body scanning as well as establishing a workable new method for using NMR to scan the human body for medical diagnosis.

For the research funding I needed to pursue the 1971 discovery, I had no choice but to write to President Nixon himself. In my letter, I wrote, "I am writing to you because I have nowhere else to turn. . . . It seems necessary to say that we feel our findings represent one of the most powerful and exciting breakthroughs in cancer in 50 years. . . . I beg of you to intercede, Mr. Nixon, and see to it that this project is funded immediately. It is too important to delay."

I previously mentioned that the president had committed $6 billion for cancer research over six years, and yet I couldn't even get a $100,000 research grant in the very field for which those funds were to be allocated — not to mention the fact that my research had birthed a major discovery regarding the probability of early cancer detection! This was inconceivable to me. To compound this irony, those who had followed up and repeated my discovery actually received the funds for their follow-up research, while the *originator* of the discovery could not get his funded. I was facing an uphill battle. One of those "obstacles" I mentioned earlier. But again, we didn't let that stop us.

I received a phone call from President Nixon's office. The caller stated, "You wrote to President Nixon." He then stated that an additional grant

Figure 25 (on the following three pages). Dr. Damadian's original MRI patent, the '832 patent filed in 1972, issued in 1974, the first of ultimately 4,552 patents issued by the United States Patent Office for MRI (as of February 2013)

3789832

THE UNITED STATES OF AMERICA

TO ALL TO WHOM THESE PRESENTS SHALL COME:

Whereas, THERE HAS BEEN PRESENTED TO THE

Commissioner of Patents

A PETITION PRAYING FOR THE GRANT OF LETTERS PATENT FOR AN ALLEGED NEW AND USEFUL INVENTION THE TITLE AND DESCRIPTION OF WHICH ARE CONTAINED IN THE SPECIFICATION OF WHICH A COPY IS HEREUNTO ANNEXED AND MADE A PART HEREOF, AND THE VARIOUS REQUIREMENTS OF LAW IN SUCH CASES MADE AND PROVIDED HAVE BEEN COMPLIED WITH, AND THE TITLE THERETO IS, FROM THE RECORDS OF THE PATENT OFFICE IN THE CLAIMANT (S) INDICATED IN THE SAID COPY, AND WHEREAS, UPON DUE EXAMINATION MADE, THE SAID CLAIMANT (S) IS (ARE) ADJUDGED TO BE ENTITLED TO A PATENT UNDER THE LAW.

NOW, THEREFORE, THESE **Letters Patent** ARE TO GRANT UNTO THE SAID CLAIMANT (S) AND THE SUCCESSORS, HEIRS OR ASSIGNS OF THE SAID CLAIMANT (S) FOR THE TERM OF SEVENTEEN YEARS FROM THE DATE OF THIS GRANT, SUBJECT TO THE PAYMENT OF ISSUE FEES AS PROVIDED BY LAW, THE RIGHT TO EXCLUDE OTHERS FROM MAKING, USING OR SELLING THE SAID INVENTION THROUGHOUT THE UNITED STATES.

In testimony whereof, I have hereunto set my hand and caused the seal of the Patent Office to be affixed at the City of Washington this fifth *day of* February, *in the year of our Lord one thousand nine hundred and* seventy-four, *and of the Independence of the United States of America the one hundred and* ninety-eighth.

Attest:

Edward _____ Jr.

Attesting Officer.

Rene D. Tegtmeyer

Acting Commissioner of Patents

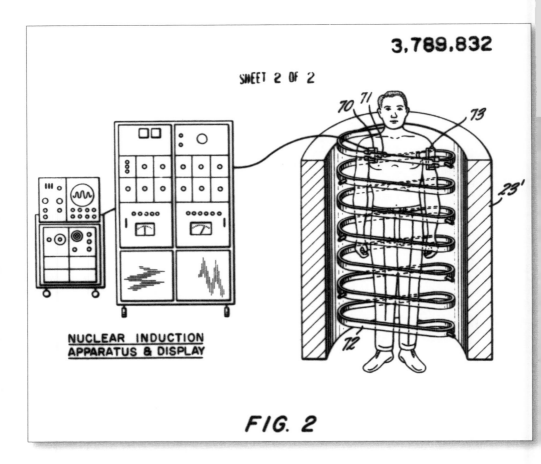

FIG. 2

was going to be created as a result of my letter. The following month, in July, I applied again to the National Institutes of Health from which we received a $20,000 grant, much less than my original request. With that money, however, together with money from private philanthropists, we bought our first NMR machine from NMR Specialties, and our first magnet, a superconducting magnet, from Westinghouse.

This superconducting magnet was comprised of tightly wound niobium-titanium wire, cooled in a bath of liquid helium to 4 degrees above absolute zero. The cooled liquid helium is necessary in order to cool down the superconducting magnet coils in MRI scanners. This allows for continuous "superconducting" of the magnet wire, which permits higher electrical current to flow through the superconducting electrical wire

United States Patent [19]

Damadian

[11] **3,789,832**

[45] **Feb. 5, 1974**

[54] **APPARATUS AND METHOD FOR DETECTING CANCER IN TISSUE**

[76] Inventor: **Raymond V. Damadian,** 64 Short Hill Rd., Forest Hill, N.Y. 11375

[22] Filed: **Mar. 17, 1972**

[21] Appl. No.: **235,624**

[52] U.S. Cl. .... **128/2 R, 128/2 A, 324/.5 R**
[51] Int. Cl. **A61b 5/05**
[58] Field of Search .... 128/2 R, 2 A, 1.3; 324/.5 A, 324/.5 B

[56] **References Cited**
UNITED STATES PATENTS

3,691,455	9/1972	Moisio et al.	324/.5 R
3,557,777	1/1971	Cohen	128/2 R
3,530,371	9/1970	Nelson et al.	324/.5 AC

OTHER PUBLICATIONS

Singer, J. R., Journ. of Applied Physics, Vol. 31, No. 1, Jan., 1960, pp. 125–127,

Primary Examiner—Kyle L. Howell
Attorney, Agent, or Firm—Brumbaugh, Graves, Donohue & Raymond

[57] **ABSTRACT**

An apparatus and method in which a tissue sample is positioned in a nuclear induction apparatus whereby selected nuclei are energized from their equilibrium states to higher energy states through nuclear magnetic resonance. By measuring the spin-lattice relaxation time and the spin-spin relaxation time as the energized nuclei return to their equilibrium states, and then comparing these relaxation times with their respective values for known normal and malignant tissue, an indication of the presence and degree of malignancy of cancerous tissue can be obtained.

16 Claims, 3 Drawing Figures

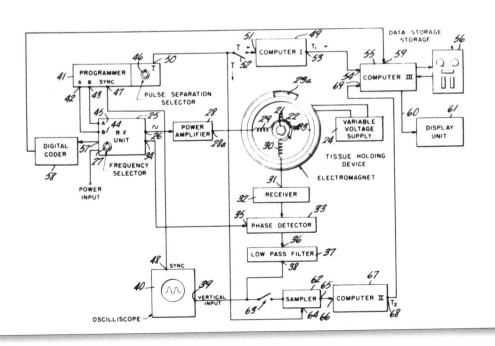

without encountering the electrical resistance that an ordinary copper wire possesses that limits the amount of current and therefore the strength of the magnetic field that could be generated by a copper wire magnet.

Liquid helium is the only medium cold enough to promote this superconductivity in superconducting metal alloys such as niobium-titanium.

This enabled the superconducting wire to generate the higher magnetic field we needed to proceed with the cancer NMR scanner. Our superconducting ("supercon") magnet for our first T_1 measurements of human tumor specimens (figures 27 and 28) created an installation problem for our space at Downstate. The magnet needed to be three feet off the floor so we could insert the NMR probe with its test tube tumor sample into the bore of the magnet from the bottom of the vertical cylindrical magnet. The liquid helium itself had to be transferred into the magnet from the top, and we didn't have a ceiling high enough to do this. To accommodate this need, Downstate kindly provided me a 5th-floor

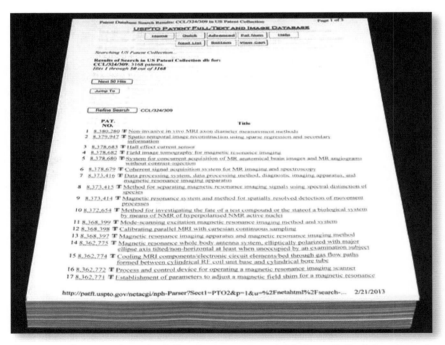

Figure 26 (here and on the following two pages). Listing of all of the United States Patent Office (USPTO) 4,552 patents (as of Feb. 2013) of MRI, listing Dr. Damadian's '832 patent as the first

Patent Database Search Results: CCL/324/309 in US Patent Collection

USPTO PATENT FULL-TEXT AND IMAGE DATABASE

| Home | Quick | Advanced | Pat Num | Help |

| Next List | Bottom | View Cart |

Searching US Patent Collection...

Results of Search in US Patent Collection db for:
CCL/324/309: 3168 patents.
Hits 1 through 50 out of 3168

Next 50 Hits

Jump To

Refine Search   CCL/324/309

PAT. NO.	Title
1 8,380,280	Non-invasive in vivo MRI axon diameter measurement methods
2 8,379,947	Spatio-temporal image reconstruction using sparse regression and secondary information
3 8,378,683	Hall effect current sensor
4 8,378,682	Field image tomography for magnetic resonance imaging
5 8,378,680	System for concurrent acquisition of MR anatomical brain images and MR angiograms without contrast-injection
6 8,378,679	Coherent signal acquisition system for MR imaging and spectroscopy
7 8,373,416	Data processing system, data processing method, diagnostic imaging apparatus, and magnetic resonance imaging apparatus
8 8,373,415	Method for separating magnetic resonance imaging signals using spectral distinction of species
9 8,373,414	Magnetic resonance system and method for spatially resolved detection of movement processes
10 8,372,654	Method for investigating the fate of a test compound or the stateof a biological system by means of NMR of hyperpolarised NMR active nuclei
11 8,368,399	Mode-scanning excitation magnetic resonance imaging method and system
12 8,368,398	Calibrating parallel MRI with cartesian continuous sampling
13 8,368,397	Magnetic resonance imaging apparatus and magnetic resonance imaging method
14 8,362,775	Magnetic resonance whole body antenna system, elliptically polarized with major ellipse axis tilted/non-horizontal at least when unoccupied by an examination subject
15 8,362,774	Cooling MRI components/electronic circuit elements/bed through gas flow paths formed between cylindrical RF coil unit base and cylindrical bore tube
16 8,362,772	Process and control device for operating a magnetic resonance imaging scanner
17 8,362,771	Establishment of parameters to adjust a magnetic field shim for a magnetic resonance

Patent Database Search Results: CCL/324/309 in US Patent Collection

USPTO PATENT FULL-TEXT AND IMAGE DATABASE

| Home | Quick | Advanced | Pat Num | Help |

| Prev. List | Bottom | View Cart |

Searching US Patent Collection...

Results of Search in US Patent Collection db for:
CCL/324/309: 3168 patents.
Hits 3151 through 3168 out of 3168

Prev. 50 Hits

Jump To

Refine Search   CCL/324/309

PAT. NO.	Title
3151 4,318,043	Method and apparatus for rapid NMR imaging of nuclear densities within an object
3152 4,315,216	Imaging systems
3153 4,307,344	Imaging systems
3154 4,307,343	Moving gradient zeugmatography
3155 4,300,096	Imaging systems
3156 4,297,637	Method and apparatus for mapping lines of nuclear density within an object using nuclear magnetic resonance
3157 4,290,019	Methods of deriving image information from objects
3158 4,284,948	Imaging systems
3159 4,280,096	Spectrometer for measuring spatial distributions of paramagnetic centers in solid bodies
3160 4,254,778	Imaging systems
3161 4,165,479	Nuclear magnetic resonance apparatus and methods
3162 4,115,730	Nuclear magnetic resonance apparatus and methods
3163 4,070,611	Gyromagnetic resonance fourier transform zeugmatography
3164 4,045,723	Two dimensional gyromagnetic resonance spectroscopy
3165 4,021,726	Image formation using nuclear magnetic resonance
3166 4,015,196	Analysis of materials
3167 3,932,805	Method of obtaining internal information of a measuring target from the out-side by the application of a nuclear magnetic resonance phenomenon
3168 3,789,832	APPARATUS AND METHOD FOR DETECTING CANCER IN TISSUE

| Prev. List | Top | View Cart |

| Home | Quick | Advanced | Pat Num | Help |

laboratory immediately below my primary 6th-floor lab. Taking in the above-ceiling duct space, I now had the contiguous vertical height of two 11-foot laboratories to enable the necessary liquid helium transfers into our 5th-floor Westinghouse supercon. But to facilitate the liquid helium transfer, we needed to cut a hole in the floor joining the two floors to enable the required daily liquid helium transfers from the portable liquid helium supply containers down into the Westinghouse magnet. Unfortunately, the floor was poured granite, a foot thick, with reinforcing rods.

That's when Mike Goldsmith attempted to open the needed hole in the floor with a sledge hammer and a concrete chisel, but even this big man's efforts proved inadequate. Then I heard the sound of jackhammers down below on the street in Brooklyn pounding away. So I went down and approached the workmen, asking if they would like to earn some extra money. And because money talks, they eagerly agreed, bringing their jackhammer tools up to 6th floor. Once there, they began jackhammering a hole through our laboratory floor. Of course, not everyone in the University hospital received the pounding jackhammer salvos with the same enthusiasm we did.

Arriving the morning the jackhammers were to commence the 5th and 6th floor "adjoining" process, I found the machines silent and the workers packing up their equipment to go home. When I asked the reason for this, they reported that shortly after they had gotten started "digging" on the 6th floor concrete to open it to the floor below, a tall doctor with white hair appeared, "ordering us to stop immediately," and even threatening to call the police. I immediately knew who they were referring to. It was Dr. Ludwig Eichna, chairman of our Department of Internal Medicine. I knew Dr. Eichna walked each morning past my 6th floor laboratory on his way from Downstate's elevator to his 6th floor office in the university hospital, so I went straight to see him (figure 29). I explained to Dr. Eichna that Downstate had already formally approved the ongoing construction, with construction drawings having been provided to Downstate's Construction and Engineering Department by the well-known New York City architectural firm "Haines Lundberg, Waehler and Djerejian." I further explained that we had received authorization from the Engineering and Maintenance department to proceed with construction. Once verified and assured that a university hospital "cave in" was not a prospect, Dr. Eichna authorized continuation of the construction.

Figure 27. Raymond Damadian, Larry Minkoff, and Ken Zaner with the Westinghouse superconducting magnet used to make the first image of a tumor in a live animal (mouse) as it was featured on the cover of *Science* in 1976.

Proc. Nat. Acad. Sci. USA
Vol. 71, No. 4, pp. 1471–1473, April 1974

Human Tumors Detected by Nuclear Magnetic Resonance

(spin-lattice relaxation/pulse nuclear magnetic resonance malignancy)

RAYMOND DAMADIAN*, KEN ZANER*, DORIS HOR*, AND THERESA DiMAIO†

* Department of Medicine and Program in Biophysics, State University of New York at Brooklyn, and †Department of Pathology, Sloan-Kettering Institute for Cancer Research, Memorial Hospital, New York, N.Y.

Communicated by Albert Szent-Gyorgyi, December 18, 1973

1472   Biochemistry: Damadian *et al.*   *Proc. Nat. Acad. Sci. USA 71 (1974)*

TABLE 1. T_1 *relaxations in normal and malignant human tissues*

Tissue	T_1 tumor	T_1 normal	Probability that the difference in the means are not significant
Breast	1.080 ± 0.08 (13)	0.367 ± 0.079 (5)	0.52×10^{-4}
Skin	1.047 ± 0.108 (4)	0.616 ± 0.019 (9)	0.55×10^{-4}
Muscle (malignant)	1.413 ± 0.082 (7)	1.023 ± 0.029 (17)	0.50×10^{-5}
(benign)	1.307 ± 0.1535 (2)		
Esophagus	1.04 (1)	0.804 ± 0.108 (5)	
Stomach	1.238 ± 0.109 (3)	0.765 ± 0.075 (8)	0.40×10^{-3}
Intestinal Tract	1.122 ± 0.04 (15)	0.641 ± 0.080 (8) (small bowel)	0.27×10^{-5}
		0.641 ± 0.043 (12) (colon)	
Liver	0.832 ± 0.012 (2)	0.570 ± 0.029 (14)	
Spleen	1.113 ± 0.006 (2)	0.701 ± 0.045 (17)	
Lung	1.110 ± 0.057 (12)	0.788 ± 0.063 (5)	0.25×10^{-3}
Lymphatic	1.004 ± 0.056 (14)	0.720 ± 0.076 (6)	0.52×10^{-2}
Bone	1.027 ± 0.152 (6)	0.554 ± 0.027 (10)	0.74×10^{-3}
Bladder	1.241 ± 0.165 (3)	0.891 ± 0.061 (4)	0.36×10^{-1}
Thyroid	1.072 (1)	0.882 ± 0.045 (7)	
Nerve	1.204 (1)	0.557 ± 0.158 (2)	
Adipose	2.047 (1)	0.279 ± 0.008 (5)	
Ovary	1.282 ± 0.118 (2)	0.989 ± 0.047 (5)	
Uterus (malignant)	1.393 ± 0.176 (2)	0.924 ± 0.038 (4)	
(benign)	0.973 (1)		
Cervix	1.101 (1)	0.827 ± 0.026 (4)	
Testes	1.223 (1)	1.200 ± 0.048 (4)	
Prostate	1.110 (1)	0.803 ± 0.014 (2)	
Adrenal	0.683 (1)	0.608 ± 0.020 (5)	
Peritoneum	1.529 (1)	0.476 (1)	
Malignant melanomas	0.724 ± 0.147 (6)		
Tongue	1.288 (1)		
Pericardial layer (mesothelioma)	0.758 (1)		
Kidney		0.862 ± 0.033 (13)	
Brain		0.998 ± 0.016 (8)	
Pancreas		0.605 ± 0.036 (10)	
Heart		0.906 ± 0.046 (9)	

Probability values are reported for series with sample size ≥ 3. Errors reported are standard error of the mean (SEM). Number of cases analyzed are indicated in parentheses.

Figure 28. Dr. Damadian and colleagues K. Zaner, D. Hor, and T. DiMaio's publication in the *Proceedings of The National Academy of Science* of the first NMR measurements of human tumors

After the construction workers successfully blasted through the thick floor, we built a platform for the magnet and an elevator to lower it so we could replenish it with liquid helium as needed. Many years later, this, for many, is a favorite story regarding the overcoming of scientific obstacles. In the years that followed, I've wondered how many research scientists have jackhammered huge holes through their laboratory floor. But had we not pushed through and overcome this barrier to our progress, we wouldn't have been able to do research on 28 different kinds of tissue, cancerous and normal.

By November 1973, our funds were exhausted, mostly due to the high cost of liquid helium. So we applied for additional funding to NIH, American Cancer Institute, and National Cancer Institute, but were sadly turned down each time.

So much was against us — lack of funding, ridicule, others getting money that we felt we should have. It seemed at times like the deck was stacked against us.

But we had a friend, Paul Dreizen, MD. Dr. Dreizen, a SUNY (State University of New York) professor at Downstate. A professor of profound intellect and scholarship, Dr. Dreizen was Dean of the Graduate School of Downstate where all of Downstate's PhD doctorates are awarded, and Chairman of the Department of Biophysics where the university's PhD program in biophysics was conducted. Dr. Dreizen received his baccalaureate degree in mathematics with distinction from Cornell University and his doctorate in medicine (MD) at New York University School of Medicine. As dean of the graduate school and therefore a key advisor to the president regarding the university's scientific curriculum and ongoing scientific research, Dr. Dreizen recognized immediately the value of our

Figure 29. Dr. Ludwig Eichna. While Dr. Damadian was a professor working with Dr. Ludwig Eichna who was Chairman of the Department of Internal Medicine, Dr. Eichna was a strong endorser throughout the university community for the construction of *Indomitable* and its immense potential benefits in the care of patients.

new tissue NMR T_1 and T_2 discovery and its prospects of generating a new scanner for the human body, which would be of immense potential value to the practice of medicine. Thus, throughout the Downstate community among the faculty and administration wherever questions were raised about the rationality of such a scanner and the large commitment of the university's scarce space and limited finances to the construction of such an outlandish project, Dr. Dreizen scholastically articulated the overwhelming medical benefits of such a scanner if it could actually be built. Our R&D team believed that if SUNY Downstate was the university that actually succeeded in constructing the first-ever MRI, it would establish Downstate as *the university that gave the world the MRI.*

True to form, we continued on with the research, undeterred. Despite all these setbacks, we never, ever gave up. I won't lie. We often had our doubts, but we kept pressing on. The work we were doing was simply too important. We could sense it. This guiding passion enabled us to eventually achieve our goal, constructing a full-body scanning machine.

We christened our new creation *Indomitable*, named so as a testament to its character and spirit of those who brought it to life.

The machine everyone thought impossible was now reality.

Endnotes

1. The T_1 relaxation time measures the time for the stimulated nuclei to discharge their excitation energy to the surroundings (lattice). The T_2 decay rate (the T_2 relaxation time) is the time rate of decay of the live NMR signal actually observed on the oscilloscope. It is the time for the destructive interferences of the phase incoherencies of all of the NMR signals generated by the individual atoms within the sample to reduce the magnitude of the observed ('observed' underlined) composite signal to zero.
2. http://www.fonar.com/pdf/doc1.1a.1d.1c.pdf. "Tumor Detection by Nuclear Magnetic Resonance" *Science*, 1971, vol. 171, p. 1151–1153.
3. "Tumor Detection by Nuclear Magnetic Resonance" *Science*, 1971, vol. 171, p. 1151–1153.
4. This involved (1) the correct magnetic field strength needed to generate a signal, (2) the necessary magnet homogeneity of the spatially localized magnetic field to generate a detectable signal and (3) spatial localization of the necessary amplitude of the magnetic component of the rf at the location to generate a signal.

CHAPTER
5

IT'S ALIVE!

The completion of *Indomitable* was one of the most thrilling moments of my life. But it wasn't easy. Not by a long shot. It represented the culmination of a long journey, the crescendo of satisfaction following long hours of desperation, doubt, and disagreements. There were almost insurmountable roadblocks blocking our paths, and lack of funding along with internal frustration. There were even some pretty heated verbal fights. But the creation of the world's first MRI machine also came with its own unique set of concerns and questions. At that time, we did not yet know the effects of the high radio frequency and magnetic field upon the body and on the necessary conduction of electricity within the heart.

Looking back, it is clear to me that we couldn't possibly have accomplished the creation without a great team. I wanted the best people on the project, and this often meant convincing someone to stay when they were ready to bolt out the door for one reason or another. But all of us persevered, working through our occasional differences and difficulties. And when the dust settled, we had successfully built the first full-body scanner in the history of medicine.

I had originally thought we could build the machine in 6 months. It took 18.

Mike Goldsmith and Larry Minkoff had been there almost from the beginning, but didn't always get along, developing what at times was a tempestuous and adversarial relationship. Mike was a big man while Larry is on the slender side. Some say Larry could be a prima donna while describing Mike as having a charming personality. Mike was a large man, and he could eat. And eat he did. A lot. Contrastingly, Larry often picked at what little food he ordered, whether it be from the Downstate cafeteria or a nearby Brooklyn restaurant. Larry's involvement in the project had begun one day in 1969 when he walked into my office expressing interest in the cell research I was doing at the time. Mike, on the other hand, my "tech" from the outset, joined the work later on.

One of their infamous fights has become legendary among the team. Egged on one day by incessant put-downs in the lab, Larry picked up a hammer and threw it at Mike, narrowly missing his large frame. According to Larry, the throw was meant to send a tangible message to his teammate. When I expressed concern about the incident, Larry remarked, "If I had wanted to hit him, I would have." However, despite their differences — and fights — both men were tireless co-workers who logged many, many hours in the lab doing research and building *Indomitable*. I appreciate them working through their constant battles, and the nitpicking that wore on each other's nerves. But they moved on for the sake of the work we were doing. They understood what was before us and what was at stake. They are a rare breed of men, as dedicated and determined as I was to see our project through to the end. Both men remain dear friends to this day.

There were, of course, others involved with the project as well, including Ken Zaner and Joel Stutman. When I originally arrived at Downstate, Stutman was a professor in the medical computer science program. He would become one of our biggest proponents, even after taking a position at Hunter College.

But rewinding for a moment, prior to building *Indomitable* in February of 1976, we had built a magnet that could scan a mouse using the FONAR method. We did this by moving the animal across a focused spot at the center of the magnet. This method applies the signal systemically throughout the whole interior of a live animal, thus producing a scan. Unfortunately, our first attempt at producing a live specimen scan resulted in frying the subject. We had put a coil around the chest of "Pioneer Mouse #1," and while attempting to secure the proper focus of the sweet spot, we inadvertently overheated the coil and lost the mouse.

He gave his life for science.

On March 11 of that same year, Larry conducted the next experiment — on Pioneer Mouse #2. In doing so, he was able to obtain the crude image of a tumor — an Ehrlich ascites solid neoplasm — in the anterior chest wall of the mouse. Larry wrote a paper (co-authored by the mouse, of course) for *Science* magazine. The story made the cover of the December 24, 1976, issue.

Some may have wondered if what we were doing was simply duplicating the CT scan in another form. But *Indomitable* was much different from a CT (CAT) scanner. CAT (computed axial tomography) originated in the 1970s and was developed by Godfrey Newbold Hounsfield, an electronics engineer at EMI and Allan MacLeod Cormack, a physicist at Tufts University in Medford, Massachusetts. For their work, the pair was awarded the Nobel Prize in Medicine in 1979. In a CT scan, a single x-ray beam rapidly rotates around the head or torso. The projections of each rotated beam are then "reconstructed" by a computer into a cross-sectional picture. As in a regular x-ray, bone obstructs the passage of the x-ray beam, thus providing the image contrast needed to make detailed images of bony structures. In the CT, the computer resolves the acquired data into image *slices*, instead of producing the whole body projection images of conventional x-rays where the body's organs overlay each other in the final image. The CT scan thereby provides additional image detail of the body's soft tissue organs not discernable with regular x-rays.

But for us, we remained focused on our goal to take scanning of the living body to a whole new level. We purchased a magnet with a 5" center bore big enough to scan a live monkey, as opposed to the 2" center bore magnet used on the much smaller mouse. With the monkey fully anaesthetized and asleep inside, and our rf antenna encircling his girth, we positioned him within the cylindrical bore of the 5" superconducting magnet. Immediately, we got the NMR signal from his torso that we needed! We were also pleased that there appeared to be no immediate technical obstacles preventing us from successfully completing his image. On this success, we proceeded with optimization of the rest of the NMR apparatus to maximize signal to noise (SNR).

Then, in the midst of our NMR "tune-up," the monkey's NMR signal suddenly, and for no apparent reason, disappeared. We searched the electronics high and low for the cause, but could find none. Then we heard an outburst of hilarity from Larry Minkoff. Searching for the cause of the missing signal, Larry had gotten down on his hands and knees to look up into the magnet bore. Upon doing so, he discovered that our NMR "signal source" had awakened from his anesthesia, climbed up out of the antenna, and perched himself on top of it with his arms folded. As far as the monkey was concerned, our experiment was officially over!

But soon I grew tired of scanning animals. I wanted to move forward with a machine big enough to scan a human. The machine in my mind had been birthed the moment the Lord gave me the idea in New Kensington in 1969. Now here I was, years later, finally beginning to see that idea become a reality.

Driven by a competitive spirit within, I wanted to be sure we achieved the first human scan before Paul Lauterbur. I knew in speaking with other members of the scientific community that Peter Mansfield, as well as Waldo Hinshaw and E. Raymond Andrew, were also heading up teams in the race to see who could build and scan the first human being.

This was one race I did not want to lose.

But despite my passion, every member of my team didn't always share the same level of enthusiasm and competition. While Minkoff was excited, Goldsmith initially wasn't.

As usual, we didn't have the money to buy a bigger magnet. So in April 1976, we made a bold decision. We would build our own!

I contacted the physics department at Brookhaven National Laboratory and, using "Mag Map" the magnet design computer software they gave me, I designed a Helmholtz pair (two magnet coils) to optimize the magnetic field homogeneity of the magnet that would optimize our chances of succeeding with a human scan. The two-coil design, according to my "Mag Map" calculations, called for 30 miles (158,400 ft.) of the niobium-titanium (NbTi) superconducting wire we needed to make a magnet big enough to encompass a human being. In terms of stored energy, this would represent the ninth largest stored energy magnet in the world at that time. The other eight were being used to *split atoms*! No one could say we didn't dream big.

Pricing the NbTi wire, I learned the cost of this Westinghouse wire was one dollar per foot, i.e., $158,000 for the 5 Tesla (5,000 gauss) magnet we had in mind: a sum way beyond our reach financially. I had only $15,000 in my research budget. Unsure I would ever be able to raise such a sum to build a human body-enclosing magnet in a medical school for the first time ever, I decided that in the interim, while I was pondering this challenge, I had the additional need to learn how to make the necessary superconducting joints between successive lengths of wire. Thirty miles of wire did not come on one spool and I was going to have to learn how to join successive lengths of spool wire into a single 30-mile length without introducing resistances at each of the joints and destroying the magnet's "superconductivity." Perhaps I could persuade my friend at Westinghouse, Steve Lane, the sales engineer I had been working with, to teach me how to make the NbTi superconducting joints in the interim while I was deliberating over a source to secure the needed $150,000.

Steve had been the one who had provided our original Westinghouse test-tube supercon (see figure 27). Upon my inquiry, Steve pressed me on why I wanted to make these joints. "Dr. Damadian," he said, "are you going into competition with Westinghouse?"

"No, Steve," I said. "Our intention is to build a 5,000 gauss superconducting magnet large enough to make an NMR scan of the live human body."

Steve responded, saying, "I'm glad you leveled with me, Dr. Damadian. No one knows it yet, but Westinghouse has decided to go out of the business of making superconducting magnets. As a result, Dr. Damadian, I have about 30 miles (150,000 feet) of superconducting wire in our warehouse that I can let you have for 10¢ on the dollar" (i.e., $15,000).

What Steve Lane did not know was that $150,000 was way beyond any sum in my budget. Moreover, he had no way of knowing that $15,000 was *precisely* the amount I had left in my budget. I said, "Yes, Steve, I would be glad to take you up on your offer." Steve then asked when I would like to come for the wire.

I said, "Is right away okay, Steve?"

"That's fine," Steve replied.

The following day, Mike and Larry drove out to pick up the Westinghouse wire. I meanwhile remained astounded by the "coincidence" that, after all these years, Westinghouse would suddenly decide to go out of the superconducting magnet-superconducting wire business at the *precise instant* I needed the wire! On top of that, I couldn't believe it was available at 10¢ on the dollar, equaling the *exact* amount we had in our budget. Moreover, and miraculously, it was precisely the wire length (150,000 feet) I had calculated with "Mag Map" that we needed to make the human body MRI magnet. Neither our prospect of constructing a human-sized "superconducting" magnet nor the wire needed to construct it had ever been discussed with Steve Lane! This was almost beyond belief. A few days later, I recounted this story to my mother- and father-in-law, both strong evangelical Christians. My mother-in-law, Amy Terry (figure 11), confidently responded, "*That's no coincidence, Raymond, that's an answer to prayer!* Your father and I have been praying continually for your project since the moment we first learned of it." I was stunned, to say the least! There was no other explanation for this amazing "coincidence." The providence and guiding hand of God once again was steering my life. And this was just one of the obvious, overt examples of His work. I wonder what other things He had done for me that I didn't see, notice, or even acknowledge as coming from Him. It reminds me of the importance of seeing God's hand in our lives beyond those "miracle moments" to the everyday mercies and provisions He graciously gives. The same God who parts the sea provides the daily manna for life. We only have to notice and acknowledge this provision with grateful and humble hearts.

That experience proved to be a pivotal turning point for me in my relationship with God. I had been away from Him for some time, having embraced a godless theory of origins and even seriously questioned God's very existence. But though I had forgotten Him, He had not forgotten me. I am reminded of the Lord's words to Israel while suffering under Assyrian captivity:

> But Zion [Israel] said, The LORD hath forsaken me,
> and my Lord hath forgotten me.
> Can a woman forget her sucking child,
> that she should not have compassion on the son of her womb?
> Yea, they may forget, yet I will not forget thee.
> Behold, I have graven thee upon the palms of my hands;
> thy walls are continually before me (Isaiah 49:14–16).

Like ancient Israel, I had been taken captive by a foreign power. The atheism of evolution denied the existence and power of the true God, and I had become its willing subject. But, upon hearing my dear mother-in-law's words, I knew that the Lord was speaking to me. He was communicating to His wayward child through her wisdom and prayer. And He was sending me a clear signal through His orchestration of circumstances in my favor. This was His way of letting me know that He was not only still there, but also still committed to me. The sheer miracle of that moment convinced me that I was not ultimately in control of my work or my personal life. It showed me that God had been working behind the scenes, not only for my benefit, but more importantly for His glory.

John 14:14 was brought to mind: *"If you ask me anything in my name, I will do it."* Even today, I chuckle in amazement whenever I think of the fact that at the precise instant I needed to build the first-ever MRI magnet and the superconducting niobium-titanium (NbTi) wire to make it, Westinghouse spontaneously decided to close down its magnet factory and sell all of its remaining wire for 10¢ on the dollar. What were the odds of that happening? As far as I knew, they possessed the only superconducting wire in existence at the time, and certainly in an amount that large. Why would their entire inventory suddenly be available at the exact instant I needed it? There was only one rational explanation: God. It became more clear than ever to me that destiny's favorable hand was on me. I was *meant* to construct the world's first MRI scanner!

Needless to say, this changed everything, and my perspective on my life was forever altered. Spiritually, this experience reconnected the dots to that night in Madison Square Garden when I had first believed totally in Jesus. I would have been a fool to deny the reality of God and His wonder-working power in that moment. Not long after this I read Henry Morris's book, *Biblical Basis for Modern Science.*[1] Then I read the *Genesis Flood* by John C. Whitcomb and Henry M. Morris[2] These books had a profound impact on me as a scientist as well as a Christian. Shortly afterward, I began to speak openly and unapologetically against evolution. My eyes had been opened, and I would never be the same.

Now that we had the wire needed to make our superconducting magnet, Goldsmith practiced by making smaller magnets first. The first measured four inches by two inches. That one held steady without collapsing. Then he made one twelve inches high and eight inches across. That one didn't collapse either. His original plan was to continue his tests by building a slightly larger magnet each time, but because of my impatience, I denied him that opportunity. I was anxious for him to immediately start on the magnet sufficiently large enough for a full-body scanner (figures 30–33).

But there was another problem. The full-size human body magnet we were envisioning was too large for our laboratory on the 5th floor (figure 27). We needed a much larger laboratory space in an already intensely space-limited and space-contested university facility to accommodate

Figure 30. Mike Goldsmith, Michael Stanford, and Raymond Damadian winding the 30 miles of NbTi wire on the first of the two solenoid magnets used in the first-ever MRI scanner of the live human body, *Indomitable*

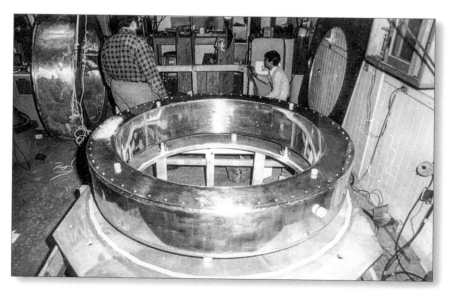

Figure 31. Mike Goldsmith and Nean Hu with the liquid helium cryogen used to cryocool the NbTi coil being wound in figure 30

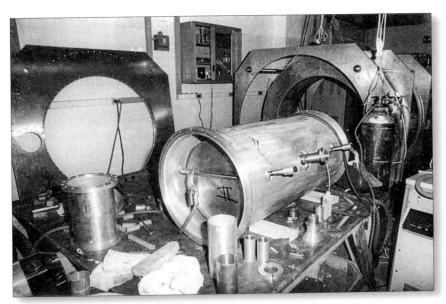

Figure 32. The liquid helium, liquid nitrogen storage vessel of *Indomitable*

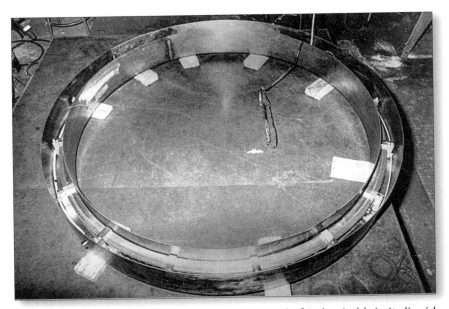

Figure 33. The NbTi superconducting magnet coil of *Indomitable* in its liquid He container

Figure 34. Dr. Calvin H. Plimpton, president of Downstate Medical Center when *Indomitable* was built, and an enthusiastic supporter of its immense potential benefits in the care of patients, if it could be successfully constructed

the much larger human-sized NMR (MRI) magnet we were envisioning, and also to contain the machine tools (e.g., lathes, milling machines, drilling machines, etc.) we needed to construct a magnet big enough to house a human body, the NMR we had named *Indomitable*. So I went to see Dr. Calvin Plimpton, MD (figure 34), our university president. I explained to Dr. Plimpton that we had reached the point in our NMR (MRI) research, which he was aware of, that we wanted to proceed with the construction of a full-sized NMR magnet and electronics to scan a human body, but that we needed additional laboratory space, which we estimated at 1,000 square feet, to enable its construction. Dr. Plimpton's immediate response was, "Take the animal laboratory space (where university experimental rats and mice were housed) across the hall from your fifth floor lab."

I answered, "But that's the space currently utilized by Eli Friedman."[3] I doubted that he would readily relinquish such a sizeable portion of his space to a simple request from me. I said to Dr. Plimpton, "Can you handle that?"

He said, "I believe I can!" With the space allocated to commence construction of the first-ever human-sized NMR (MRI) magnet, we commenced the construction of *Indomitable*.

To construct a magnet of this size, we first had to build the two hoops out of channel bar to contain the Niobium-titanium magnet wire. Mike called in a favor from the Brooklyn Navy Yard to machine the hoops on a lathe. After the hoops were made, we attached a thimble with a hole in it to wind the wire around the hoop. These two magnets were comprised of *30 miles* of niobium-titanium superconducting wire, precisely and tightly wound into the hoops. Each was wound in 52 layers, and each layer was comprised of 76 to 91 turns. This painstaking process took six weeks to complete. Unfortunately, we had no way of testing the magnet during construction.

While Mike kept busy working on the hoops, Larry and I built the *dewars* — ten feet tall, six feet wide and 18 inches deep, and each weighing 1½ tons! A dewar is basically a highly sophisticated thermos bottle that prevents heat from being transferred to the contents of the dewar, in this case, the niobium-titanium superconducting wire which was immersed in liquid helium. The liquid helium was required to maintain the "super-cooling" to absolute zero temperatures of the superconducting wire.[4] This liquid helium also enabled the magnet to super conduct thousands of amperes of current. By doing this, it could produce the high magnetic field strength we believed we needed to generate enough of an NMR signal from the human body to complete an actual scan.

Larry and I ran into numerous problems while building the dewars. What made matters worse was that I had convinced myself that other labs must be making better progress then we were (I later learned this was not the case). Nevertheless, our work was slow and tedious, causing us to be at the lab far more weekends than I can remember. This meant more time away from the kids, and more responsibility at home for Donna.

When Mike finally finished the magnets, he used an instrument called an "ohmmeter" to look for electrical shorts (malfunctions). Had he found even one malfunction inside those magnets, we would have had to scrap six weeks' worth of work. Meanwhile, the dewars Larry and I were working on were not close to being finished.

Of the issues we faced, one was the outermost vacuum can of the dewar containing the magnet doughnut. We knew that once the magnets were placed inside the dewar we might have to check on the magnet itself. We figured we could create an O-ring to allow accessibility. But it leaked. A lot. So we bent it, re-welded it, and twisted it. Then we tried to pump it down. Nothing! The leaks continued. We used soapy water to locate the leaks and discovered we had numerous ones that needed to be welded and sealed. This meant more work. And more time. But time, I believed, was not on our side. Every week that passed made me feel like we were falling behind in this race to build the world's first MRI scanner for the human body.

All told, it took us a full year to complete the two magnet doughnuts needed for the scan. But when we had problems with vacuum leaks that we couldn't find and correct (particularly on dewar number two), I decided in the interest of time to go with just magnet number one.

Ferreting out "leaks" in our magnet dewar was a frustrating challenge. We used a special device to detect those leaks.[5] And of course we found more. It took weeks to fix them. This was exhausting and often deflating preparatory work.

Another thing we needed was a spectrometer, so I bought one from Donald Vickers, a former co-worker of Lauterbur's. After the demise of NMR Specialties in New Kensington, Pennsylvania, Vickers founded Seimco. When he brought the spectrometer to Downstate, he pressed me until I eventually told him what we were doing.

As usual, money once again was an issue. Urged on by my father-in-law, Bo Terry, I sought help from President-elect Jimmy Carter. Who better to ask a favor from than the President of the United States, right? This man was about to be sworn in as the president and leader of the free world. If he didn't posses the power to do something, who could? Plus, he was entering his "honeymoon" phase of Congress, a time when he might have a better chance at obtaining funding. So I made the long trip down south to Plains, Georgia, in December 1976. Once there, I met President-elect Carter and many members of his family, including his cousin Hugh, brother Billy, and even his mother Lillian. Nevertheless, I was unsuccessful in drumming up any financial support. Cousin Hugh was the most sympathetic, but simply couldn't get me the necessary audience with Jimmy. Hugh even promised things would be better once Jimmy actually took office, but nothing ever materialized.

Then, on a chance meeting, God sent us an angel from Nashville, Tennessee, by the name of Bill Akers. After spending two hours with us in the lab, Akers said he was confident he could raise the $10,000 needed to continue our work. He promised that in the event he was unable to raise the money, upon his return to Nashville he would write us a personal check for $10,000. And he did just that, keeping his word and issuing a personal check for that amount. Then Bill went even beyond this, persuading his brother Clark Akers and two friends — James Stewart and John Rich — to donate money as well. All told we received a total of $40,000. Akers had saved the day for us.

The last piece of the puzzle was building the antennae, the rf receiver coil that would receive the NMR signals from the body. The original plan was to build a coil that measured four feet in diameter. But through trial and error over months, Mike came up with a 14-inch coil that worked. When he increased the size to 16 inches, it didn't work. So we

Figure 35 (left). Raymond Damadian, Lawrence Minkoff, and Michael Goldsmith with liquid helium-cooled *Indomitable*

Figure 36 (below). R. Damadian, M. Goldsmith, and L. Minkoff with *Indomitable* electronics

stayed with the 14-inch coil for the time being.

We were now done, but still needed a name for the machine. After bantering around a few names, I suggested the name *Indomitable* (figure 35). We had invested a lot of hard work in building this monster machine. We'd overcome enormous obstacles. We'd refused to be conquered or defeated in our relentless pursuit of our goal. Besides, our creation *looked* "indomitable." The

Figure 37. Joel Strutman, Lawrence Minkoff, Raymond Damadian, and Mike Goldsmith.

magnet opening was a giant wheel with a storage chamber on top and a narrow board laying horizontally through the magnet wheel. The name fit.

We tested signal strength (figure 36) and discovered the signal drifted when the strength of the magnetic field was set at 1,000 gauss.[6] Eventually we found a steady signal at around 500 gauss, ten times lower than I had first wanted. But at this point, there wasn't much more that we could do. We were too close to tinker further.

Our first scan was of a turkey from a local market, obtained via a last-minute decision with a little help from a local butcher who was about to close up shop for the day. I persuaded him to stay open long enough for me to get a fresh specimen. We scanned the turkey for 26 minutes with great results.

Then it was my turn.

For weeks I wondered and worried over the safety of the machine. There was still so much we didn't yet know. Over the years, we had tested numerous specimens in preparation for building *Indomitable*. But no matter how many successful tests you perform on animals, the first test on a human is the most nerve-racking. Every imaginable horror runs through your mind. Will there be health risks or dangers? My mind raced back to Pioneer Mouse #1 who lost his life for the cause of science. Would I be "Pioneer *Man* #1" and suffer the same fate?! And even outside of being

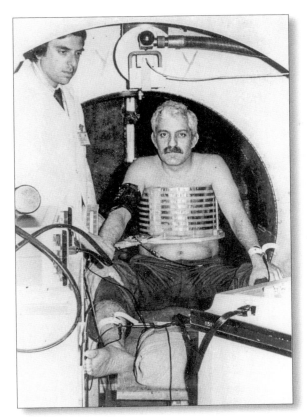

Figure 38. Raymond Damadian with Michael Goldsmith's first-ever live body (thoracic) NMR antenna, seated in *Indomitable* with EKG monitoring, defibrillator shock paddles, and skilled cardiologist in the event of a magnetically induced cardiac arrhythmia. The outcome was a normal EKG and no NMR signal.

"fried" like the mouse, what other kind of damage might be done? Internally? Externally? Short-term? Long-term? All these thoughts bounced around in my mind, and at times they dominated my every thought. But at the end of the day, there was only one way to find out.

On June 24, 1977, I entered *Indomitable* (figure 38).

My goal was to stay in the magnet for just 30 minutes for the expressed purpose of simply seeing if we were going to be able to get an NMR signal at all from my body, given the major concerns we had. Were we going to be able to achieve the necessary signal to noise ratio from Mike's first-ever human body NMR coil? Was there going to be sufficient magnet homogeneity from our first-ever human-sized NMR magnet to produce a signal from a small focused spot within the body? Would the human body, when placed within Mike's coil impedance, load Mike's coil to the extent that no signal could be generated by the coil? I entered the machine with a blood pressure cuff on my arm and

Figure 39. Larry Minkoff in *Indomitable* for the first-ever MRI scan of a human being, 1977 — "Mink 5"

EKG wires attached to my chest. An oxygen tank was ready in case I should need it, and a cardiologist was standing by as well. I sat down on the narrow board in the middle and slipped the coil-wrapped cardboard vest over my chest.

The tension was so thick you could almost see it. Certainly we all felt it. But the moment would not wait. We had to go forward. Human testing inside *Indomitable* was *inevitable*!

At 8:55 p.m. the machine was turned on and we all held our breaths. And nothing happened. Nothing!

After carefully searching for the problem, Mike and Larry found a broken wire, subsequently fixing it. Once again, I returned to my seated position inside *Indomitable* at 10:07 p.m.

And nothing happened . . . *again!*

For hours we tried to get a signal, but to no avail. Finally, we gave up for the night. The doctors and graduate students who had gathered to watch the test also packed up and left. Add another perplexing disappointment to our already long list.

The next day, we reconvened to discuss numerous reasons why we were unable to get a signal. Mike, who was substantially more rotund than me (figure 30), had the audacity to suggest that I was "too fat for his coil." How dare he! We later dubbed this the "Goldsmith Hypothesis" or the "Too Fat Hypothesis." Mike surmised that I was loading it down with my insurmountable "impedance." If there was ever a case of the pot calling the kettle "black," this was it!

"We need someone smaller," he argued. And as if scripted, Mike and I both turned and looked at Larry. Of the three of us, Larry was our only option, being the thinnest.

Thus we began trying to talk Larry Minkoff into the scanner.

Finally, on July 2, 1977, after much persuasion, Larry reluctantly agreed. This immediately prompted me to began compiling a two-page, pre-scan checklist that included 50 items, such as:

- producing a field on the *Indomitable* magnet and making sure it was stable,
- verifying that the vacuum was holding,
- establishing that the liquid helium level was adequate, and, of course,
- making sure all electronics were working properly, etc.

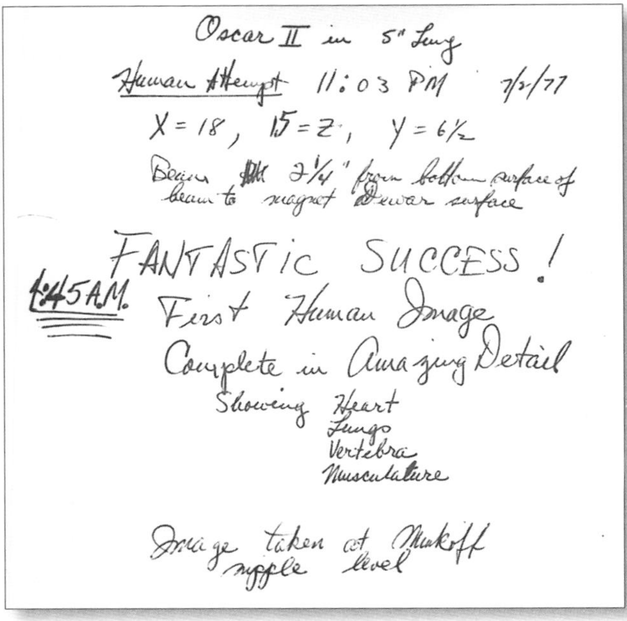

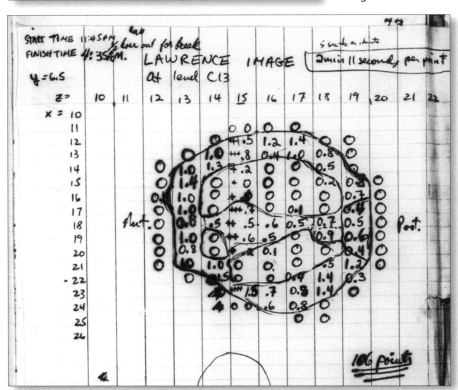

Figure 40 (left). Team *Indomitable's* jubilation on the achievement of the first-ever MRI scan of a human being — "Mink 5"

Figure 41 (below). Hand-drawn data of the 106 points of the first-ever scan of a human being — "Mink 5"

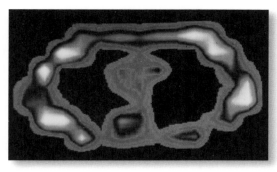

Figure 42. "Mink 5" — first-ever scan of a human being. Completed on Larry Minkoff in *Indomitable* at 4:45 a.m. the morning of July 3, 1977, with the image visualization of the heart, lungs, aorta, cardiac chamber, and chest wall at the thoracic level of T-8

This process took about 14 hours!

Finally, just before midnight, Larry took a deep breath and entered *Indomitable* (figure 39). Our initial "focused spot" was positioned in the "water rich" (NMR signal rich) location of Larry's heart. To our delight, we immediately got a signal! Then came the pivotal moment. The "focused spot" would be moved by moving Larry across the fixed position "focused spot" in the center of the magnet. When Larry was moved off-center to scan location #2, the "focused spot" would be within the "air sacs" of Larry's lung alveoli where the NMR signal should disappear because the signal generating hydrogen atoms of Larry's heart water were now replaced by the non-signal generating oxygen and nitrogen gas atoms of

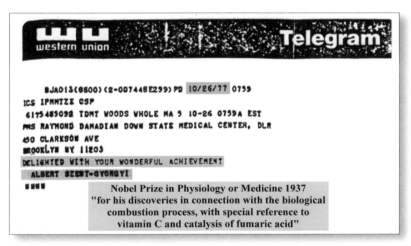

Figure 43. Congratulations from Dr. Albert Szent-Gyorgyi on the achievement of "Mink 5"

Larry's lungs. The hydrogen generated NMR signal should go away if our "focused spot" was genuinely focused. The transport seat was moved, positioning the "focused spot" in Larry's lungs where the signal should not exist. The hydrogen NMR signal vanished! Internally and silently I screamed, "Holy Smokes — it's actually gonna work" (figure 40). Over and above the entire whole stockpile of potential pitfalls, "It's actually gonna work!" The NMR scan of the live human body is going to *be* reality! We then moved the "focused spot" to the rest of his chest, namely his vertebra, musculature, and chest wall. The scan of Larry's torso produced 106 picture elements (pixels) (figure 41) in just under five hours. By comparison, an MRI today will generate more than 65,000 pixels in mere minutes. Slowly moving Larry inch by inch, we carefully watched as data appeared on the oscilloscope. Goldsmith took graph paper and colored pencils, sketching an image as he saw it (figure 41).

"Visionary nonsense" had become reality!

We called that first successful scan, "Mink 5" (figure 42). After Larry, of course.

At 2 a.m. and again at 3, we paused to give Larry a break, who was glad not to have suffered the same fate as the mouse. He had also not escaped from the coils like the monkey did! Elated, but exhausted, we finished at 4:45 a.m.

At last we'd done it. This would prove to be a red-letter date in all our lives (figure 43), and we hoped it would do the same in the medical world as well. We celebrated by opening a bottle of wine, toasting our success. I added to the celebration by triumphantly smoking a cigar. As I did, I paused to ponder the long and winding road that had led to this moment. Though others doubted, I had never wavered in my belief. I was secure and confident it could be done and I knew we were the ones to do it. Eight long years had passed since the original idea had first come to my mind. After climbing what at times seemed like insurmountable mountains, all our hard work had finally paid off.

God had intervened, and the world had an actual first scan of a live, breathing human being.

And we were the ones who had the privilege of making it happen.

But that wouldn't prove to be the end of the story for us. Far from it. There would be much more ahead, including additional hidden obstacles and as well as unforeseen enemies. Little did we know at the time, but our success would not go unchallenged.

Soon after we successfully built *Indomitable* and accomplished the first-ever scan (image) of the live human body, we got word about a setback Lauterbur was reporting regarding his own effort to construct a human-sized scanner and achieve the first image of the live human body. Lauterbur reported that the dimensions of the magnet the manufacturer had shipped to him had a bore size too small to scan a human. Because of my paper in *Science* that originated the idea of a full-body medical NMR scanner, we received Lauterbur's report of the delivery of a magnet inadequately sized to scan an adult human being, which he was reporting *after* the public announcement of our accomplishment on

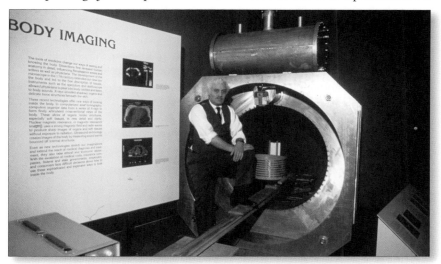

Dr. Damadian standing by *Indomitable* when it was on display at the Smithsonian.

Indomitable of the first-ever scan (image) of the live human body, as a concession that he had been unable to actually accomplish this herculean task. Indeed, to the best of our knowledge, this was a massive task that Lauterbur never accomplished even *after* our report of the first-ever NMR human body image on Larry Minkoff — "Mink 5." No such image of the human body or of a lesser-dimensioned child that would accommodate the lesser dimension of his magnet was *ever* published (to the best of our knowledge) by Lauterbur.

Having birthed the original idea of the NMR body scanner, we were intent on being the first to accomplish it. Failing to do so meant we might be denied the recognition for the original idea. The person who performed the first human scan was likely to go down in history as *the* inventor of the MRI.

I wanted that distinction to go to our team.

There was much more of the MRI story to be written.

Endnotes

1. Henry Morris, *The Biblical Basis for Modern Science* (Green Forest, AR: Master Books, 2002).
2. John C. Whitcomb and Henry M. Morris, *The Genesis Flood* (Phillipsburg, NJ: P & R Publishing, 1982).
3. Professor Eli Friedman was a very distinguished and influential professor at Downstate and was the director of nephrology in charge of patient kidney dialysis. He was currently housing his laboratory animals in that space.
4. Absolute zero is minus 273.15° Celsius. Helium had to be kept below minus 269° Celsius or it would boil off to useless gas.
5. This device is called the Veeco model MS17-AM.
6. A gauss is a unit of magnetic induction, and is one ten-thousandth of a *tesla*, another unit measuring magnetic strength.

CHAPTER

6

THE BACKLASH / TOO SOON TO QUIT

I am quite sure that when Thomas Edison finally achieved success in inventing the practical incandescent light bulb, there was a wave of excitement and relief that swept over both himself and those in his laboratory. After failing repeatedly on numerous occasions, the famous inventor reportedly said, "I have not failed. I've just found 10,000 ways that won't work."

With any pioneering work in any field, whether it be technology, medicine, or both — success is typically the result of thousands of failed experiments. At times you chase "ghost theories" which later prove to be only apparitions of the truth. You often find yourself wandering through a maze of mind games where test after test, experiment after experiment, can lead you back to the place from which you began. You become very familiar with "square one." Discovery is a demanding work, and it can be a cruel taskmaster.

At times, you want to quit. Circumstances, critics, and work associates may give up on the work. They may even give up on you, walking away and abandoning you to the task. But we who are in the field are not alone in this experience. Missionaries know this loneliness. So do pastors and other Christian workers who labor tirelessly to advance God's Kingdom. Many, like Paul, know the feeling of being abandoned by a younger, more inexperienced Timothy. Soldiers deployed to the battlefield have often wondered in the long months of duty whether their mission was really worth the sacrifice. Parents become weary in the long walk of raising children, and many lose focus and energy before their children are released into the world. Perhaps you've experienced repeated failure in your own life, and that has left you deflated and defeated, unable to carry on.

But carry on you must.

For it is only by taking the next step in our journey that we draw closer to the finish line and success. I must confess, at times my own heart seemed to call for my surrender. But where would humanity be if we were a race of quitters? Edison. Bell. Franklin. Pasteur. Carver. Ford. Gutenberg. The list goes on and on. These were all men who faced enormous roadblocks on their journey to discovery and success. They all heard the call to quit. But not one did. And the names of those who did are forgotten, washed down the drain of history.

I shudder to think of where I would be today had not my father (figure 9) and his family persevered when driven from their home in Armenia, a donkey and a cart as the only means of transportation. Even upon his arrival in the United States, his refusal to quit and his determination to find a good job eventually enabled him to provide for his family. I believe that struggle for survival and fierce work ethic was faithfully instilled within me.

The career path I chose was not an easy one. But it takes no real effort to lose. Winners know that victory comes, not by luck, but by hard work and a bulldogged refusal to give up.

I am reminded of the poem that reads:

> When things go wrong as they sometimes will,
> When the road you're trudging seems all uphill,
> When funds are low and the debts are high,
> And you want to smile, but you have to sigh.
> When care is pressing you down a bit.
> Rest, if you must, but don't you quit.
> Life is queer with its twists and turns
> As every one of us sometimes learns.
> And many a failure turns about
> When he might have won had he stuck it out:
> Don't give up though the pace seems slow —
> You may succeed with another blow.
> Success is failure turned inside out —
> The silver tint of the clouds of doubt.
> And you never can tell how close you are.

It may be near when it seems so far:
So stick to the fight when you're hardest hit
It's when things seem worst that you must not quit.
— Anonymous

In life, there are those who triumph and those who simply entertain romanticized ideas of success. The latter are soon cast by the wayside, shipwrecked on the rocks in their efforts to achieve. Like a marathon race, the course itself often weeds out those who ultimately fall short. Many aspire, but few attain. The triumphant, however, have a quality that makes them unique, setting them apart from the rest. This quality allows them to break free from the pack, elevating them to another level of competition. It's a trait so rare today that you hardly see it anymore. And what is this nearly extinct attribute?

Perseverance.

It's the ability to keep moving when others say it's okay to quit. It's the will to go forward when all manner of obstacles and enemies attempt to stop you and drive you back. Without perseverance, Edison could never have realized his revolutionary, world-changing invention. Neither could Orville and Wilbur Wright. But I have learned that the arena where perseverance is most needed is in life itself. It's required in relationships, and most importantly in our relationship with God Himself. And it sure comes in handy when obeying the often difficult and demanding tasks He calls His children to. I know the Apostle Paul developed it throughout his missionary journeys and the trials associated with his calling. Shipwreck. Beatings. Death Threats. Riots. Imprisonment. All these were a part of the "marathon race" set before him. The course itself to which he was called threatened to weed him out.

But it didn't.

This is one of those God-given "truths" I spoke of earlier, and it's a great example of how His principles go beyond mere facts and knowledge, to filtering down into where real life happens. Right down to where the rubber meets the road.

During the period of time we were feverishly working on making *Indomitable* a reality, I needed a heavy dose of this perseverance. But I learned in my experience that life's long journeys are simply a series of shorter races. I came to realize that I can only do what I can do *today*. And that's exactly what we did, arriving to work each day to face whatever obstacles and uphill climbs awaited us.

One. Day. At. A. Time.

And over the course of several years we found ourselves at last reaping the rewards of our labor.

Not only had we built the first full-body scanner, but we had successfully achieved the first-ever NMR (MRI) image of the live human body. This proved to be a major pioneering breakthrough in science and medicine. There was no doubt in our minds that this technology would radically change people's lives all over the world.

In the coming months, we scanned Larry Minkoff four more times in an effort to shorten our scan time. We were onto something big, and everyone could sense it. Unfortunately, the jubilant celebration resulting from our groundbreaking discovery didn't last very long.

Although we had celebrated that first night, what we had no way of knowing was that trouble and ridicule lurked right around the corner. Because of my fear of getting beat, I opted to forego the traditional route of getting a paper published about Larry Minkoff's original scan (Mink 5) before publicly announcing it so humanity could know immediately what had just been accomplished for the benefit of mankind. Instead, I decided to hold a press conference at Downstate to let the world know that NMR scanning of the live human body had finally become reality. The public relations person at our university had just left so I hired an independent firm to handle the announcement. They prepared a press release and put it out.

The next day, a number of news media showed up at Downstate and visited our lab to see *Indomitable* with Larry seated inside of it as we described how his scan had been accomplished. The attending media included local television stations and a reporter for *The New York Times*. We made our announcement and followed it up with several interviews. I thought this would put an end of the mockery and the ridicule. I reasoned that this would at last earn us the respect I felt we deserved for all our hard work, becoming the first-ever to scan a live human being by NMR.

I was wrong.

We got hammered.

To our complete shock, perhaps the result of undermining from our disappointed competitors, the local news stations did not report our achievement in a favorable light. Instead of praise, *The New York Times* story focused on the fact that we hadn't actually detected a cancer in our first-ever healthy human being (for which I, and especially Larry

Minkoff, were grateful!). The article ignored the grand importance of this monumental discovery, focusing instead on the fact that we had successfully produced the first-ever scan of a live human being. This was unbelievable to me. What I thought would be a triumphant moment acknowledging our near-miraculous accomplishment somehow turned into a public relations nightmare. How ironic that a discovery of such magnitude, which has since saved thousands (if not millions) of lives, detecting cancer, would be treated with such contempt.

Thankfully, there were also scores of congratulatory phone calls and telegraphs. But we likewise found ourselves subject to more ridicule and frustration than earlier with our initial test-tube efforts and promotions of it for financing. I thought our conclusive MRI scan would put an end to the race, silencing the critics once and for all. Unfortunately, it did not. Donald Hollis and Paul Lauterbur, not surprisingly, became two of our biggest opponents. For years following our first scan, both these men were quite vocal against its validity and significance, even though we had

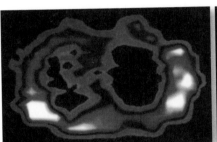 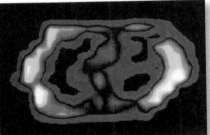

Figure 44. FONAR scan at the level of 1¾ inches below the Angle of Leaves, by the method of *Indomitable* in a man 46-years-old with pulmonary cat cell carcinoma. Tumor indicated by light blue infiltrate in the left lung field, which should be black, as it is in the right lung cavity. Midline structure (red) separating the two lung cavities is the cross section through the arch of the aorta. (*Philosophical Transactions of the Royal Society of London B*, 1980, vol. 289, p. 498, plate 2, figure 13)

Figure 45. FONAR cross-sectional scan through the thorax at the level of the 3rd intercostal space, by the method of Indomitable, in a patient with an adenoma carcinoma of the breast that metastasized to the right lung. The tumor is seen as a band of signal-producing tissue (light blue) bridging the right lung cavity. The tortuous structure separating the right and left lung cavities is the aortic arch. (1978, scanning time 36 minutes) (*Philosophical Transactions of the Royal Society of London B*, 1980, vol. 289, p. 497, plate 3, figure 15 color version)

Figure 46. The first-ever commercial MRI, the FONAR QED 80. The FONAR QED 80 was equipped with a computer-driven patient transport system (vertical white bed mount pictured at the front of the QED 80 scanner) to automate the manual three-dimensional step-wise scanning procedure utilized by *Indomitable*.

followed Larry Minkoff's initial scan with multiple publications of MRI images of patients with cancer (figures 44 and 45). In addition, we utilized our focus spot technology in the first-ever commercial scanner, the "QED 80" (figure 46) and sold and installed four of the FONAR QED 80 focused spot scanners.[1] We introduced the QED 80 at the 1980 annual meeting of the RSNA (Radiological Society of North America).

Though I shouldn't have been surprised at this continual criticism, I was. Since my days of testing cancer samples in New Kensington, Pennsylvania, back in July 1970, the possibility of an MRI scan of the human body was considered either to be a joke, not that important, or simply beyond reality. Some had called our work "visionary nonsense" even "science fiction." And there were also those, who after examining the evidence and deciding that our work was indeed credible, proceeded to blatantly rip off the idea, claiming credit for it themselves! I never cease to be amazed at brazen acts like this. There is something fundamentally wrong with a person taking something that does not rightfully belong to him. But according to the Bible, such is the nature of man (Jeremiah

17:9). God obviously knows this about His wayward creation, which is why He had to remind His own covenant people, *"Thou shalt not steal"* (Exodus 20:15). He even engraved it in *stone* so there would be no missing it, mistaking it, or misinterpreting it. A part of His infamous *Ten Commandments*, the Lord issued these moral parameters on His creation's character and behavior in order to teach mankind something about Himself and about *themselves*. I find it interesting how humanity finds it nearly impossible to uphold even the most rudimentary levels of this basic morality. However, fed by pride, jealousy, envy, and greed, man would rather take that for which he did not work than to sweat and toil to produce a work of his own hands.

I suppose it was inevitable this would happen. The potential for fame, scientific and technological notoriety, and of course financial gain perhaps made our discovery too tempting for some. But despite such efforts by unscrupulous men and companies, we have been able to prove time and again that we were first with the idea — first in its origination, first in its development, first in its invention and patent, first in its construction, and first in its commercialization as a product. However, I would be less than honest if I did not admit that such scientific piracy made me feel frustrated and angry.

In addition to stealing our intellectual property, many in the media, along with various competitors of ours, refused to give us the credit we deserved. The NMR community in particular was resentful of the fact that the "visionary nonsense" idea of NMR scanning of the live human body had come from an M.D., not a "real scientist." Worse yet, its actual construction and reduction to practice (proving its reality) had also come from an M.D. named Damadian. Lauterbur's attempt to build a scanner had been unsuccessful and Mansfield's attempt was not accomplished until *a year after Indomitable* produced its first-ever image of a live human body.

So you can understand my surprise when I saw a December 5, 1977, headline in the *Medical Tribune* that read:

New Body Scan Technique Gives Pictures In Living Color

I had submitted an article earlier that year but was told our scan of Larry was not "newsworthy." We had also submitted (unsuccessfully) Larry Minkoff's live body image to the *Medical Tribune* and others six months earlier. This particular story from Nottingham (England) detailed the "non-invasive" scan of Peter Mansfield's team. His pictures, however, were in reality nothing more than *hand-drawings* from an x-ray picture, *not* an actual image acquired from a live human body as we had done!

Nonetheless, though clearly we had made the first scan, our work was far from done. First and foremost among our goals was to reduce the scan time. We knew that nearly five hours in a machine would be far too much for a patient to endure. So on February 1, 1978, we successfully scanned Larry in 38 minutes. Lowering that time was yet another pioneering breakthrough and meant more viability for future commercial use of our machine.

So we set our sights on building machines for commercial use, and proceeded with great enthusiasm. Since we were used to primarily being concerned with concepts and creating, the issue of how we would actually *pay* for all this somehow became an afterthought. However, it soon proved to be the unavoidable and proverbial elephant in the room, and we were forced to address it. Finances, it seemed, were always an issue. What complicated things a bit was that by this point, I already owed Downstate hundreds of thousands of dollars, including twenty thousand for the phone bill alone! This didn't particularly sit well with the new Department chairman, who had replaced Dr. Eichna. He promptly had my phone shut off. For a while, I played a game of cat and mouse where I would have the phone secretly turned back on and he would respond by having it turned off. This went on for a while until I was finally able to pay the bill.

Another issue we faced was the exorbitant price of liquid helium, which would make commercial NMR units cost-prohibitive for hospitals and patients. Despite huge protests by the staff, I made the call to build a permanent magnet for the first commercial scanner instead of using a "supercon." Mike didn't think it could be done. So I found myself striving again to prove yet another critic wrong, even if that critic happened to be a member of my own team!

However, nine months after the success of Mink 5, we built our first scanner using a permanent magnet. The money issue continued to plague us like a nagging backache, and we were forced to shut down *Indomitable* and any further scanning from it.

Then one day in 1978, while doodling in my office, I came up with the idea to start a new company. I decided to call it FONAR (Field Focused Nuclear Magnetic Resonance). This was the name of the technique we used to scan Larry Minkoff as well as acquire other images from the body. Because of the continuing difficulties over our work at Downstate, I didn't need much time to convince Larry, Mike, and Joel to leave with me. We needed to spread our wings and fly with this thing, without any corporate hindrances or obstacles.

All we needed, again, was more money.

Yet again, the almighty dollar. It's been said that money makes a great slave, but a horrible master. And I would agree. Paul the Apostle also said that the "love of money is the root of all evil" (1 Timothy 6:10). He was right, of course. However, in medical research, it's a "necessary evil." We were well aware of how critical funding is, and though forced to keep locating new financial resources, we were also confident that if given the chance we could turn that money into a good servant, using it as a tool to better mankind. So we pressed on, and two years later, in April 1980, through much testing and fundraising, we took the world's first-ever commercial MRI — FONAR QED 80 — to the annual meeting of the American Roentgen Ray Society. Later that year we showcased it at the Radiological Society of North America (RSNA). Ironically, one of the first two scanners we eventually sold and installed was to Drs. Ross, Lie, Thompson, and Associates in Cleveland, Ohio (figures 47 and 48), not far from where Paul Lauterbur, our greatest competitor, was born. The other was sold to the University of Mexico in Monterrey, Nuevo Leon, Mexico.

Subsequently (and as expected) other companies copied us and began introducing their own commercial MRI scanners. To make matters even worse, the magnets they introduced had higher field strengths and were achieving better image quality. This led me to increase our magnet field strength from 500 gauss to 3,000 gauss (.3 Tesla). The increased strength meant we had to build a bigger and heavier magnet.

In 1982 we rolled out the Beta 3,000, which featured a markedly quieter magnet and generated images with much greater detail. Our first installation of the new model was at Brunswick Memorial Hospital on Long Island. Our next unit was installed at UCLA. We then began taking orders on a regular basis.

By 1983, we also had some stiff competition, with some 13 companies producing MRI scanners at that time. Sadly, not only were companies using our technology, they were also infringing all of our patents!

Later I would be quoted in a *Wall Street Journal* story following our eventual lawsuit with Johnson & Johnson: "The patent system is designed to provide the young inventor and the young company the

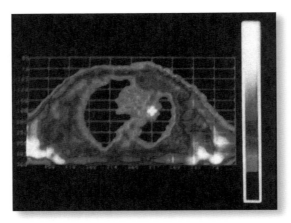

Figure 47. "Carcinoma of the left upper lobe with peripheral consolidation." Images published by Drs. Ross, Lie, Thompson & Associates from their FONAR QED 80 MRI scanner installed in their radiology practice in Cleveland, Ohio. QED 80 images were acquired by the step-wise 3D patient translocation method of Indomitable (*Radiology Nuclear Medicine Magazine*, June 1981 cover). The 3D step-wise translocation of the patient across the magnetically focused resonance aperture. The resonance aperture was achieved by focusing the "near field" magnetic component of the transmitted rf (U.S. Patent 3,789,832) in combination with the shaping of the static magnetic field of the region of interest to generate a spatially localized NMR signal.

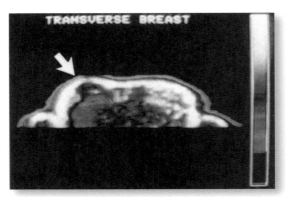

Figure 48. "NMR image of the breast shows a large mass (dark area) in the central position of the right breast. T_1 data are consistent with the diagnosis of cyst. (mean: 151, width: 239)." Images published by Drs. Ross, Lie, Thompson & Associates from their FONAR QED 80 MRI scanner installed in their radiology practice in Cleveland, Ohio. QED 80 images were acquired by the step-wise 3D patient translocation method of *Indomitable*. (*Radiology*, vol. 143, no. 1, April 1982, p. 202.)

protection needed to offset the resources available to huge competitors. This decision shows that there is justice for the little guy in America."

It's true. Without a patent system, people and corporations will shamelessly steal your ideas. To date more than 4,550 patents have been issued for the MRI. Our MRI patent was the first (figure 26). A patent is not cheap, costing the patentee between $10,000 and $12,000 by the time it is issued.

But our patent system is essential for converting new ideas to reality and generating new inventions. Without this patent system, innovators would have no protection for their inventions. Additionally, without patents they would have no means to finance companies to produce these inventions. Further, patents help generate the manufacturing companies that result in the enrichment of our economy and out nation. It's a domino effect of invention, patenting, funding, and progress. And all this leads to prosperity.

The patent principle came into existence in the U.S. Constitution, Article one, Section 8 (8), which reads:

> *The Congress shall have power . . . To promote the progress of science and useful arts, by securing for limited times to authors and inventors the exclusive right to their respective writings and discoveries.*

In recent years, "shell" companies have emerged, seriously threatening the critical viability of the American patent and the United States patent system. These companies manufacture nothing and contribute nothing, but are created solely to mine profits from the users of patents they have acquired licenses to. They are like trolls, lurking in the shadows beneath the bridges of commerce, waiting to pounce on their next victim to rob and drain away his assets. Even so, patents are critical in the creation of new products and technology. Without a patent system, I believe the number of inventions would decline drastically.

Not surprisingly, we had to fight and contend vigorously in order to protect our patents. However, we had no idea just how brutal the battle would become. However, I did not enter those battles without hope. And that hope was born, not from wishful thinking or romantic ideas of success, but rather from hope itself.

When the author of Hebrews wrote to encourage believers facing the struggles and challenges of life and faith, he instructed them to cast off anything that would hold them back. He then urged them to fix their eyes on Jesus, who is the "author and finisher of our faith" (Hebrews 12:2).

In other words, direct your faith and focus on the One who pioneered the greatest example of perseverance in history. Consider Jesus, who "endured the cross, despising the shame. . . . endured such contradiction of sinners against himself" (Hebrews 12:2–3). He goes on to remind them that none of them have shed blood in their resistance of sin (like Jesus did).

As such He is able to give *us* that same enduring spirit, enabling us to " not grow weary" or "lose heart." Jesus became my ultimate example, inspiring me to press on, both in my work as well as in my personal life. He didn't quit. And He didn't stop until He had fulfilled the mission of salvation for which His Father had sent Him.

C.W. Longenecker's poem "The Victor" says it well.

If you think you are beaten, you are.
If you think you dare not, you don't.
If you like to win but think you can't,
It's almost a cinch you won't.
If you think you'll lose, you're lost.
For out in the world we find
Success begins with a fellow's will.
It's all in the state of mind.
If you think you are outclassed, you are.
You've got to think high to rise.
You've got to be sure of yourself before
You can ever win the prize.
Life's battles don't always go
To the stronger or faster man.
But sooner or later, the man who wins
Is the man who thinks he can.

Endnotes

1. "QED" is an acronym for the Latin *Quid Erat Demonstrandum*, meaning "that which was meant to be proved" or "that which had to be demonstrated."

CHAPTER

7

80 MILLION REASONS TO COMPROMISE

O ne of the things I have come to love about Scripture is how brutally honest it is. It never soft sells or sugarcoats its characters or ever glosses over their faults and failures. In other words, the men and women of the Bible have no halos. Instead, the raw, uncut nature of God's Word records the accounts of ordinary men and women who often stepped outside of their comfort zones, and by faith attempted great things for God. And thousands of years later, their feats of faith continue inspiring people like me.

Of the many stories in Scripture that inspire me, the well-known account of David and Goliath is among my favorites. It's the historical account of an unlikely boy who defeated a formidable enemy. David, a young man, small and inexperienced in battle, finds himself facing a seasoned, professional Philistine warrior. Oh, and he's also 9'6" tall! It's the quintessential tale of the intimidating and the powerful threatening the frail and the weak. The classic underdog story. And yet, in an unusual twist of battlefield irony, David prevails and defeats the giant.

One of the reasons that story impresses me is because not for one minute is there any doubt in David's mind whether or not he's going to win. This, in spite of the fact that no one else seems to believe he can, not even his own brothers! I believe David's confidence stemmed from a high view of God and a firm sense of justice. This shepherd boy knew the difference between right and wrong: between honor and disrespect. His motivation was to bring recognition to Israel's God by conquering

Goliath. Had David not stepped out in courageous faith, Israel would have suffered certain bloody defeat and ended up as Philistine slaves (1 Samuel 17:8–9). That is, for the ones who actually survived the inevitable battle, it was a "winner-take-all" proposition, and everyone knew it.

And though that historical episode occurred thousands of years ago, similar battles continue to this day. These battles are not fought with slings and swords, but rather with suits and words. Little did I know I would soon find myself right in the middle of such a fight.

Soon after we had put the first-ever commercial MRI (FONAR QED 80) into the market, we discovered to our dismay, that bigger corporations began infringing on our patent. By 1983, 13 companies were manufacturing MRI machines and infringing on our patents. Not content to merely stand idly by while others pirated what was rightfully ours, we decided to let the courts settle the issue.

We decided to take on Goliath.

Actually a whole army of Goliaths.

Two of our biggest patent infringement lawsuits were against Johnson & Johnson and General Electric (then the largest corporation in the world).

Of course, we were forced to seek out our own patent attorneys, which we finally did, securing the services of the firm Lerner, David, Littenberg, and Samuels for our Johnson & Johnson litigation and a firm out of Minneapolis — Robins, Kaplan, Miller and Ciresi — to litigate the General Electric infringement. To be sure, going to court and suing some of the nation's largest and most powerful companies was *not* in my original plan when I secured my patents and founded FONAR.

As an additional part of protecting our patent, we also had to proceed with ligation against other major companies as well — Hitachi, Siemens, Toshiba, Shimadzu, and Philips. These corporate giants are recognized worldwide, household names with nearly impeccable reputations. But being a multimillion-dollar corporation also means you have plenty of money with which to retain some of the country's finest patent lawyers. In other words, Goliaths representing Goliaths! To the casual observer, they all appeared undefeatable. But had we not done this, we would have surely risked facing extinction as a company. We simply had no choice. It would be a showdown between the small, young company who invented *Indomitable* and the country's most *indomitable* corporations!

This whole experience for me proved to be a crash course in litigation and the court system. I had spent the better part of three decades doing laboratory work, not litigation. In that sense, I was in way over my head. Emotionally, I prepared for the worst, while at the same time hoping and praying for a victory. I knew I had truth on my side, and trusted that the courts would also see it that way.

Through this process I quickly learned that lawsuits were very time-consuming and enormously expensive, not to mention being a big distraction from the needs of work and business. But in order to preserve our company, defend our patent, and protect invention, we were forced to take these companies to court. Aside from the integrity issue and the justice we felt was due us, we also firmly believed people needed to know the truth.

The first of these giants we took on was Johnson & Johnson in 1982.[1] Some of Johnson & Johnson's patented products include Acuvue, Benadryl, Bengay, Johnson's Baby (shampoo), Listerine, Lubriderm, Motrin, Mylanta, Neosporin, Neutrogena, Nicoderm, Pepcid, Rogaine, Rolaids, Sinutab, Splenda, Sudafed, Tylenol, and Visine (the list goes on and on). Their name and brand is well established and ingrained in world commerce.

So we sued Johnson & Johnson, then waited as it took *three years* to go to trial! That's another thing I learned about our court system. The so-called "wheels of justice" do indeed grind exceedingly slowly. We knew Johnson & Johnson had infringed on our patent for the magnetic resonance imaging system they were selling. Put bluntly, they stole our idea, made their own machines and then took both the profit and the credit for it. They had sold close to 100 machines by the time we had to initiate litigation in order to survive. At the time, only about 250 machines were on the market worldwide, and fewer than 50 of those machines were made by us.

In the suit, we argued that there had been a blatant infringement on our patents.[2] Among the claims our lawsuit contended was that in the late 1970s, I had constructed an NMR apparatus large enough for a human being to be placed within it. Since then, a whole medical NMR industry (now called Magnetic Resonance Imaging or MRI) had been developed. The suit explained how doctors use NMR machines to help them decide what is wrong with their patients and subsequently what to do about it.[3] We further argued that these detailed MRI images did not exist in medical images (e.g., x-ray pictures) *before* my discovery of the pronounced tissue T_1 and T_2 differences that enabled them, the pronounced T_1 and T_2 differences in the body's healthy and diseased tissues that make more than 90 percent of all the MRI images produced today; MRI's "T_1 weighted" and "T_2 weighted" MRI images.

Thus, our argument in the district court was that Johnson & Johnson was using *our* patented claims on T_1 and T_2 in *their* T_1 and T_2 images to generate the pixel contrast needed to visualize cancers in MRI images. They were also using our patent to generate the pixel contrast needed to visualize anatomic detail in the body's critical life-giving soft tissue vital organs (brain, heart, liver, kidney, spleen, pancreas, and key non-bony spinal structures [discs, ligaments, etc.]). Prior to our discovery, all these previously were visualized by *x-ray* technology, which for these purposes were inferior and inadequate.

The trial in Federal District Court in Boston lasted for two months, during October and November of 1985. Thankfully, the jury ultimately ruled in our favor. Their positive verdict meant two things: (1) we had successfully slayed our first "giant," and (2) Johnson & Johnson would have to pay us millions in damages and royalties *plus* be forced to stop using our technology. Needless to say, this was a huge victory for us. Up to this point we had not turned a profit in seven years of existence.

In *The New York Times* article about the verdict, Lorraine Schwarz, an analyst at Salomon Brothers, had this to say:

> "Winning the suit could change the dynamics in the industry. If it is upheld, FONAR could collect money from everybody that currently manufactures the machine. The numbers get almost embarrassing." She added that "as a result of the suit, FONAR could receive upward of $50 million in damages and royalties."

I was quoted in the *Times* article as saying, "This was the test case for us. And we are making plans to file similar suits or to negotiate royalty arrangements with the six other companies that sell the machines."

As Scripture says, there is a time for everything (Ecclesiastes 3). Jesus even said there is a time to turn the other cheek (Matthew 5:39; Luke 6:29). However, this was *not* one of those times. Rather it was more appropriately a time to fight like David. It was also a time to argue the veracity of our case like Paul did his before the Roman courts in Acts 25–26. Through contending for what was rightfully ours, we were fighting for the principle of *truth* itself, and the integrity of other inventors like us in the future who would surely suffer similar victimization of their patents.

In that same *Times* article, Robert Kniffen, a Johnson & Johnson (J&J) spokesman commented from a prepared statement which read: "Johnson & Johnson firmly believes that its magnetic resonance imaging equipment has never infringed any claims of the Damadian/FONAR patent and that the entire patent is invalid. We believe that the jury's finding against us is entirely unwarranted and will be rejected."

Johnson & Johnson stated that it planned to immediately appeal if the judge upheld the jury's verdict.

Obviously, we felt confident Judge Robert E. Keeton would uphold the jury verdict and award us the appropriate damages and royalties.

He didn't!

In a stunning and surprising move, Judge Keeton overruled the jury's verdict. In his summary on January 31, 1987, he wrote:

> Plaintiffs having withdrawn with prejudice their Second Cause of Action (for unfair competition), and having waived at the commencement of trial all claims in R. Damadian Patent No. 3,789,832 other than Claims 1, 2, 7, 8, and 10, the case having been tried before a jury, and the court having ruled on post-trial motions, for the reasons stated in the Opinion of January 10, 1986, it is hereby ORDERED, ADJUDGED AND DECREED:
>
> 1. Defendants Johnson & Johnson and Technicare Corporation have not infringed or induced infringement of Claims 1, 2, 7, 8, or 10 of the Damadian Patent No. 3,789,832;
>
> 2. Claims 7, 8, and 10 of the Damadian Patent No. 3,789,832 are invalid;
>
> 3. As to Claims 1 and 2 of the Damadian Patent No. 3,789,832, defendants have failed to establish any of their asserted defenses of invalidity, unenforceability or patent fraud.
>
> 4. The complaint is hereby dismissed; and
>
> 5. Defendants are awarded their costs in this action."

This is referred to as J.N.O.V. (Judgment Notwithstanding the Verdict). In other words, the judge essentially ignored the jury's decision and overruled them in order to pronounce his own verdict in the case.

Lawrence G. Foster, a spokesman for Johnson & Johnson, said in *The New York Times* story that the decision "relieved the great concern that we would be locked out of this magnetic imaging."

It goes without saying that this reversal left us in utter shock, not to mention being very upset. We could never have imagined that a judge could or would so arbitrarily and completely reverse a jury's verdict, especially in light of the clear evidence that had been presented. Of course, our first clue should have been when we observed Judge Keeton jovially lunching each day in the courtroom cafeteria with J & J's attorneys while we sat alone at our table.

This same judge also gave specific instructions to the jury regarding claim 7 of the '832 patent upon which J&J had infringed. Specifically, during the trial, J&J's attorneys argued they were not performing clause 7f, the parenthetical clause at the end of claim 7, and therefore were not using (infringing) my company's patent. The patent attorney, however, who wrote the '832 patent, testified at trial that he had deliberately set off this terminal phrase of claim 7 by a *comma*, thereby making it a "hoped for result" under patent law and not a required step. In spite of the testimony of the patent's legal author, Judge Keeton in his instructions to the jury, ordered the jury that while deliberating the '832 patent, they must *remove* the comma in claim 7 and replace it with the word "and," thereby making it a required step of the claim.

We couldn't believe that our life's work was being decided by a *comma*!

Notwithstanding Judge Keeton's order to replace the comma in claim 7f with the word "and," the jury nevertheless ruled in our favor, attributing infringement by Johnson and Johnson of our '832 patent.

Attempting to overcome this catastrophic ruling by Judge Keeton regarding our invention of the MRI, we appealed to the United States Court of Appeals for the Federal Circuit (CAFC). In our filing, we claimed that Judge Keeton had committed "prejudicial error" in his "rewording" of clause (f) of claim 7 in its instructions to the jury *instead of* quoting that clause directly. Claim 7f read "comparing the values obtained in (e) with predetermined like values for normal and cancerous tissue, said comparison indicating the existence and degree of malignancy."

The Appellate Court unfortunately upheld the District Court judge and dismissed the case, stating, "We conclude that the district court correctly determined that no evidence, and thus no substantial evidence, supports a finding that users of J & J's machine practice the method of claims 1 and 2 of the (Damadian) '832 patent. The jury's verdict that J & J infringed and induced infringement of those claims therefore cannot stand. The district court's judgment that claims 1 and 2 are not infringed is affirmed. FONAR's request that this court order a new trial is *denied*. The judgment that J & J has not proven claims 1 and 2 invalid or unenforceable is vacated and the appeal from that judgment is dismissed as moot, *affirmed in part, vacated in part*."

So we had victory with the jury but defeat with the judge. In essence we won, but we also lost in the end, the part that ultimately mattered.

The giant remained alive and at large, emboldened perhaps to seek someone else to conquer and devour.

As for us, we limped off the battlefield, wounded and bleeding. We had to move on, as there were other battles to fight. In 1995, we settled a patent dispute with Hitachi Ltd. Opening arguments began in a federal jury trial in Hauppauge, Long Island, New York. We had sued Hitachi and a subsidiary, Hitachi Medical, for $62 million over four patents related to our MRI technology. However, considering the financial pressure we were under due to attorneys, court costs, and simply to keep FONAR floating, we were forced to settle for far less. Disappointed, we soldiered on.

A year later we reached an agreement with Siemens Medical Systems Inc., but again with the continued financial stress, we settled again for a much smaller amount than their actual infringements should have paid out. Siemens released a one-time payment for past and future royalties. We also agreed to issue licenses to each other allowing the use of various components of magnetic resonance imaging technology. Again, not the "best case scenario" we had hoped for, but we were at least moving forward and gaining some positive momentum. Being in court was a distraction and an irritation, albeit a necessary one at the time. However, all those court battles to date would prove to be relatively minor compared to what awaited us. They were mere sideshows leading up to the "main event." The ultimate "Goliath," and biggest giant of all, waited for us just over the next hill.

General Electric was the largest of all the colossal, corporate titans we faced. Contrary to my desire after the despairing J&J result and its fruitless and expensive outcome, we filed suit against General Electric on September 1, 1992, after my son, Timothy's, relentless urging. Tim volunteered to take over the management of the litigation to spare me the fruitless agony I perceived it to be following the J&J experience. Suing over U.S. Patent 4,871,966 issued in 1989 for the use of MRI equipment to obtain multiple image slices at different angles (multi-angle-oblique imaging), we also brought suit regarding U.S. Patent 3,789,832 for the use of our original invented T_1 and T_2 scanning technology, based on the pronounced T_1 and T_2 differences we had discovered between cancer tissue and normal tissue and between the normal tissues themselves.[4]

We were well aware that taking on a corporation of General Electric's size could literally make or break us. GE had a long and storied history that included an impressive list of financial and corporate successes, including being named by *Forbes* as the fourth largest company in the world.[5] Though we certainly appeared as grasshoppers in their sight, I believed that nothing was impossible with God. Others may have been too intimidated to even consider such a challenge, given the sheer magnitude and financial resources at the disposal of such a corporation like GE. To charge into a battle like this seemed like suicide, or at the very least, madness. But again, we had no choice but to proceed by faith. While GE was fighting for one more avenue of income among hundreds they possessed, we were fighting for survival! Our existence as a company hung in the balance. My Armenian and French perseverance was now kicking into overdrive. I was determined we would fight to the end and survive!

What made this epic court case even more dramatic was that GE had one more advantage in their favor — a Chief Executive Officer by the name of Jack Welch. Welch was a very powerful and savvy man, not to mention world famous. He was, in essence, the "Giant within the Giant." When he eventually left the company in 2001, his retirement package was worth more than $400 million. They don't give $400 million to losers. Welch had established himself as a proven winner and a seasoned business warrior. He was not a man to be taken lightly and he had every intention of defeating us. Having begun his tenure at GE in 1981, the company's revenue rose from just under $27 billion to approximately $130 billion in the year before he retired. Welch knew how to make business grow and expand. He didn't get to be the CEO of one of the largest corporations in the free world by being passive. Instead, Jack Welch was a veteran leader.

And he wanted to win this case.

I began to sense a bit of what David may have felt as he walked into the Valley of Elah to face his taunting Philistine foe. Conventional wisdom would have predicted our chances of winning this thing to be "slim to none." Closer to "none," actually.

Three years later, when the trial finally came to a conclusion, I found myself in the United States District Court for the Eastern District of New York. I was there because the jury had reached a verdict in our case. Needless to say, we all waited with tense anticipation for the jury's announcement. The tension mounted as the female juror stood and began reading their decision. However, the language was so technical that I found it hard to understand which direction she was going! When she finally finished, Judge Wexler, noting the confused look on my face, said, "Dr. Damadian, I can tell from your face that you don't understand the verdict. So let me put it to you plainly. You *won* on all counts."

The jury had determined GE to be *guilty* of infringement of patents '966 and '832, ordering them to pay FONAR $128.7 million in damages! I could hardly believe what I was hearing! Later, one of the female jurors saw me in the hallway and remarked, "So clear was the evidence against GE, if it hadn't have been for some of the men on the jury, the ladies would have given you *400* million!"

We were obviously overjoyed at the jury's decision in our favor. However, that joy would prove to be short-lived as, predictably, GE appealed the decision of the District Court to the U.S. Appellate Court for patents, the Court of Appeals for the Federal Circuit (the CAFC). But on February 25, 1997, the CAFC upheld the District Court's 1995 decision of infringement. Upon receiving the news, Welch, obviously not happy with the CAFC's decision, immediately called for a private meeting with me in Manhattan.

"Well," he said to me over the phone, "I should have made this call a long time ago. I'll meet you anywhere. Tell me when and where."

I was talking on the phone with one of the most powerful businessmen in the world. Though I knew he was just a man, there was still an intimidation factor present. I knew it, and I'm pretty sure Welch knew it. Even so, I also knew that courage isn't the *absence* of fear, but rather *doing what you fear*.

I declared to Welch, "I'm not meeting you without my lawyers."

So I called two of my brilliant patent lawyers, Ron Schutz and Marty Lueck. Ron was a former electronics engineer who decided to go into law and become a patent attorney.

The three of us met Welch at GE's headquarters at 30 Rockefeller Place in Midtown Manhattan. We were ushered into a boardroom, and once we were all there, Jack Welch announced, "Dr. Damadian, I'm ready to make you an offer. I'm prepared to give you a check today for *$80 million*. But I'm *not* going to pay you for damages on your '832 patent" — my original patent that originated MRI.

GE was offering to pay FONAR $80 million for FONAR's second patent, the '966 multi-angle-oblique patent. In doing so, this would set aside my original '832 patent, which would then be licensed to GE. If FONAR refused GE's $80 million offer, Welch threatened to file for a second hearing by the CAFC and request what is called an "en banc" hearing. This would mean *all* of the CAFC judges (8 total) would be participating in place of the 3 judges who had been a part of the original decision. It meant we would roll the dice and take our chances that the judges might rule in GE's favor.

$80 million.

There are a lot of things people will do for money, and a lot more things they would do for a *lot* of money. How would you respond if someone offered your company a check for $80,000,000? Eighty million for something invented by your own company? And yet, accepting this check would mean I would no longer own the rights to the original '832 patent that had founded the entire MRI industry.

It was in that moment I suddenly found myself in a different kind of valley. Only this time it wasn't a valley of battle but rather a valley of *decision*. Sitting before me was one of the most powerful men in the corporate world. His bold leadership and persuasive personality were legendary. And Welch was not used to being told "no." The decision I faced that day was a test for me. My response in that moment would reveal what kind of man Vahan and Odette Damadian had raised all those years ago. And I knew I would remember it the rest of my life.

Our company was being offered $80 million.

Just walk away, Damadian. Cut your losses and move on. That's all I had to do. It would all be over in a matter of minutes with the signing of a check and my signature on an agreement. Simply accept the handshake of compromise and walk out of that boardroom $80 million richer. Sounds simple. Easy. Even a "no-brainer," right?

But it wasn't the right thing to do. It wouldn't have been a *truthful* decision for me. And not only would it have invalidated my entire life's work in the disabling of my original invention and patent, but it also would have violated my own personal integrity. Having been on this earth a few years, I knew what God wanted me to do in that moment. Those grey hairs on my head weren't just there because of countless hours of labor spent in the laboratory. There were a few strands of wisdom also woven in there as well. And that wisdom counseled me not to throw my life's investment and work down the drain. Accepting that check meant that all I had accomplished to date would be wiped away, exchanged for an expensive piece of paper.

This life can rob you of many things — material possessions, position, physical health, etc. — but one thing they can't take away from you is your integrity. That's something that you alone control. It is yours to develop and protect. You can give it away or trade it for something less valuable, but those who do so eventually regret it, if not in this life then surely in the next.

So I decided that I would not and *could* not concede, compromise, and accept his offer, no matter how attractive or lucrative it was. Looking into the eyes of GE's CEO, I said, "Mr. Welch, you are asking me to take my heart and soul, my invention, and surrender it as irrelevant. I can't do that."

Upon hearing those words, the blood drained from the faces of my two attorneys. Ron and Marty had taken this case on 100 percent contingency for 40 percent of the award (presuming we would win). They were dying on the inside because I was walking away from their $32 million. You should have seen the look on my attorneys' faces when I turned Welch down. "Stunned" doesn't even come close to describing it. But I just couldn't take the offer.

Therefore, I did what few people had ever done.

I said "No" to Jack Welch.

And as promised, GE proceeded to file with the CAFC for an "en banc" hearing by all the judges.[6] Fortunately, the "en banc" CAFC upheld the original 1995 decision of the U.S. District Court in our favor, ordering GE to pay FONAR the $128 million judgment. GE responded by requesting the CAFC postpone the $128 million payment to FONAR until *after* their further appeal to the United States Supreme Court. However, the CAFC denied their request and ordered GE to pay FONAR "Now."

And the stone sank into Goliath's forehead.

FONAR CORPORATION and Dr. Raymond V. Damadian, Plaintiffs/Cross–Appellants,

v.

GENERAL ELECTRIC COMPANY, and Drucker & Genuth, Mds, P.C., d/b/a South Shore Imaging Associates, Defendants–Appellants.

Nos. 96–1075, 96–1106 and 96–1091.

United States Court of Appeals, Federal Circuit.

Feb. 25, 1997.

Rehearing Denied; Suggestion for Rehearing In Banc Declined May 8, 1997.*

VERDICT

On May 27, 1997 the Honorable Wm. H. Rehnquist, Chief Justice, the United States Supreme Court, enforced the Order of the Federal Circuit Court of Appeals and ordered G.E. to pay Fonar. G.E. paid Fonar $128,705,766 for patent infringement. G.E. was further restrained from any use of Fonar technology.

The Court found that G.E. had infringed U.S. Patent 3,789,832, MRI's first patent, which was filed with the U.S. Patent Office in 1972 by Dr. Damadian. The Court concluded that MRI machines rely on the tissue NMR relaxations that were claimed in the patent as a method for detecting cancer, and that MRI machines use these tissue relaxations to control pixel brightness and supply the image contrasts that detect cancer in patients.*

The Court also found infringement of U.S. Patent 4,871,966 concerning a technique of obtaining MRI images at multiple angles.

AFFIRMED BY THE UNITED STATES SUPREME COURT

* The patent also discloses the first ever *comparison* study of the tissue NMR relaxations of the *normal* tissues thus demonstrating for the first time that the discovery by Dr. Damadian of the dramatic *differences* in the NMR relaxations of living tissues disclosed in the patent is true for living tissue in *general*. The discovered relaxation differences of *both* the cancerous and *normal* tissues are an integral part of the Court enforced 1972 patent claims (Claim 1a,1b,1c) establishing *standards* for the *normal* tissues and malignant tissues of the same type. The NMR relaxation differences disclosed in the patent for normal tissues as well as for cancers are used throughout MRI imaging to supply and *control* pixel contrast. *The tissue NMR relaxation, which does not exist in any other imaging modality, provides the exceptional contrast of MRI (10 to 30 times that of x-ray) and is responsible for the extraordinary beauty of the MRI image.*

Figure 49. May 27, 1977, verdict FONAR vs. GE, U.S. Supreme Court, Wm. Rehnquist, Chief Justice, enforcement of FONAR's first-ever patent on MRI, U.S. Pat. 3,789,832, and U.S. Pat. 4,871,966 concerning a technique for multi-angle oblique MRI imaging and the U.S. Federal Court order of $128,705,766 for patent infringement

General Electric did write the check, but then went ahead and appealed to the Supreme Court. The final blow was dealt when GE's Cert Petition to the United States Supreme Court to reverse the CAFC's decision was denied by Chief Justice William Rehnquist on October 6, 1997 (figure 49). It was officially (and finally) over.

I was in Washington with Lou Bonanni, our executive vice president, when the Supreme Court decision came down. We were making a presentation of FONAR's UPRIGHT® MRI and its benefits for servicemen to some U.S. Army generals, when, in the midst of my presentation, one of the generals' secretaries entered the room insisting I take a critical phone call. And I'm supremely glad I did. Our attorney had called to relay the news that the U.S. Supreme Court had *denied* GE's Cert Petition to vacate the Court of Appeals for the Federal Circuit's decision upholding our patents. Relaying the good news to Lou, the two of us began dancing up and down, screaming with joy, to the shock and surprise of the Army generals. I can now check this off my bucket list: dancing before generals!

We had won!

Later that same year, Jack Welch retired from GE, and Jeff Immelt became its CEO. Assuring me, "My word is my bond," Immelt promised me GE would never manufacture an UPRIGHT® MRI. And he was indeed true to his word. GE did, however continue to make conventional MRI's, for which they also paid us $10 million for licensing fees! We gave thanks to God, and in turn invested all that money back into FONAR. While some of the amount could have been distributed to me because of my retained rights under my '832 patent, *all* of the award was directed to FONAR for the benefit of FONAR's shareholders and for the further advancement of our company's mission.

Our persistence had prevailed, our integrity remained intact, and my heart overflowed with gratitude to God. The truth was triumphant! As Shakespeare's Launcelot Gobbo put it in the "Merchant of Venice" "the TRUTH WILL OUT."David had overcome Goliath . . . *again*!

Endnotes
1. Johnson & Johnson is a U.S multinational medical devices, pharmaceutical, and consumer packaged goods manufacturer founded in 1886. It was ranked at the top of Harris Interactive's National Corporate Reputation Survey for seven consecutive years up to 2005. J&J was also ranked as the world's most respected company by *Barron's Magazine* in 2008, and was the

first corporation awarded the Benjamin Franklin Award for Public Diplomacy by the U.S. State Department in 2005 for its funding of international education programs.

2. Our lawsuit stated:

Claims 1 and 2 of the '832 patent read:

1. A method for detecting cancer comprising:

a. measuring and establishing standard NMR spin-lattice relaxation times and spin-spin relaxation times for both normal and cancerous tissue of the type under analysis using as an indicator nuclei at least one nuclei which exhibits deviant behavior in cancerous tissue;

b. measuring the NMR spin-lattice relaxation times and spin-spin relaxation times for the suspected tissue to determine the extent of deviant behavior of the indicator nuclei; and

c. comparing the values obtained in (b) against the standards obtained in (a).

2. The method of claim 1, wherein the indicator nuclei are cell water protons.

3. Specifically, NMR imaging machines use the amplitude of the NMR signals from points in the body to set the pixel (picture element) brightness of the pixels that form the image. NMR signal amplitude depends on three factors, of which T_1 and T_2 are the major contributor of T_1 and T_2 NMR images. T_1 and T_2 images constitute more than 90% of the MRI images acquired. The marked T_1 and T_2 differences discovered by myself between cancer and healthy tissues and between the healthy tissues themselves provide the differences in pixel brightness (pixel contrast) that generate exceptional detailed images.

4. Raymond Damadian, "Tumor Detection by Nuclear Magnetic Resonance," *Science*, 171: 1151–1153, 1971). T_1 and T_2 images constitute 80–90% of all MRI scans performed today for the human body.

5. Other indicators of GE's success include being ranked in 2011 among the Fortune 500 as the 26th largest firm in the U.S. by gross revenue; being ranked in 2011 among the Fortune 500 as the 14th most profitable; being listed in 2011 as the 4th-largest in the world among the Forbes Global 2000; in 1896, being one of the original 12 companies listed on the newly formed Dow Jones Industrial Average. After 117 years, it is the only one of the original companies still listed on the Dow index.

6. There were seven judges since one had removed himself from the case.

CHAPTER
8

NOBILITY WITHOUT THE NOBEL

In life, there are no guarantees, and I have found that there are but a few things you can really count on. The love of God and the truth He provides are the sure foundation upon which any wise person should build their lives (Matthew 7:21–29). Even so, we all carry on in life with the hope (and assumption) that justice and equity usually win. And in the case of our suit against GE, this proved to be true. Fairness is one of the guiding principles by which society exists and conducts business. We earn a week's wage and expect our employer to give us that which we have earned — a week's salary. We answer questions correctly on a school exam and rightfully anticipate (even predict) the resulting grade. Even in science, we can forecast certain experimental results based on chemical combinations and the laws of nature.

But at times this fairness and equity isn't quite so "cut and dried." When outcomes are ultimately decided by human judgment, results are not always so predictable. As a scientist, I am trained and experienced in dealing with reliable end results. The whole point of "experimenting" is so you can ultimately reach a dependable and consistent conclusion. In other words, you arrive at a point where you can confidently proclaim, "The facts don't lie." That's when unmistakable truth becomes crystal clear to everyone who encounters it, regardless of previous bias, perspective, or presupposition. All science depends on this process. It's what moves a postulate to a hypothesis, and what transforms a theory into actual *fact*.

When it came to the Nobel Prize for Physiology or Medicine in 2003, I leaned heavily on my clear record of discovery being validated. For some ten years previous to this, I had become aware that I was being considered for the prize. It was time for me to receive my just due from the worldwide scientific community. Additionally, I also had experienced firsthand the words of the wisest man who ever lived:

> There is nothing better for a man, than that he should eat and drink, and that he should make his soul enjoy good in his labour. This also I saw, that it was from the hand of God (Ecclesiastes 2:24).

That same Solomon also wrote:

> A man shall be satisfied with good by the fruit of his mouth: and the recompence of a man's hands shall be rendered unto him (Proverbs 12:14).

The Apostle Paul echoed Solomon's spirit when he instructed the Ephesians: "Let him that stole steal no more: but rather let him labour, working with his hands the thing which is good, that he may have to give to him that needeth" (Ephesians 4:28).

Indeed, I had labored, and "with my own hands," built the first-ever human-size MRI scanner and produced the very first MRI image of a human being (figure 42). I had done this with the intention of sharing with "him who is in need." My hands. My labor. My work. My invention. My contribution to the world. And *all* for God's glory.

In a deliberation process that had been going on for a decade, those who make the decision regarding the prestigious Nobel Prize award came to the conclusion that someone other than me deserved to be recognized. In the early hours of October 6, 2003, I awoke to check the Nobel Prize's website. What I learned was not only had the award been given to two other men, but also that I had been *excluded* (figures 50–52). It was as if I and my pioneering work and discovery had never existed.

The 2003 Nobel Prize in Physiology or Medicine was awarded to Paul Christian Lauterbur (a chemist from the University of Illinois) and

The Nobel Prize in Physics 1981
Nicolaas Bloembergen, Arthur L. Schawlow, Kai M. Siegbahn

"for their contribution to the development of laser spectroscopy"

Damadian published his idea under the title, "Tumor Detection by Nuclear Magnetic Resonance" in the March 1971 issue of *Science* magazine. "In principle," he wrote, "nuclear magnetic resonance (NMR) techniques combine many of the desirable features of an external probe for the detection of internal cancer."[221]

"T_1 and T_2, everybody uses those quantities," said Professor Bloembergen. "Dr. Damadian's contribution was to apply it to living tissues. That's the big step and that's not so easy."

"I knew that Damadian was talking about it and working on it in the early '70s. And, you know, we sort of wished him luck and waited to see what would come out. I was very fascinated to see that cancerous tissue would have different relaxation times [from non-cancerous tissue].

Dr. Damadian deserves credit for calling attention to the fact that differences in NMR relaxation times T_1 and T_2 in human cells existed and he used this to determine whether the cell was normal or diseased (cancerous). He further demonstrated that such measurements can be made on a living human body. He produced the first body scans.

A second important step was that of Dr. Paul Lauterbur who combined Damadian's results and faster data acquisition with CAT scanning techniques. The latter had been developed by Professors Hounsfeld and Cormack, who received the Nobel Prize for its application in X-ray diagnostics.

In my opinion, Dr. Raymond Damadian's contribution is as important and as significant as the second step made by Lauterbur."[1]

Nicolaas Bloembergen

Nobel Prize in Physics (1981)
"for their contribution to the development of laser spectroscopy"
Professor of Physics, Harvard University

[1] The Pioneers of NMR and Magnetic Resonance in Medicine - The Story of MRI, James Mattson, Merrill Simon, Bar-Ilan Univ. Press, p 461-462

Figure 50. Professor Nicholas Bloembergen's acknowledgement of Dr. Damadian's priority in the invention of the MRI

"We are perplexed, disappointed and angry about the uncomprehensible exclusion of Professor Raymond Damadian M.D. from this year's Nobel Prize in Physiology or Medicine. MRI's entire development rests on the shoulders of Damadian's discovery of NMR proton relaxation differences among normal and diseased tissues and his proposal of external scanning of NMR relaxation differences in the human body, published in Science in 1971"

Eugene Feigelson, M.D.
Dean of the College of Medicine
SUNY Downstate Medical Center
Distinguished Service Professor
Senior Vice President for Biomedical Education and Research

Figure 51. Dean Feigelson's distress regarding Downstate's heartbreak resentment at being denied the recognition by the Nobel Committee that they eminently deserved for their faculties' creation and construction of the first-ever MRI

Dear Ray:

I couldn't believe the news on Monday morning. It is outrageous that you were not selected as the winner of the Nobel Prize for Physiology or Medicine for your pioneering basic research and development that led to modern MRI!

Paul dropped by my office yesterday. It's a sad time for him too. He worked so hard every year for the past several years to see that all the forms and supporting letters for your nomination were written and sent in on time.

Personal regards,

Robert F. Furchgott

Nobel Prize in Physiology and Medicine 1998
"discovery of the role of nitric oxide
as a signalling molecule"

Figure 52. Professor Robert Furchgott's outrage at the injustice done by the Nobel Committee's decision for the 2003 Nobel Prize for MRI.

Sir Peter Mansfield (a physicist from the University of Nottingham) "for their discoveries concerning magnetic resonance imaging."[1]

Of course, I was well acquainted with Lauterbur and Mansfield. Lauterbur was a PhD chemist who was on the Board of Directors of

NMR Specialties Corporation in New Kensington, Pennsylvania, where I had made my original MRI discovery and where I had previously done my experiments with Dr. Cope. A lot had happened since those days. What's intriguing is that today the whole NMR machine I made my discovery on (figure 19) has been converted through technology down to one chip on a motherboard. Indeed, a lot has changed!

But specifically, my experience with Dr. Lauterbur began when the president of NMR Specialties, Paul Yajko, came to me and said, "Dr. Damadian, your discovery is very interesting. If we can get Dr. Lauterbur to endorse your discovery, that would help you gain rapid acceptance of your discovery and recognition around the world."

I responded, "That sound's great, Paul. Let's do that."

A potentially great idea, to be sure. And one which he followed up on. The only problem was that Lauterbur's response to the suggestion was less than compliant. "I'm not interested in that," was his curt reply. His unexpected response was not only frustrating to me, but also not a good first impression of Dr. Lauterbur.

I've always felt there was a general underlying resentment in the nuclear magnetic resonance community against me because I wasn't a PhD like others, but rather merely a "lowly MD." NMR technology had been in use for 24 years, and here comes some MD from the "outside" who makes this groundbreaking medical discovery. And they didn't like that. Lauterbur's PhD was actually in NMR, and someone not in the "fraternity" like me had made the discovery. It's as if my discovery itself wasn't merit enough to earn me a place among the research community "elite." But apparently this general snubbing of my discovery was not entirely universal. A graduate student at Johns Hopkins at the time, Leon Saryan, read my 1971 *Science* paper and went to his thesis adviser, Dr. Hollis, and asked him if he could repeat my tissue NMR experiments and follow up on it. Hollis agreed and Saryan proceeded to repeat my experiments. Lauterbur later remarked, "It was measurements I observed Saryan carrying out in September 1971 that caught my attention."[2] This led me to the conclusion that it wasn't my experiments that Lauterbur objected to, but rather the fact that I, a non-chemist MD, was the man behind them.

Lauterbur reasoned that if he could make projections with a magnetic field gradient using the distribution of the signal intensities, he could reconstruct an actual picture image from the tissue signal differences *discovered* by me that were not known to exist prior to my 1970 discovery.

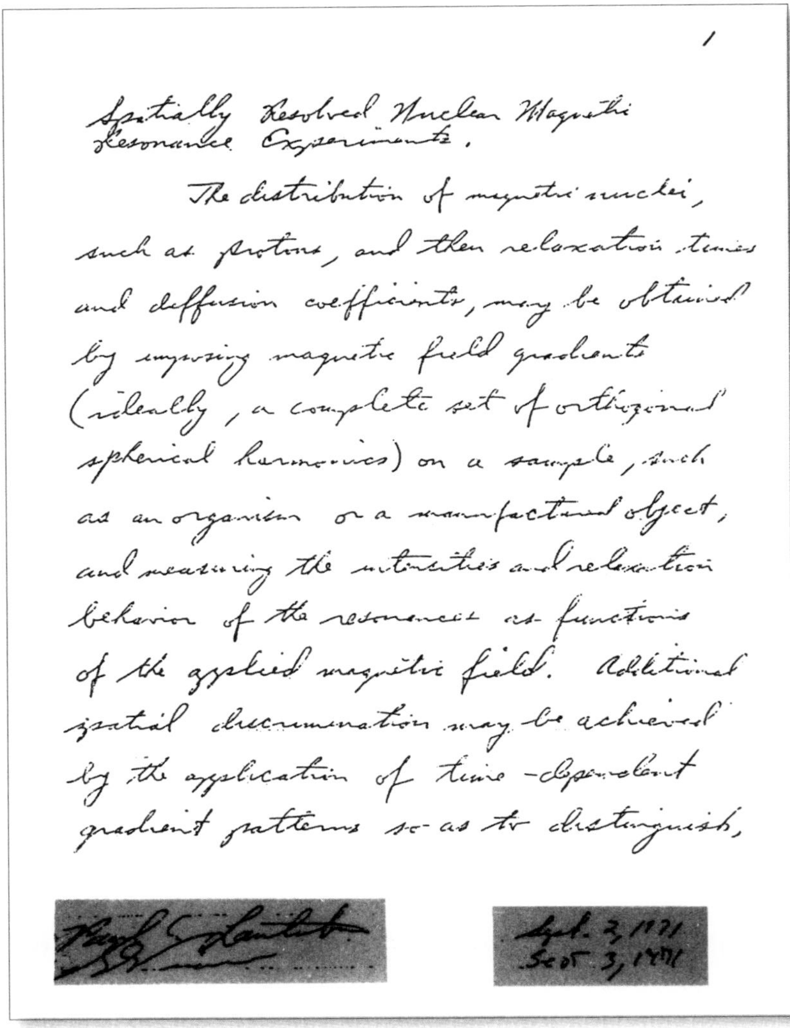

1

Spatially Resolved Nuclear Magnetic Resonance Experiments.

The distribution of magnetic nuclei, such as protons, and their relaxation times and diffusion coefficients, may be obtained by imposing magnetic field gradients (ideally, a complete set of orthogonal spherical harmonics) on a sample, such as an organism or a manufactured object, and measuring the intensities and relaxation behavior of the resonances as functions of the applied magnetic field. Additional spatial discrimination may be achieved by the application of time-dependent gradient patterns so as to distinguish,

Sept. 3, 1971
Sept. 3, 1971

Figure 53 (here and on following two pages). Lauterbur's notebook acknowledgment of Damadian's priority in the invention of the MRI

In 1973, Paul Lauterbur published a paper to this effect in *Nature*, and did so without referencing me or conceding that the experiments that made this possible were first done by me. *Nature* initially rejected his article, but then when Lauterbur explained that this technology will enable us to make detailed detection and pictures of cancer because of the discovery of the difference in the cancer signals made by me (figure 53), *Nature* relented and agreed to publish the paper. When the article appeared, Lauterbur cited how it can be used for cancer visualization and cancer discovery, but did not reference me at all. The paper he *did* cite, however, is one that referenced *my* previous work as the first discovery. In other words, he went out of his way to leave us out.

Naturally, that caused us to be very upset — and not just us, but also many other scientists as well. Lauterbur ended up taking a lot of heat for that. But all this happened back in '73. It wasn't until many

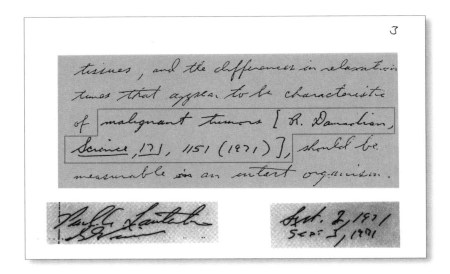

years later that he conceded that all this original work was done by me. In 1986, *13 years* after Lauterbur published his original paper, *Cancer* magazine (figure 54) published a speech by Dr. Lauterbur where he acknowledged my pioneering accomplishments.[3]

The Nobel Committee 2003, in order to eliminate the only *genuine discovery* (my *discovery* of the abnormal NMR [MRI] signals of diseased tissue [figure 22] that make the image) in the development of the MRI, found it necessary to contort the contributions of Lauterbur and Mansfield into *"discoveries" of "methods* (techniques)" (figure 55), when they were *exclusively "methods"* that were developed specifically to implement my *genuine discovery* of the signals that make the image.

The Nobel Committee stated that both Lauterbur and Mansfield made "seminal discoveries concerning the development of the *technique*," and cited that "Paul Lauterbur discovered . . . that could not be visualized by other *techniques*." Peter Mansfield was cited as having made "an essential step in order to obtain a practical *method*." Both citations were *contorted into* **discoveries** to overcome Nobel's *explicit exclusion of "methods" (or techniques)* (figure 55) as qualifying for his Nobel Prize in Physiology or Medicine, while at the same time, and remarkably, the only *genuine discovery* that did qualify for Nobel's Prize in Physiology or Medicine, my *discovery*, was *excluded* (figure 57).

As the Nobel statutes specify (§4) (figure 57), "If a work that is being rewarded has been produced by two or three persons, the prize shall be

Raymond Damadian had obtained in his 1970 experiments and which he had published in *Science* in March 1971.[12]

In 1986, *Cancer* magazine published a speech by Lauterbur in which he recalled that:

> "the attention of the medical community was first attracted by the report of Damadian that some animal tumors have remarkably long proton NMR relaxation times. Efforts to reproduce these results and to explore their significance were soon underway in other laboratories."[13]

One of those efforts took place right before Lauterbur's eyes at NMR Specialties, with the experiments conducted by Leon A. Saryan, a graduate student in biochemistry from Johns Hopkins University. "It was measurements that I observed Saryan carrying out in September of 1971 that caught my attention,"[14] said Lauterbur.

Lauterbur's Idea for Visualizing the Different T_1s and T_2s of Normal and Cancerous Tissue

Saryan did his research at NMR Specialties because he was not in a position to duplicate the experiments on his own NMR machine at Johns Hopkins University.[15] When Lauterbur watched Saryan successfully repeat the Damadian experiments, he viewed the procedure with great interest and was impressed by the results. He stated:

> "Even normal tissues differed markedly among themselves in NMR relaxation times, and I wondered whether there might be some way to noninvasively map out such quantities within the body."[16]

If there was a way to tell exactly which locations these NMR signals were coming from within an intact complex object like the human body, there might be a way to devise a map using the information-packed tissue signals Damadian had uncovered.

That evening Lauterbur went to a local fast-food restaurant, the "Eat 'N Run," sat down with his hamburger and intensely pondered the intriguing and difficult problem. In the case of hydrogen proton imaging of a living object, it was clear that the intact object contains a host of hydrogen protons. With every one of them simultaneously emitting NMR signals that contain information about the structure in which they reside, how could one determine what information is coming from where when all you have to work with is one composite, garbled NMR signal? Was there

Figure 54 (here and on the following three pages). Lauterbur's acknowledgment of Damadian's priority in the invention of the MRI

a way to somehow encode the NMR signals emitted from each part of an object so that they would disclose their spatial location? Before Lauterbur finished his meal, he came up with the key to a technique that would help do just that.

Having worked with NMR spectrometers for years, Lauterbur was very familiar with both magnet homogeneities and inhomogeneities— the former preferred, the latter despised. From this, he realized that inhomogeneous magnetic fields actually labeled NMR signals according to their spatial coordinates! By deliberately imposing an ordered system of magnetic inhomogeneities on the magnetic field, he could use these inhomogeneities to extract valuable NMR tissue information otherwise lost in the composite NMR cacophony. This idea would be the basis upon which Lauterbur would develop his technique to spatially encode NMR signals and create images.

Spatial Encoding

Basically, the NMR signals emitted by hydrogen protons in a homogeneous magnetic field are all of the same frequency, the Larmor frequency for hydrogen corresponding precisely to the strength of the magnetic field. Although the intensity of the emitted NMR signals may vary from location to location, depending on such factors as proton density, for example, the frequencies of all the hydrogen NMR responses are identical. However, if there is a certain spot in the field where the strength of the magnetic field is different, i.e. where there is an inhomogeneity at that location, the frequency of the NMR signals emitted by hydrogen protons residing in that spot is different from the frequency of those in the properly-calibrated region. More specifically, if the strength of the field in that region is lower than that of the homogeneous region, the frequency of the NMR signal from that spot will be lower, too, and vice versa.

The following are Lauterbur's recollections of his thoughts that evening while sitting in a Pennsylvania diner.

> "I got to thinking that magnetic field gradients provide a general solution to the problem. The reason you couldn't tell the different tissues in a normal NMR machine is that you make a magnetic field that's the same everywhere. If you have a magnetic field that is different on one side of the sample from the other side, then the frequencies of the spectra are different, too. In a uniform field, if you have a little bit of tissue here and a little bit of tissue there, then the

signal is the same. If you plot that out, the signals would be right on top of each other and you couldn't distinguish one from the other. Now, if you have a smoothly varying field, then you would have different frequencies and so you could study the signals and distinguish the differences.

"Now this is 1-dimensional. We're dealing with a 3-dimensional object. So the question was, 'Could you extend this idea to resolve completely the 3-dimensional object?' I thought if you could . . . you should be able to go all the way."[17]

The next day Lauterbur went out and bought himself a notebook in which to record his idea for making NMR images.

On *September 2, 1971,* Lauterbur wrote the following in his notebook under the title of "Spatially Resolved Nuclear Magnetic Resonance Experiments:"

"The distribution of magnetic nuclei, such as protons, and their relaxation times and diffusion coefficients, may be obtained by imposing magnetic field gradients (ideally, a complete set of orthogonal spherical harmonics) on a sample, such as an organism or a manufactured object, and measuring the intensities and relaxation behavior of the resonance as functions of the applied magnetic field. Additional spatial discrimination may be achieved by the application of time-dependent gradient patterns so as to distinguish, for example, protons that lie at the intersection of the zero-field (relative to the main magnetic field) lines of three linear gradients.

"The experiments proposed above can be done most conveniently and accurately by measurements of the Fourier transform of the pulse response of the system. They should be capable of providing a detailed three-dimensional map of the distributions of particular classes of nuclei (classified by nuclear species and relaxation times) within a living organism. For example, the distribution of mobile protons in tissues, and the differences in relaxation times that appear to be characteristic of malignant tumors [R. Damadian, *Science,* **171,** (1971), 1151], should be measurable in an intact organism."[18] (See pages B1 through B3 of appendix to this chapter.)

See figure 53

Lauterbur discussed his ideas with G.D. Vickers, then Vice President of Applications at NMR Specialties, and, as scientists do to protect their ideas, had Vickers witness his three-page entry in the notebook by signing his name and entering the date—*September 3, 1971*—at the bottom of each page.[19] (See pages B1 through B3 of appendix to this chapter.)

See figure 53

The Gradient and the Fourier Transform

Using gradients to provide spatial discrimination in one dimension had been described a couple of decades earlier, back when Lauterbur was still finishing up his undergraduate work at Case Institute of Technology. Robert Gabillard in France and Herman Carr* and Edward Purcell at Harvard had all described and used such a concept. One of those researchers, Professor Herman Carr of Rutgers University, writing in a letter to the editor of *Physics Today* in 1993, stated:

> "A radically new component *was* introduced in the 1970s, but it was not the basic concept of spatial localization and spin maps, which had already been introduced for one (spatial) dimension in the early days of NMR. . . .
>
> "To the best of my knowledge the idea for superimposing a magnetic field gradient onto the main homogeneous magnetic field had its origin in the self-diffusion effects Erwin L. Hahn observed on his spin-echo envelopes as nuclei diffused through the small residual inhomogeneity of his main magnetic field. Based on this clue, Edward M. Purcell and I intentionally superimposed a strong magnetic field gradient onto the main field, giving a linear dependence of the resonant frequency on the spatial position of the diffusing nucleus. The enhanced diffusion effect then enabled us to make accurate quantitative measurements of the self-diffusion coefficient for suitable fluids. . . .
>
> "The new component of the 1970s is perhaps best described as the vision that a useful spin map as complicated as an interior medical image was in principle obtainable and was a goal worth pursuing."[20]

That it was a goal worth pursuing was proven by the discovery that cancers could be detected with NMR. That a useful spin map could be achieved had been perceived by both Damadian and Lauterbur with their respective NMR scanning and mapping spin localizing methods. (See A5, A10 through A19 of appendix to Chapter 8; see pages B1 through B3 of appendix to this chapter.)

---

* Carr was completing his doctoral thesis in NMR physics under Professor Edward Purcell at the time.

awarded to them jointly. In no case may a prize be divided between more than three persons." In the category of Physiology or Medicine the Nobel Committee has made the award to three persons 34 times before. Because of this, it became obvious to me that my exclusion must have been deliberate. But why? Why would an esteemed and respected entity such as Nobel generate such a deliberate distortion of Alfred Nobel's will directive? Why would they omit the very person who was primarily responsible for these "*discoveries* concerning magnetic imaging"? Why would they give this coveted award to men who had not discovered anything, but provided only *methods* to implement my actual ***discovery*** (figures 21 and 22)?

Unfortunately, deliberations of the committee are kept secret for 50 years, so I will never know the exact reasons that led to their decision. However, I do know this: committees are made up of people, and people can make intentional omissions as well as unintentional mistakes. In fact, past Nobel Prize committees made decisions that history would later judge with some skepticism. In 1948, Paul Hermann Müller was awarded a Nobel for his discovery of *dichlorodiphenyltrichloroethane*, or DDT. This pesticide was used to kill insects that carry and spread malaria and typhus. However, today we know it also kills birds, fish, and assorted other wildlife. The following year, the committee awarded the coveted Nobel Prize to a Portuguese neurologist named Egas Moniz, the man who pioneered the "prefrontal leucotomy" — later called a *lobotomy*. Used to treat a host of psychiatric disorders, the procedure today is viewed with great disdain by modern medical and psychiatric communities. Other unforeseen errors by the committee are more blatant and embarrassing.[4] There is at least one additional case where the award actually excluded a key figure in the discovery of insulin. In that instance, those who received the Nobel "nobly" chose to share their monetary awards with their collaborators.

That would not be the case with me, though I had actually predated Lauterbur and Mansfield's advancements with my original and foundational discovery and development.[5]

It goes without saying that I was devastated by this news. I felt like I had been sucker-punched in the gut. And I was unprepared for such blatant disregard for my life's work. But even beyond my disappointment, this deliberate snub was an outrage and disgrace to the integrity of the Nobel organization itself. Historians had for many years referred to me as the "Father of the MRI," and yet the recognition went to two

THE WILL OF ALFRED NOBEL

The Nobel Foundation was established under the terms of the will
of ALFRED BERNHARD NOBEL, Ph.D.h.c., dated Paris, November 27, 1895, which in its relevant parts runs as follows:

The whole of my remaining realizable estate shall be dealt with in the following way: the capital, invested in safe
securities by my executors, shall constitute a fund, the interest on which shall be annually distributed in the form
of prizes to those who, during the preceding year, shall have conferred the greatest benefit to mankind. The said
interest shall be divided into five equal parts, which shall be apportioned as follows: one part to the person who
shall have made the most important discovery OR invention within the field of physics; one part to the person who
shall have made the most important chemical discovery OR improvement; one part to the person who shall have
made the most important discovery (no OR) within the domain of physiology or medicine; one part to the person
who shall have produced in the field of literature the most outstanding work in an ideal direction; and one part
to the person who shall have done the most or the best work for fraternity between nations, for the abolition
or reduction of standing armies and for the holding and promotion of peace congresses. The prizes for physics
and chemistry shall be awarded by the Swedish Academy of Sciences; that for physiological or medical work
by the Caroline Institute in Stockholm; that for literature by the Academy in Stockholm, and that for champions
of peace by a committee of five persons to be elected by the Norwegian Storting. It is my express wish that
in awarding the prizes no consideration whatever shall be given to the nationality of the candidates, but that the
most worthy shall receive the prize, whether he be a Scandinavian or not.

Figure 55. Violation of Alfred Nobel's will in the awarding
of the 2003 Nobel Prize for MRI

Press Release: The 2003 Nobel Prize in Physiology or Medicine

development of nuclear magnetic resonance spectroscopy for determination of the three-dimensional structure of biological macromolecules in solution.

Discoveries of importance to medicine

This year's Nobel Laureates in Physiology or Medicine are awarded for crucial achievements in the development of applications of medical importance. In the beginning of the 1970s, they made seminal discoveries concerning the development of the technique to visualize different structures. These findings provided the basis for the development of magnetic resonance into a useful imaging method.

Paul Lauterbur discovered that introduction of gradients in the magnetic field made it possible to create two-dimensional images of structures that could not be visualized by other techniques. In 1973, he described how addition of gradient magnets to the main magnet made it possible to visualize a cross section of tubes with ordinary water surrounded by heavy water. No other imaging method can differentiate between ordinary and heavy water.

Peter Mansfield utilized gradients in the magnetic field in order to more precisely show differences in the resonance. He showed how the detected signals rapidly and effectively could be analysed and transformed to an image. This was an essential step in order to obtain a practical method. Mansfield also showed how extremely rapid imaging could be achieved by very fast gradient variations (so called echo-planar scanning). This technique became useful in clinical practice a decade later.

Rapid development within medicine

The medical use of magnetic resonance imaging has developed rapidly. The first MRI equipments in health were available at the beginning of the 1980s. In 2002, approximately 22 000 MRI cameras were in use worldwide, and more than 60 million MRI examinations were performed.

Figure 56.

A great advantage with MRI is that it is harmless according to all present knowledge. The method does not use ionizing radiation, in contrast to ordinary X-ray (Nobel Prize in Physics in 1901) or computer tomography (Nobel Prize in Physiology or Medicine in 1979) examinations. However, patients with magnetic metal in the body or a pacemaker cannot be examined with MRI due to the strong magnetic field, and patients with claustrophobia may have difficulties undergoing MRI.

Especially valuable for examination of the brain and the spinal cord

Today, MRI is used to examine almost all organs of the body. The technique is especially valuable for detailed imaging of the brain and the spinal cord. Nearly all brain disorders lead to alterations in water content, which is reflected in the MRI picture. A difference in water content of less than a percent is enough to detect a pathological change.

In multiple sclerosis, examination with MRI is superior for diagnosis and follow-up of the disease. The symptoms associated with multiple sclerosis are caused by local inflammation in the brain and the spinal cord. With MRI, it is possible to see where in the nervous system the inflammation is

http://www.nobel.se/medicine/laureates/2003/press.html

men who had simply read about my *discovery* from *Science* and made method improvements to my scanning invention. With all due respect to Lauterbur and Mansfield, this, to me, was a gross injustice. Still, the nagging question remained.

Why?

Some have suggested it had something to do with the fact that I was technically a *physician* and not an *academic scientist*. The Nobel Assembly is the body that awards the Nobel Prize in Physiology or Medicine. This assembly itself is made up of 50 professors, which at that time was chaired by Dr. Bjorn Nordenstrom. In a letter Dr. Nordenstrom wrote to me a few years earlier, he indicated that he wanted me to get the Nobel Prize. This was hugely significant because he was the chairman of the Nobel Assembly at the time he wrote to me. However, I later learned the committee became nervous when controversy arose involving Lauterbur. What really got their attention was something Lauterbur had said.

Nobel Statutes
§4

A prize may be equally divided between two works each of which may be considered to merit a prize. If a work which is to be rewarded has been produced by two or three persons, *the prize shall be awarded to them jointly.* In no case may a prize be divided by more than three persons.

Work produced by a person since deceased shall not be considered for an award; if, however, a prize-winner dies before he has received the prize, then the prize may be presented.

Each prize-awarding body shall be competent to decide whether the prize it is entitled to may be conferred upon a institution or association.

Figure 57. Exact reproduction of Nobel Statutes Section 4 (§4). Nobel Statutes specify the Nobel Award is to be given to "no . . . more than three persons."

He had told them that if Raymond Damadian gets the Nobel along with him, he would refuse it! That made no sense whatsoever. No one *refuses* the Nobel Prize. But the mere threat and thought of such an act could have cast a dark shadow of embarrassment on the committee since this, to my knowledge, had never happened before. They simply did not want the controversy that Lauterbur promised to stir up should I be awarded the prize with him.

This was beyond comprehension to me.

Prior to all this, a number of groups from Stockholm came to visit me. One of those who interviewed me was a man by the name of Dr. Hans Ringhertz. Ringhertz had been a student of Dr. Nordenstrom, having earned his degree under him. Not long after this, I was invited to Sweden to speak to some faculty members at the Karolinska Institute. At that point in time, I hadn't seen Dr. Nordenstrom in 2 or 3 years. As I was walking around the Karolinksa, I saw a giant portrait of Dr. Nordenstrom hanging on the wall, flanked on either side by some two dozen other portraits of faculty members. Not knowing the significance of the portraits (since I hadn't spoken to Dr. Nordenstrom in a couple of years), I was worried that, perhaps unknown to me, my good friend had passed away and that this portrait photo was a memorial to him. So I said to Dr. Ringhertz, "Is Dr. Nordenstrom not still alive? Has something happened to him?"

And for some strange reason this question appeared to delight Ringhertz. What my question revealed to him was that I hadn't spoken to Nordenstrom for several years. He knew, therefore, that I hadn't had much recent communication with Dr. Nordenstrom, and by Ringhertz reporting to Dr. Nordenstrom that I was asking if he was still alive that might overcome resistance he might get from Dr. Nordenstrom for excluding me from the Nobel in order to gain Lauterbur's acceptance. As it turns out, this visit occurred just a few months before the 2003 prize was announced.

Some speculated that I was excluded from the Nobel because chemists didn't want this kind of prestigious recognition to go to a non-chemist medical doctor. Imagine this kind of schoolyard jealousy among grown men. Ironic as it is, it's the MD, not the chemist, who's the one with the specific painful experience of taking care of patients and watching them die from cancer. Because of those experiences, he is much more sensitive when a discovery is made that might have a life-saving benefit. Contrast this with a chemist who never takes care of

VIOLATION OF THE WILL OF

ALFRED NOBEL:

Eradication of Nobel's EXPRESS DISTINCTION

BETWEEN "DISCOVERY" and "METHOD" (or

"technique")

and

Elimination of NOBEL's Confinement of HIS PRIZE

in the DOMAIN of PHYSIOLOGY and MEDICINE to

DISCOVERY ONLY (figure 55)

For his Prize in Physics Nobel specifies it is to be

given for an

Important "DISCOVERY" **OR** "Invention" (figure 55).

For his Prize in Chemistry Nobel specifies it is to be

given for

the Most Important "DISCOVERY" **OR**

"Improvement" (figure 55)

while

For his PRIZE in Physiology or Medicine

NOBEL SPECIFIES

it shall be given "one part to the person who shall

have made the most

important "DISCOVERY" ONLY **(NO OR)** within the

domain of

Physiology or Medicine (figure 55)

NOBEL SPECIFIES that his PRIZE

in Physiology or Medicine is to be restricted to

"DISCOVERY" ONLY

patients. How could he recognize the benefit that a particular technology might have for the care of patients? Surely this couldn't have been the reason for passing over me.

But regardless of the reason(s), it has always been my belief that the committee had to directly violate Nobel's will in order to do what they did. In other words, they made a specific violation of the statutes of the Nobel Foundation in awarding the prize to Lauterbur and Mansfield and excluding me. In the Nobel statutes it states, "For his prize in Physics, (Nobel specifies) it is to be given for the most important *discovery* or *invention*" (figure 55). For his prize in Chemistry, (Alfred Nobel specifies) it is to be given for the most important chemical *discovery* or *improvement*." So you can get the Nobel Prize in Physics or Chemistry for a *method*, a *technology*, OR a *discovery*.

However, in *medicine* (the category for which I was denied the prize) Nobel's will specifies "one part to the person who shall have made the most important *discovery* within the domain of physiology or medicine" (figure 55). It specifically excludes a method or a technique as a condition for a Nobel Prize in Physiology or Medicine. The Nobel Prize in Physiology or Medicine under Nobel's will is restricted to a *discovery* alone. It is not allowed for a *method* or a technique, which is the only component Lauterbur (and the other recipient, physicist Peter Mansfield) provided.

The *discovery* designated by Nobel's will was provided by me, not Lauterbur or Mansfield. I made the *discovery* of the abnormal NMR signals of diseased tissue and the marked differenaces of these signals within the normal tissues themselves (figures 21 and 22) that are used to *make the MRI image,* and without which *there is no image!* Thus it is clear that the committee explicitly violated Alfred Nobel's will in this matter. They made their award in Physiology or Medicine for the two *methods* contributed by Lauterbur and Mansfield while *intentionally excluding* the only contribution qualified for the prize in Physiology or Medicine under Nobel's will, the genuine *discovery* provided by me. In fact, they had to go out of their way to do this by *intentionally excluding* the man who had made the *discovery* so they could award the prize to two men who had *exclusively added* **methods** to picture the tissue discriminating signals **discovered** by me, and without which signals there is *no picture.*

Others surmised I was snubbed due to the fact that I had actively lobbied for the prize, but then again, so had the winners. Some have ventured to say that the omission was due to a much more *concrete* reason. Even those who staunchly stand behind evolution have speculated that the reason I was passed over was due to my outspoken views on creationism.[6] When it was first proposed to me that I might be excluded from the Nobel because of my creation views, I rejected that likelihood, and indeed I had been assured by Dr. Nordenstrom that that would be of no consequence. I gave it a second thought when I heard Lauterbur's response in the time before the 2003 Nobel Prize was awarded when he was asked by the press what scientific research he expected to be pursuing in the future. He answered, and the press reported, that in the future he would be carrying out research in molecular *evolution*. I was stunned when I read Lauterbur's response in the newspaper. Lauterbur, an inorganic boron chemist with no background in biology or biochemistry would suddenly be devoting his future life *to evolution* research. It was hard for me not to conclude that his public enthusiasm for a future of *evolutionary research* was being directed at ears that wanted assurance that he would not be engaging in creation science research in the future like his competitor.

I am not an evolutionist.

Being an outspoken creationist, I hold to a literal 6-day creation scenario as described in Genesis. But in a post-Christian world, someone in the field of science who believes in intelligent design is the equivalent of a "scientific heretic," and such a view is considered blasphemy against Darwinian thought. It may as well be sandblasted above the doorways of higher education that refusing to pay homage to Darwin and his misguided theory of origins puts you on a "black list" of sorts. This loyalty to the biblical account of how the universe, earth, animal kingdom, and humankind came to be is often equivalent to a death sentence with regard to respect and credibility in most academic and scientific circles. They cling to the perceived security of evolution like a toddler clutching a stuffed animal. It's often the "acceptable sacrifice" required if you aspire to climb the ladder of scientific success. Like the theory so many blindly follow, one must be willing to "adapt" and "evolve," morphing oneself in order to conform and receive desired recognition. To those who have been brainwashed by the Darwinian template, a creationist may as well also claim to be from Mars. This may also be the reason a man like Fritz Schaefer, a leader in the field of computational quantum mechanics who, though nominated five times, has been consistently passed over by the Nobel Committee. Schaefer is a creationist.

This is strange, because according to history, others who have supported intelligent design have been awarded the Nobel Prize in categories ranging from Physics to Chemistry and even in the field for which I was denied — Physiology or Medicine.[7] I, along with famous British astronomer and mathematician Sir Fred Hoyle, are referred to as "runner ups."[8]

Such is the world in which you and I live.

Merely writing off such injustices as "God's will" is unacceptable to me. In my mind, it's simply a matter of man-caused injustice, and difficult to sweep under the rug or ignore. For what kind of world would it be if we simply ignored every untruth, unfair practice, or injustice, looking the other way while allowing them to continue? Where would racial equality be? What about slavery? Sex trafficking? Human rights violations? Granted, we can't right every wrong on the planet, but it would be irresponsible not to try to at least draw attention to the blatant disregard for the truth and for impartiality and justice.

Soon after the Nobel announcement, a group calling themselves "The Friends of Raymond Damadian" protested by taking out full-page advertisements in the *New York Times, Washington Post,* and the *Los Angeles Times.* Their article was titled, "The Shameful Wrong That Must Be Righted." Particularly painful was the reality that after originating the idea and after all the years of laboring to overcome the ridicule of critics and bringing the idea of NMR scanning of the living human body to reality, the Nobel Committee had granted me the agony of being written out of the history of MRI. It called on the Nobel's two winners to "help right this wrong." This article certainly created some public awareness, but it also engendered some unintended resentment from the scientific community. "Who is Damadian to complain about the Nobel Prize?" some argued.

You may wonder, what's the big deal? Why keep talking about it? Am I obsessed with this injustice? No. Does it still bother me? Yes, and here's why.

First of all, the way I look at it, the committee deliberately transgressed the truth. And as you know by now, I am very passionate about the truth. The truth is unequivocal, and they were trashing both it and history. Apart from my own personal stake in this issue, the other reality is that truth is the foundation of science. If you trash the truth, there *is* no science. To not tell the truth with regard to the Nobel Prize was a slap in the face to science itself.

Secondly, those of us who have a high sense of justice have their "moral radar" alerted when inequality, discrimination, or blatant bias is used against people who deserve fair treatment. It's bigger than me not getting the Nobel Prize, and it certainly isn't "whining," as one *New York Times* writer suggested.[9] If a writer, musician, or artist had his/her work pirated, augmented, and then published under another's name, his or her protest against such an act wouldn't be considered "whining," but rather it would be embraced, especially if the one who took credit for it won a Grammy or literary award.

In 1972, the United States Olympic basketball team was robbed of their gold medal, as biased officials kept resetting the game clock until the Soviets came away with the victory. To this day, some 43 years later, not one of those American basketball players has accepted that second place (silver) medal. Those medals have since resided in a safety deposit box somewhere in Lausanne, Switzerland, where they remain to this day. Their "stolen glory" still stands as one of the worst moments in sports lore and the biggest farce in Olympic history.

I originated the idea of scanning the human body by NMR. Without the *idea* you have nothing. But beyond this, I also discovered the *signal* that makes the MRI image. No signal. No image. Then I built *the very first scanner!* So understandably, it was painful to live through all that. I had dedicated my life to the development of the MRI, withstanding ridicule and every other kind of criticism along the way, only to be written out of the history of the MRI, at least in the Nobel version of that history. And yet I, as well as most others, know that history would not exist without my part in generating it.

Immediately following this bad news, I was driven to prayer. The Bible says you should be "casting all your cares upon him; for he careth for you" (1 Peter 5:7). And I certainly had a lot of "cares" regarding this issue. But there was a psychological effect on me as well. Because of all the years I had spent in academia, I had developed a certain awe and respect for the Nobel Prize. Now, as a result of all I went through, that respect has greatly been diminished to almost zero. Today, the Nobel Prize in some categories is even given to people who haven't done anything at all! This comes as no surprise in a world where we give trophies to childhood sports teams whether they win or lose!

You see, when you lose Christ, you no longer can perceive the truth, even when it's right in front of you. Or perhaps you willingly deny that truth, as Paul points out in Romans 1. Either way, truth and integrity is lost.

Ultimately, I fully understand that the greatest reward for my work is not through some public recognition, but rather through the millions of lives helped by MRI. Not being awarded the Nobel Prize doesn't diminish in the least the much greater gratitude I experience knowing the many lives my invention has helped save and that it has given humanity a new tool with which to successfully battle disease.

But even beyond this is the assurance that a far greater reward awaits me. I am confident in what God's Word promises — "an inheritance incorruptible, and undefiled, and that fadeth not away, reserved in heaven for you" (1 Peter 1:4). This is the prize I aspire to receive. God's approval through Christ's accomplishment on the Cross and His guarantee of eternal life through His Resurrection — *that* is what inspires me. For the believer in Jesus, the past does not define us nor does it deter us. Instead, it's our future that motivates us to press on, longing for that day when we will hear Him say, "Well done, thou good and faithful servant: thou hast been faithful over a few things, I will make thee ruler over many things: enter thou into the joy of thy lord" (Matthew 25:21).

Though it is often a difficult lesson to learn, we, as followers of Jesus Christ, must gain our greatest fulfillment not in fame or finances, but rather in a future kingdom. It's this eternal perspective that guards our hearts against the things of this world that would overwhelm us. It's this very attitude that motivated Paul to encourage the Colossian Christians to "seek those things which are above, where Christ sitteth on the right hand of God. Set your affection on things above, not on things on the earth. For ye are dead, and your life is hid with Christ in God. When Christ, who is our life, shall appear, then shall ye also appear with him in glory" (Colossians 3:1–4). Glory.

How ironic that this is what most men seek today. Whether by professional achievement (as in sports, academia, medicine, or the arts) or by public praise (given to celebrities who have done nothing to deserve it), being *recognized* carries with it a certain level of human exaltation. And rightly so, for there are honorable achievements that merit such praise.

And yet the glory this world gives through accolades and awards is represented by money that is soon spent and trophies that will ultimately tarnish and rust. The Corinthians were exhorted to run the race of this life "that ye may obtain" (1 Corinthians 9:24). He then reminds believers that those who compete in earthly pursuits "do it to obtain a corruptible crown; but we an incorruptible" (1 Corinthians 9:25). Rome would award her military heroes and athletic champions, adorning them with a laurel or olive leaf crown. But no such Roman wreaths remain today for the very reason Paul mentioned. They're perishable. Temporary. They don't last. They're "faded glory." Contrast those earthly rewards with the ones given to those whose lives are dedicated to Jesus Christ. Though we are honored, the honor belongs to Him alone, so much so that we will cast our crowns at His feet one day in tribute to His supreme greatness (Revelation 4:10). No, I did not receive the Nobel Prize.

But that does not mean others haven't seen fit to recognize me for my achievements. The Smithsonian National Museum of American History in 1986 installed my *Indomitable* in its exhibit. Two years later, in 1988, President Ronald Reagan awarded me with the National Medal of Technology (figure 58), the highest award for applied science. The next year I was inducted into the National Inventor's Hall of Fame along with John Deere (founder of the John Deere Tractor Company), Irving Langmuir (inventor of the high-vacuum electron tube and gas-filled incandescent light) and George Westinghouse (founder of Westinghouse Corporation and inventor of the air brake) (figures 59–61). There, I now gratefully keep company with the likes of Thomas Edison, Samuel F.B. Morse, and the Wright Brothers. My great-grandfather Marcel (figure 62) would be proud.

My induction ceremony was presided over by President George H.W. Bush. Referencing the program, "Invent America!" which was created to encourage inventiveness among our nation's youth, Bush remarked,

> I have seen Dr. Damadian at work, captivating young imaginations with the fires of his own. I would not be surprised to see him joined in the Hall of Fame by some of those promising young minds. All it takes is imagination and encouragement, and he is an ideal source of both. He is living, reassuring proof that the spirit of invention continues to thrive in our great Nation.

There would be many more accolades and awards in the coming years. But upon reflection, prizes, awards, and recognition were not what had originally motivated me to begin my research all those years ago. Those long hours spent toiling in the laboratory weren't fueled by dreams of glory and ceremony, but by a passion to know and discover for the benefit of healing patients suffering from mortal diseases. Medals and praise were not what kept me working, even when faced with failure and seemingly insurmountable opposition. And being passed over for an award that should have rightfully been mine does not today deter me

Figure 58. 1988 — Dr. Damadian is awarded the nation's highest honor in technology, the United States National Medal of Technology for his invention of the MRI by President Ronald Reagan

from continuing in my efforts to help millions through what God has allowed me to achieve.

When I first formed FONAR, out of the blue one day I received a call from a member in my community by the name of Bill Judson. I

Dr. Raymond Damadian at his induction into the National Inventors Hall of Fame, February 12, 1989, for the invention of magnetic resonance scanning.

Figure 59. February 12, 1989, Dr. Damadian's induction into the National Inventors Hall of Fame for his invention of the MR scanner (MRI)

knew Bill since we had grown up together in the same community. Bill called to say, "Damadian, I want to invest in your company."

Naturally, I was glad to have a strong and enthusiastic supporter of the company. But interestingly enough, one of the partners in his own company was a Swede and a close friend of his. Bill wanted that friend to recommend me to the Nobel Committee. It turns out this Swede's close friend happened to be Michael Nobel, grand-nephew of Alfred Nobel, and head of the Nobel family. He eventually came here to visit me, and

Figure 60. The 1989 Inductees into the National Inventors Hall of Fame

Figure 61. Raymond Damadian's father, Vahan Krikor Damadian, congratulating his son on his induction into the National Inventors Hall of Fame

Figure 62. Marcel Pénot Sr., father of Dr. Damadian's grandmother, Jeanne Victoria Pénot, and a pioneer of the French Internal Combustion Engine

we became friends. As he worked with us in the field of MRI, he also bought a FONAR MRI scanner.

As a follower of Christ, I know that a future glory awaits me. But until that time I humbly pursue the immense satisfaction that comes in this life from seeing lives helped and saved by our invention.

And *that* is nobility greater than any earthly prize.

In addition, and gratefully, Dr. George Kauffman has recently published "Nobel Prize for MRI Imaging Denied to Raymond V. Damadian a Decade Ago" that addresses the "injustice done to Dr. Damadian" by the Nobel Committee.[10]

Endnotes

1. http://www.nobelprize.org/nobel_prizes/medicine/laureates/2003.
2. James Mattson, *The Pioneers of NMR and Magnetic Resonance I Medicine: The Story of MRI* (Israel: Bar-Ilan University Press, 1996), p. 712.
3. Ibid., p. 712, 714.
4. See http://www.smithsonianmag.com/science-nature/prize-fight-95652491/?-no-ist for specific examples of this.
5. Some have made a convincing argument that the Committee interprets Alfred Nobel's will as it suits them best. See http://www.fonar.com/pdf/31120-NY-TimesNobel-Will.pdf for more info.
6. http://www.smithsonianmag.com/science-nature/prize-fight-95652491/?no-ist=&page=2.
7. http://www.uncommondescent.com/intelligent-design/seven-nobel-laureates-in-science-who-either-supported-intelligent-design-or-attacked-darwinian-evolution/.
8. Ibid.
9. http://www.nytimes.com/2003/10/20/opinion/no-nobel-prize-for-whining.html.
10. Dr. George Kauffman, "Nobel Prize for MRI Imaging Denied to Raymond V. Damadian a Decade Ago," *Chemical Educator*, vol. 19, 2014, 73–88; http://www.fonar.com/pdf/NOBEL%20PRIZE%20FOR%20MRI%20DAMADIAN,%20GBK,%20CHEM%20EDUCATOR,%2019,%2019,73-90%20%28MARCH%2021,%202014%29.pdf.

CHAPTER

9

THE RETURN TO
TRUTH

It has often been said, "If you aim at nothing, you'll hit it every time." That's not only true in sports and business, but also in life as well. I believe one of the greatest discoveries a person can make in this life is to find his or her purpose. To ask, "Why am I here?" and then to find a meaningful answer to that question. Too many people are born, exist here for a while, and go to the grave having never really experienced or accomplished anything of significance. Henry David Thoreau penned that most go on to "lead lives of quiet desperation." It's a sad commentary on a life that was lived for self and at its end has literally nothing to show for it. We mourn such lives because of something deep within telling us we were meant for *more*. More than merely *existing*. More than just living, making a living, and then dying.

As Christians, we believe God has placed us here to actually make a difference in the world, to go beyond meeting our own needs and helping make life better for our fellow man. Of course, the pinnacle of that contribution comes in showing someone the way to salvation through Jesus Christ. But it doesn't end there. There are other ways to be a genuine blessing to our friends, family, community, and country. For me, I found a way through scientific discovery. I am only one man, but I have always felt as if God's guiding hand was on me, even through a season of my life where I relegated Him to the back seat of my life. Even then, He was still sovereignly directing my path. I'm reminded of what Solomon wrote: The mind of man plans his way, but the Lord directs his steps

(Proverbs 16:9). Surely that was true for me. Whether I realized it or not at the time, the discoveries I would make in the field of magnetic resonance were not accidents of nature, but the unfolding of God's plan for my life. All truth belongs to God, no matter who happens to discover it or proclaim it. From the physical laws of nature and the universe to truth about God in creation to spiritual truth revealed by Scripture, it all originates in an eternal God and Creator of us all. And He has graciously seen fit to share much of His truth with us. But He has also allowed mankind to stumble upon that truth or to systematically uncover it through experimentation and experience. Apart from His willingness to share it, we would know virtually nothing at all.

This is one reason I remain in awe of the Bible. Though it has been attacked and mocked, especially in recent decades, the Bible remains an impenetrable rock of truth. Theologian Bernard Ramm has written:

> A thousand times over, the death knell of the Bible has been sounded, the funeral procession formed, the inscription cut on the tombstone, and committal read. But somehow the corpse never stays put. . . . No other book has been so chopped, knifed, sifted, scrutinized, and vilified. What book on philosophy or religion or psychology or *belles lettres* of classical or modern times has been subject to such a mass attack as the Bible? with such venom and skepticism? with such thoroughness and erudition? upon every chapter, line and tenet?[1]

And yet the Bible continues to defy critics and silence skeptics worldwide. It takes on all comers without fear. That's because when truth is on your side, fear is obliterated into insignificance. And one of the strong evidences of such truth is when the Bible directly mentions areas of science. What took mankind thousands of years to discover, the Bible had already stated to be true. While not written as a book of science, what we find is that every time the Bible speaks about an area of science, it is found to be 100 percent accurate.

Every. Single. Time.

For example, did you know that long before geologists and explorers declared the earth to be round, the Bible already recorded that fact? Isaiah 40:22 states:

It is he that sitteth upon the circle of the earth, and the inhabitants thereof are as grasshoppers; that stretcheth out the heavens as a curtain, and spreadeth them out as a tent to dwell in.

Job 26:7, proclaiming the suspension of the planet in space, says God "stretches out the north over the empty place and hangeth the earth upon nothing."

It wasn't until the 17th century that William Harvey discovered the life-giving circulation of the blood in the human body, something Leviticus 17:11 affirmed 3,000 years earlier.

For millennia, astronomers argued about the number of stars contained in the night sky. Ptolemy claimed there were 1056 stars, while others amended and tweaked the number. And astronomers, philosophers, and mathematicians continued to debate the topic. Today, experts estimate that there are 400 *billion* stars in our Milky Way Galaxy alone! And consider that there are some 170 billion other galaxies like ours![2] That brings the total number of known stars to be a septillion, or 1 with 24 zeros after it! In other words, they can't be counted (figure 63). Ever. Of course, God had already revealed that scientific fact to the prophet Jeremiah some 2,600 years ago (Jeremiah 33:22). Psalm 147:4 and Isaiah 40:26 add that God created every one of those stars, determines the number of them, and even calls them all by name!

Scripture also speaks of:

- Physics — space, time, force, motion, matter (Genesis 1:1)
- The first law of thermodynamics, or the law of conservation of mass and energy (Genesis 2:13; Ecclesiastes 1:9; Colossians 1:17; Hebrews 1:3)
- The second law of thermodynamics, or entropy (Genesis 3:17; Psalm 102:25–26; Romans 8:20–22)
- Meteorology, Circulation of the Atmosphere (Ecclesiastes 1:6)
- Anthropology (men lived in caves) (Job 30:5–6)
- Hydrology (Psalm 135:7; Ecclesiastes 1:7; Job 36:27–29)
- Hydrothermal vents — mentioned 3,000 years *before* their discovery by science (Genesis 7:11; Job 38:16)

Ongoing archeology continues to validate both the accuracy and historicity of biblical accounts each time a dig uncovers artifacts and sites related to Scripture. Regarding the Bible's accuracy and historicity and particularly

Figure 63.
The
conclusion
of the
world's top
astronomers
that the
only
explanation
of the
universe is
a Creator
(*Wall Street
Journal*,
December
26, 2014, p.
A11)

THE WALL STREET JOURNAL. ★ ★

Science Increasingly

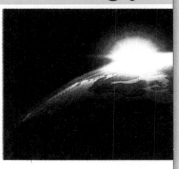

I n 1966 Time magazine ran a cover story asking: Is God Dead? Many have accepted the cultural narrative that he's obsolete—that as science progresses, there is less need for a "God" to explain the universe. Yet it turns out that the rumors of God's death were premature. More amazing is that the relatively recent case for his existence comes from a surprising place— science itself.

HOUSES OF WORSHIP
By Eric Metaxas

Here's the story: The same year Time featured the now-famous headline, the astronomer Carl Sagan announced that there were two important criteria for a planet to support life: The right kind of star, and a planet the right distance from that star. Given the roughly octillion—1 followed by 24 zeros—planets in the universe, there should have been about septillion—1 followed by 21 zeros—planets capable of supporting life.

With such spectacular odds, the Search for Extraterrestrial Intelligence, a large, expensive collection of private and publicly funded projects launched in the 1960s, was sure to turn up something soon. Scientists listened with a vast radio telescopic network for signals that resembled coded intelligence and were not merely random. But as years passed, the silence from the rest of the universe was deafening. Congress defunded SETI in 1993, but the search continues with private funds. As of 2014, researches have discovered precisely *bubkis*—0 followed by nothing.

What happened? As our knowledge of the universe increased, it became clear that there were far more factors necessary for life than Sagan supposed. His two

parameters grew to 10 and then 20 and then 50, and so the number of potentially life-supporting planets decreased accordingly. The number dropped to a few thousand planets and kept on plummeting.

Even SETI proponents acknowledged the problem. Peter Schenkel wrote in a 2006 piece for Skeptical Inquirer magazine: "In light of new findings and insights, it seems

The odds of life existing on another planet grow ever longer. Intelligent design, anyone?

appropriate to put excessive euphoria to rest . . . . We should quietly admit that the early estimates . . . may no longer be tenable."

As factors continued to be discovered, the number of possible planets hit zero, and kept going. In other words, the odds turned against any planet in the universe supporting life, including this one. Probability said that even we shouldn't be here.

Today there are more than 200 known parameters necessary for a planet to support life—every

Friday, December 26, 2014

Makes the Case for God

Corbis

single one of which must be perfectly met, or the whole thing falls apart. Without a massive planet like Jupiter nearby, whose gravity will draw away asteroids, a thousand times as many would hit Earth's surface. The odds against life in the universe are simply astonishing.

Yet here we are, not only existing, but talking about existing. What can account for it? Can every one of those many parameters have been perfect by accident? At what point is it fair to admit that science suggests that we cannot be the result of random forces? Doesn't assuming that an intelligence created these perfect conditions require far less faith than believing that a life-sustaining Earth just happened to beat the inconceivable odds to come into being?

There's more. The fine-tuning necessary for life to exist on a planet is nothing compared with the fine-tuning required for the universe to exist at all. For example, astrophysicists now know that the values of the four fundamental forces—gravity, the electromagnetic force, and the "strong" and "weak" nuclear forces—were determined less than one millionth of a second after the big bang. Alter any one value and the universe could not exist. For instance, if the ratio

between the nuclear strong force and the electromagnetic force had been off by the tiniest fraction of the tiniest fraction—by even one part in 100,000,000,000,000,000— then no stars could have ever formed at all. Feel free to gulp.

Multiply that single parameter by all the other necessary conditions, and the odds against the universe existing are so heart-stoppingly astronomical that the notion that it all "just happened" defies common sense. It would be like tossing a coin and having it come up heads 10 quintillion times in a row. Really?

Fred Hoyle, the astronomer who coined the term "big bang," said that his atheism was "greatly shaken" at these developments. He later wrote that "a common-sense interpretation of the facts suggests that a super-intellect has monkeyed with the physics, as well as with chemistry and biology . . . . The numbers one calculates from the facts seem to me so overwhelming as to put this conclusion almost beyond question."

Theoretical physicist Paul Davies has said that "the appearance of design is overwhelming" and Oxford professor Dr. John Lennox has said "the more we get to know about our universe, the more the hypothesis that there is a Creator . . gains in credibility as the best explanation of why we are here."

The greatest miracle of all time, without any close seconds, is the universe. It is the miracle of all miracles, one that ineluctably points with the combined brightness of every star to something— or Someone—beyond itself.

Mr. Metaxas is the author, most recently, of "Miracles: What They Are, Why They Happen, and How They Can Change Your Life" (Dutton Adult, 2014).

its supernatural power, especially remarkable is Isaiah's unique and literal prediction of Jesus coming by virgin birth 700 years prior to its occurrence. "Therefore the Lord himself shall give you a sign; Behold, a virgin shall conceive, and bear a son, and shall call his name Immanuel" (God with us) (Isaiah 7:14). Also, "For unto us a child is born, unto us a son is given: and the government shall be upon his shoulder: and his name shall be called Wonderful, Counsellor, The mighty God, The everlasting Father, The Prince of Peace" (Isaiah 9:6).

This is further corroborated by Matthew: "Now all this was done, that it might be fulfilled which was spoken of the Lord by the prophet, saying, Behold, a virgin shall be with child, and shall bring forth a son, and they shall call his name Emmanuel, which being interpreted is, God with us" (Matthew 1:22–23).

Again, the Bible was not written as a *science* book, but rather as a *truth* book. Science doesn't create truth. It merely discovers or uncovers it. And as it stands, it has a 100 percent accuracy and success rate in matters related to science and history. Even so, when those in the academic community attempt to malign or discredit Scripture and its claims, they usually resort to the "science" argument. They do this for two primary reasons: (1) They know that no one in their right mind would dare to disagree with science, right?, and (2) They are committed to certain presuppositions regarding the generally-accepted theories of scientific data-gathering. In other words, they often arrive at the conversation "pre-loaded" with certain conclusions based on their assumptions, opinions, beliefs, and yes, *biases.*

Nowhere is this more acutely revealed than when it comes to the topic of the origins of man. Evolution (or Darwinism) is *the* "Golden Calf" of the science world. It stands as a sort of centerpiece and cornerstone of thought in both scientific and academic culture. There is an unwritten rule, along with a sometimes not-so-subtle pressure for every doctor, researcher, scientist, anthropologist, and biology student to regularly bow and pay homage to this theoretical god of origins. Failure to do so results in swift rejection, mockery, retribution, and in some cases, even excommunication.

But while evolution is the accepted theory of origins, it is rarely ever treated as an actual theory. Darwin may as well have chiseled his book in stone and delivered it while descending from Evolution Mountain, so revered and unquestioned are its claims.

Figure 64. The evolutionist perspective that the upright-walking human being descended from the knuckle-dragging ape

Ironically though, Darwinism has yet to support itself with any real scientific evidence. Not a single "missing link" has been proven to back up the claims that mankind evolved from primordial ooze *billions* of years ago. In fact, not one archeological find has authenticated the assertion that "ape man" ever existed at all. To the contrary, much of their purported "evidence" has later been proven to be either false or even deliberate hoaxes, including Piltdown Man, Neanderthal Man, Java man, Peking Man, and others.[3] It's not that these people aren't sincere in their beliefs. They are. It's just that they are sincerely deluded and duped. Sincerely *wrong*. Like a blind man trying to describe a sunset, they speak about "scientific fact" and information that simply doesn't exist. Just like that blind man, they may feel the same warmth of the sun, but cannot accurately explain what it actually looks like. Therefore, they remain dependent on their imaginations and the descriptions of other blind men. To use an old expression, they have had the "wool pulled over their eyes."

Tragically for the evolutionist, his beloved "knuckle-dragger" (figure 64) never, ever actually walked the earth. In fact, there is so much evidence *against* evolution (biologically, scientifically, and logically) that it's a wonder that thinking people still accept it as a viable theory. Even Charles Darwin[4] himself admitted his conclusions were problematic and difficult to accept. In his *Origin of Species*, Darwin writes: "By this theory [evolution], *innumerable transitional forms must have existed. Why do we not find them embedded in countless numbers?*" (emphasis added).[5]

He admits that this glaring omission in the fossil record is a "very obvious difficulty." He goes on to wonder, "Why then is not every geological formation and every stratum full of such intermediate links? . . .

This perhaps is the most obvious and gravest objection to be urged against my theory" (emphasis added).[6]

Indeed.

Had I, when introducing my theories and findings regarding magnetic resonance imaging, been unable to produce *any* evidence whatsoever for my conclusions, I would have been laughed out of the scientific world. Or if I had "magically" produced so-called "accurate images" of internal organs of the human body with no way of verifying how I obtained these images, I would have been better suited for a career at Disney World than the scientific and medical world!

And yet, Darwinism is globally accepted as *fact*, almost without question.

Not only is there *no* evidence for intermediate life forms ("transitional links" as Darwin specifies them)[7] to support evolution's assertions, but Darwin's own "evidence" argues *against* him! In his classic example using finches with variations of beaks, we now know that this is an example of *micro*-evolution, or simply variations within the same species (i.e., biblically: within the same *kind*). There is no evidence of crossing over from one species (*kind*) to another, or *macro*-evolution (no "transitional links" or "transitional forms")."[8] There is no adaptation of one *kind* of species to another *kind*. No crossing over from fish to reptile. Reptile to bird. Primate to man. Finches remain finches. Dogs remain dogs. Primates are still primates. Instead, all his evidence points to something else, and it's not evolution. Darwin's observations validate, not evolution, but rather the *revelation* of God in Scripture.

> God made the beast of the earth *after his kind*, and cattle *after their kind*, and every thing that creepeth upon the earth *after its kind*: and God saw that it was good" (Genesis 1:25, emphasis added).

In short, Darwin (and all his subsequent devoted disciples) have failed to demonstrate the existence of Intermediate Life Forms (or ILF, "transitional links" or "transitional forms" as Darwin[9] specifies them). No ILF's = no evolution. I find it amusing that atheistic evolutionists will mock Christians for believing in a God they cannot see when *they* fanatically believe in evidence they themselves cannot see or produce! If there was even a shred of truth to evolution, there should be *trillions* of fossils, fragments, and skeletons everywhere.

Absence of Evidence for Darwin's "One Primordial Form" Conjecture[10]

As Darwin specifically concedes, regarding his theory, "The distinctness of specific forms, and their not being blended together by *innumerable transitional links* is a very obvious difficulty" (emphasis added).[11] While an almost infinite and unceasing series of molecular accidents has to occur to get from Darwin's original *one primordial form,* as he names it, to an ultimate live human being, the remains in the fossil record of such *transitional links,* as Darwin specifies them, should be *innumerable* as he states. In addition, 156 years later, in A.D. 2015, they are still not to be found, i.e., they remain *missing.* Indeed, perhaps after 156 years of extensive fruitless archeological searching that has exploited all the powers of modern technology, they should not be characterized as *missing* any longer but acknowledged for what they are: *non-existent,* particularly in light of Darwin's own concession that according to his evolutionary model they should be *innumerable.* Most importantly, their existence is foundational to any assertion of "evolution." No evolutionary hypothesis can be sustained without them ("transitional links").

The originally proposed "missing links" have, in the main, been refuted by modern scientific evidence as "missing links."[12] Neanderthal man, for example, "who was regarded as an ape-man in the days of Charles Darwin but now is often accepted as fully human. . . . The cranial capacity of the Neanderthal race of *Homo Sapiens* was, on the average, equal to or even greater than in modern man."[13] The postulate that the remains of the ape *Australopithecine,* Lucy, originally "interpreted by a number of anthropologists as indicating an erect posture and bipedal walking" is without support.[14] Therefore, a "human-like" ape has been refuted by the research findings of Dr. Charles Oxnard after "detailed three-dimensional measurements and then a computerized multi-variate statistical analysis of all the pertinent relationships" concluded "to the extent that resemblances exist with living forms, they tend to be with the orangutan."[15]

As Morris concluded, "There is no good evidence that the Australopithecines [Lucy et al.] were erect walkers at all."[16] That is, the *missing links* are still *missing,* when they should be *innumerable.* The *transitional links,* cardinal to any assertion of the existence of a progressive transition up the chain of *kinds* essential to evolution, remain absent when they should be *innumerable.*

Indeed, notwithstanding Darwin's unsubstantiated conjecture that "probably all the organic beings which have ever lived on this earth have descended from some *one primordial form,*" he further concedes, "Why . . . is not every geological formation and every stratum full of such intermediate links. This perhaps is the most obvious and gravest objection which can be urged against my theory."[17] He then acknowledges that "to suppose that the eye, with all its inimitable contrivances . . . could have been formed by natural selection, seems, I freely confess, *absurd* in the highest possible degree."[18]

Calculation of the Probability of Darwin's Acknowledged "Confession" of ABSURDITY[19]

The number of genes currently estimated to be present within the human genome are 20,000 to 25,000.[20] Utilizing the smaller number of genes (i.e., 20,000) to enhance the probability of a mutation (to its highest chance of occurrence) the statistical chance of a genetic mutation within the human genome (i.e., within the gene) that exercises control over the structure of interest (e.g. the lens of the eye) is

$$\text{one in 20,000, that is } \left(\frac{1}{2 \times 10^4} \right).$$

Regarding an anatomic structure such as the eye, its function cannot be attributed to the function of a single anatomic structure; for example, the lens of the eye on its own cannot generate vision. The final physiologic product, vision, is the composite operating in coordination, as illustrated in figure 65, the vision light path of a viewed image enters the eye at the cornea and then passes in sequence through the iris, the lens, the vitreous body, the rods and cones of the retina (figure 66), the optic nerve, and finally to the optic cortex of the brain. Most importantly, none of the individual anatomic components, for example, the lens, is independent. The final physiologic product, vision, requires the coordinated contribution of each and **ALL** of the specific functions of each component of the light path (figures 65 and 66) to produce the final visual image.

The probability of generating 20,000 genes by "chance" from Darwin's "primordial one," for example, the "slime mold"[21] further magnifies the improbability of an evolution by "chance."

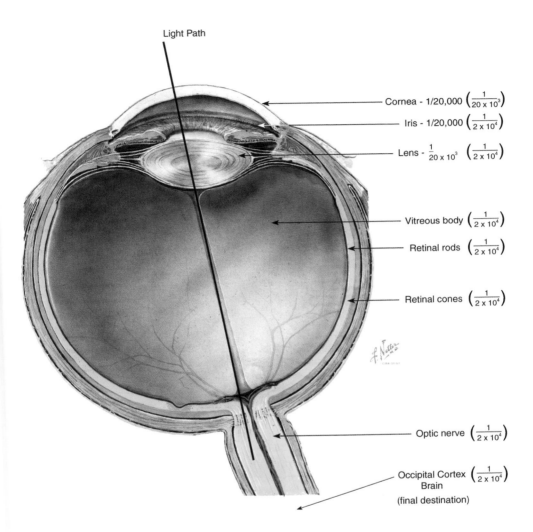

Figure 65. The anatomic lightpath to the optical cortex of a visualized image and the anatomic structures that must arise *simultaneously* by *"chance"* to generate the "selective" advantage necessary for the eye to "evolve."

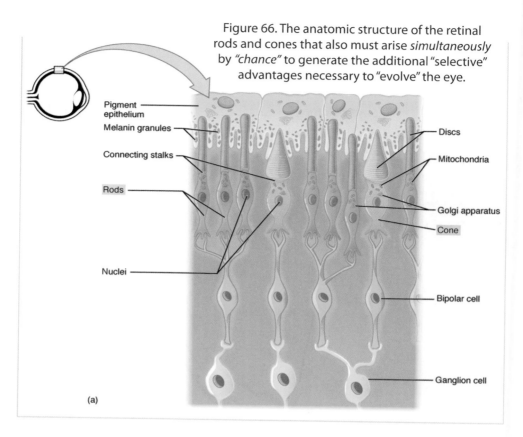

Figure 66. The anatomic structure of the retinal rods and cones that also must arise *simultaneously* by *"chance"* to generate the additional "selective" advantages necessary to "evolve" the eye.

(a)

The individual component, for example the lens, has no physiologic outcome (e.g., vision) without the remainder of the optical chain (figures 65 and 66). Thus an evolutionary "chance" mutation of a gene (i.e., 1 of 20,000 genes) to generate a lens of the eye provides no "selective advantage" by the evolutionary process of natural **selection** without the remaining seven components of the eye's light path. All eight of the light path components (cornea, iris, lens, vitreous body, rods, cones, optic nerve, optic cortex) must occur **simultaneously** by "chance" for vision to occur and provide a "selective" survival benefit. Accordingly, the probability of the "chance" occurrence of the eye is the probability of occurrence of the eight structures necessary to generate vision occurring simultaneously (individual occurrence of one of the light path components provides no selective advantage for the process of *natural* selection to proceed), which is the product of the individual probabilities of the eight anatomic structures contributing to the image light path calculated in figures 65 and 66. The computed probability of the **simultaneous** occurrence of the eight "chance" mutations within the human genome of 20,000 genes necessary to generate vision is 1 "chance" of occurrence out of 25.6 x 10^{33} (figure 65) or 1 "chance" in 25.6 decillions (figure 70).

Moreover, that is only the calculated "chance" occurrence probability for the eye. Adding the additional "chance" occurrence probability of the ear (figure 67) and the heart (figure 68) to the "chance"

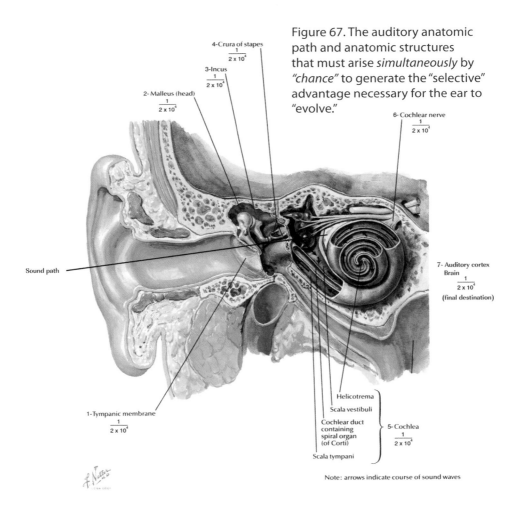

Figure 67. The auditory anatomic path and anatomic structures that must arise *simultaneously* by *"chance"* to generate the "selective" advantage necessary for the ear to "evolve."

Note: arrows indicate course of sound waves

Composite Probability of the Ear by "CHANCE"

$$\frac{1}{2 \times 10^4} \times \frac{1}{2 \times 10^4} \times \frac{1}{2 \times 10^4} \times \frac{1}{2 \times 10^4} \times \frac{1}{2 \times 10^4} \times \frac{1}{2 \times 10^4} \times \frac{1}{2 \times 10^4} = \frac{1}{(2 \times 10^4)^7} = \frac{1}{128 \times 10^{28}} = \frac{1}{1.28 \times 10^{30}}$$

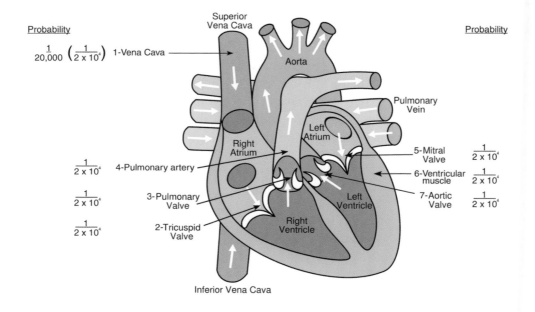

Probability

$\frac{1}{20,000}$ $\left(\frac{1}{2 \times 10^4}\right)$ 1-Vena Cava

$\frac{1}{2 \times 10^4}$ 4-Pulmonary artery

$\frac{1}{2 \times 10^4}$ 3-Pulmonary Valve

$\frac{1}{2 \times 10^4}$ 2-Tricuspid Valve

Probability

5-Mitral Valve $\frac{1}{2 \times 10^4}$

6-Ventricular muscle $\frac{1}{2 \times 10^4}$

7-Aortic Valve $\frac{1}{2 \times 10^4}$

Superior Vena Cava
Aorta
Pulmonary Vein
Left Atrium
Right Atrium
Left Ventricle
Right Ventricle
Inferior Vena Cava

Composite Probability of the Heart by "CHANCE"

$$\frac{1}{2 \times 10^4} \times \frac{1}{2 \times 10^4} \times \frac{1}{2 \times 10^4} \times \frac{1}{2 \times 10^4} \times \frac{1}{2 \times 10^4} \times \frac{1}{2 \times 10^4} \times \frac{1}{2 \times 10^4} = (2 \times 10^4)^7 = \frac{1}{128 \times 10^{28}} = \frac{1}{1.28 \times 10^{30}}$$

| Vena Cava | Tricuspid Valve | Pulmonary Valve | Pulmonary Artery | Mitral Valve | Ventricular Muscle | Aortic Valve |

Figure 68. The cardiac anatomic pathway of incoming blood and the anatomic structures encountered by the circulating blood that must arise *simultaneously* by *"chance"* for the heart to "evolve."

Composite Probability of the "CHANCE" occurrence of
the eye, ear and heart in the genesis of the human body

$$= \frac{1}{2.56 \times 10^{34}} \times \frac{1}{1.28 \times 10^{30}} \times \frac{1}{1.28 \times 10^{30}} = \frac{1}{4.19 \times 10^{94}}$$

The composite probability of just these three organs occurring by "CHANCE" (without the additional probabilities of the "CHANCE" occurrence of the remaining vital organs (brain, liver, kidney, pancreas, intestines) is one chance in 4.19 decitrigintillions (i.e. 4.19 x one with 94 zeros).

Figure 69. Composite probability of the "chance" occurrence
of the eye, ear, and heart in the genesis of the human body

occurrence probability of the eye, the Composite Probability (figure 69) of the "chance" occurrence of all three — the eye, the ear and the heart — is 1 "chance" in 4.19 decitrigintillions (i.e., 1 "chance" of occurrence out of 4.19×10^{94} possibilities) (see figure 70). In addition, this is the computed composite "chance" occurrence probability for only three of the body's vital organs (the eye, ear, and heart) and does not include the

Base -illion (short scale)	Value	U.S., Canada and modern British (short scale)	Traditional British (long scale)	Traditional European (Peletier) (long scale)	SI Symbol	SI Prefix
1	10^6	Million	Million	Million	M	Mega-
2	10^9	Billion	Thousand million	Milliard	G	Giga-
3	10^{12}	Trillion	Billion	Billion	T	Tera-
4	10^{15}	Quadrillion	Thousand billion	Billiard	P	Peta-
5	10^{18}	Quintillion	Trillion	Trillion	E	Exa-
6	10^{21}	Sextillion	Thousand trillion	Trilliard	Z	Zetta-
7	10^{24}	Septillion	Quadrillion	Quadrillion	Y	Yotta-
8	10^{27}	Octillion	Thousand quadrillion	Quadrilliard		
9	10^{30}	Nonillion	Quintillion	Quintillion		
10	10^{33}	Decillion	Thousand quintillion	Quintilliard		
11	10^{36}	Undecillion	Sextillion	Sextillion		
12	10^{39}	Duodecillion	Thousand sextillion	Sextilliard		
13	10^{42}	Tredecillion	Septillion	Septillion		
14	10^{45}	Quattuordecillion	Thousand septillion	Septilliard		
15	10^{48}	Quinquadecillion	Octillion	Octillion		
16	10^{51}	Sedecillion	Thousand octillion	Octilliard		
17	10^{54}	Septendecillion	Nonillion	Nonillion		
18	10^{57}	Octodecillion	Thousand nonillion	Nonilliard		
19	10^{60}	Novendecillion	Decillion	Decillion		
20	10^{63}	Vigintillion	Thousand decillion	Decilliard		
21	10^{66}	Unvigintillion	Undecillion	Undecillion		
22	10^{69}	Duovigintillion	Thousand undecillion	Undecilliard		
23	10^{72}	Tresvigintillion	Duodecillion	Duodecillion		
24	10^{75}	Quattuorvigintillion	Thousand duodecillion	Duodecilliard		
25	10^{78}	Quinquavigintillion	Tredecillion	Tredecillion		
26	10^{81}	Sesvigintillion	Thousand tredecillion	Tredecilliard		
27	10^{84}	Septemvigintillion	Quattuordecillion	Quattuordecillion		
28	10^{87}	Octovigintillion	Thousand quattuordecillion	Quattuordecilliard		
29	10^{90}	Novemvigintillion	Quindecillion	Quindecillion		
30	10^{93}	Trigintillion	Thousand quindecillion	Quindecilliard		
31	10^{96}	Untrigintillion	Sedecillion	Sedecillion		
32	10^{99}	Duotrigintillion	Thousand sedecillion	Sedecilliard		
33	10^{102}	Trestrigintillion	Septendecillion	Septendecillion		
34	10^{105}	Quattuortrigintillion	Thousand septendecillion	Septendecilliard		

Figure 70. Nomenclature of large numbers

computed "chance"occurrence of the body's remaining vital organs (i.e., the brain, kidneys, liver, pancreas, intestines) which would compound the calculated improbability of the "chance" occurrence of human life to a far greater magnitude.

Darwin's evolutionary presumption derives solely from his observation of "graduated finch beaks" among the finch population of the Galapagos Islands (figure 71), together with his observation of the existence of aquatic lizards (marine iguanas) on the islands. The varied finch beaks and marine iguanas solely represent a variation *within the kind* equivalent to the multiple variation of breeds *within* the dog *kind* (figure 72). They do not provide any evidence whatsoever to support the *naturally*

Figure 71. The Finch beak variations observed by Darwin that prompted his conjecture that "all the organic beings which have ever lived on this earth have descended from some one primordial form" (p. 9). The beak variations, however, represent variations solely *within the kind*, analogous to breed variations within the dog kind (figure 72) with no evidence of evolutionary "transitional links" from one kind to another kind, which Darwin concedes should be *innumerable* according to his evolutionary model, but are not, that is, they are "missing" (p. 226–227).[22]

Figure 72. Breed variations within the dog kind

occurring transition from one *kind* to another *kind* that is cardinal to sustaining any evolutionary hypothesis like Darwin's "probably *all* the organic beings which have ever lived on this earth have descended from some *one primordial form*."[23]

As specified in God's creation account, "God made the beast of the earth, after his *kind*, and cattle after their *kind*, and every thing that creepeth upon the earth after his *kind*" (Genesis 1:25, emphasis added), each living creature derives from its own *kind*. Each *kind* specifically created by God is not accidentally derived from some other *kind*. Darwin provides no evidence for "naturally" occurring transitions between one *kind* and another *kind*, the cardinal prerequisite for any "naturally" occurring evolutionary process. Darwin acknowledges these do not exist, to supply the "*innumerable transitional links*" his theory requires.[24] The skulls of our "ancestor" apes (gorilla, orangutan, chimpanzee) rise only to the upper brow, while the human skull rises an additional 2½ inches to its peak because it is housing 1200cc of brain (figure 73) instead of the 400cc of brain housed by our "ancestor's" skull. Where then is the "transitional link" who had 800cc of brain instead of our "ancestor's" 400cc of brain? Where is the "transitional" ape with an opposable thumb (figure 74)? Where is the upright walking "transitional ape" as opposed to the "knuckle walking" ape (figure 64)?

Moreover, as recently reported by Eric Metaxas in an article in the *Wall Street Journal*, "Science Increasingly Makes the Case for God" (figure 63), contrary to astronomer Carl Sagan's presumption ("given the roughly octillion — 1 followed by 21 zeros — planets capable of supporting life" he hypothesized), Congress supported SETI (Search for Extraterrestrial Intelligence) research, "discovered precisely bubkis — 0

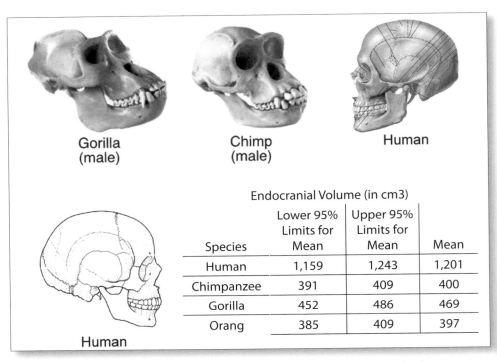

	Endocranial Volume (in cm3)		
Species	Lower 95% Limits for Mean	Upper 95% Limits for Mean	Mean
Human	1,159	1,243	1,201
Chimpanzee	391	409	400
Gorilla	452	486	469
Orang	385	409	397

Figure 73. The absence of "transitional links" from the ape kind to the human kind, which Darwin concedes should be innumerable to sustain a theory of evolution. No apes with intermediate brain or skull sizes, e.g., 800cc of brain, are known to exist when the brain size of the ancestor apes are uniformly 400cc while the human *kind* is 1200cc. (Leslie Aiello and Christopher Dean, *An Introduction to Human Evolutionary Anatomy* (San Diego, CA: Academic Press, 1990), p. 193).

followed by nothing" resulting in Congress' defunding of SETI "in 1993." Indeed, the SETI-funded research resulted, as Metaxas reports, that "The number of possible planets" (to support life) hit zero."[25] Consequently, as the Metaxas report further continues, "the odds against life in the universe are simply astonishing" and "at what point is it fair to admit that science suggests that we cannot be the result of random forces?" "Doesn't assuming that an intelligence created these perfect conditions require far less faith than believing that a life-sustaining Earth just happened to beat the inconceivable odds to come into being?" As Sir Fred Hoyle, the astronomer who coined the term "Big Bang," said, "The numbers one calculates from the facts seem to me so overwhelming as to put this conclusion (that 'a super-intellect has monkeyed with the physics, as well as with chemistry and biology') almost beyond question" (figure 63).

Metaxas further reports in his December 2014 article, "Theoretical physicist Paul Davies concluded that 'the appearance of design is overwhelming,' " and "Oxford professor Dr. John Lennox further concluded from the SETI research, 'the more we get to know about our universe, the more the hypothesis that there is a Creator . . . gains in credibility as the best explanation of why we are here.' " Further evidence for creation: another black eye for evolution. Indeed, they may as well believe in the Easter Bunny or Santa Claus.

Yet they persist, proclaiming their theory of origins with

Figure 74. There is also an absence of any other evidence for ape to human transitions, that is, the absence of an "intermediate" ("transitional link") with an opposable thumb or an "erect" "walking ape" (see figure 64).

all the glassy-eyed enthusiasm of a cult member. But there is another reason why evolutionists cling to Darwin's theory like a child to a security blanket. Consider for a moment that if evolution were exposed for what it really is — a hollow theory that is more fiction than science — atheists and scientists would be forced to concede that other theories of origins might be possible. If there is no evolution (which requires only random chance and not an intelligent Creator), then Darwin's disciples would have to admit there *could* be a God out there somewhere. Expel evolution from the classroom and what's left to humanity's origin? Aliens? Where's the evidence for that? If you intellectually acknowledge that evolution might not be true, then there may indeed be the possibility of a God. And if there is a Supreme Being who created the universe, the world, and humankind, there is a strong probability He could be the God of the Bible. And if that's true, we are all accountable to Him and His truth.

That's exactly the kind of truth that messes with your ego and threatens the right to rule over your own life.

Now you have a window into why some evolutionists vehemently defend their indefensible position on the theory of origins. I recommend visiting answersingenesis.org where you will find more research to help increase your understanding about the Bible and how science backs up creation.

Scripture is clear that it was *God* who created mankind, *not* natural selection. The Bible says He did this during one day, and not over billions of years. Genesis claims there were six literal days involved in creation. Not six ages or eras. Six *days*. That's a 24-hour period of time. Moses uses the Hebrew word *yom*, which, when combined with a number (as in "six days"), refers to a 24-hour period of time. Israel's lawgiver wrote with specificity, delineating one day from another in creation, even setting boundaries for them ("morning and evening," which elsewhere in the Old Testament refer to *literal days*). Moses could have just as easily used language to communicate that God made the world over the course of many years, ages, or periods of time.

But he didn't.

Further, Jesus, the Creator Himself (John 1:1–3) claimed that at the "beginning of the creation, God made them male and female" (Mark 10:6), meaning humankind was created at the same time as the rest of the world. If Moses was wrong about his six literal days, why didn't Jesus explain or expand on that, as He did with many other misunderstood and misinterpreted Old Testament truths? Jesus called Satan a "murderer from the *beginning*" (John 8:44), referring to his role inciting Cain's murder of his brother Abel. If man's true beginning happened billions of years ago, are we to assume that somewhere in the evolutionary chain of development, one missing link killed another missing link? Or should we take Jesus' words here more simply to mean that near the beginning of creation, one sinful man killed another?

Could God have made the world in 14 billion years? Yes. Could He have taken twice that length of time. Again, yes. Evolution is *logically* possible (because God is infinite and can do anything He desires) but *scientifically* untenable (because there is no scientific evidence to support it).

Besides, nowhere in Scripture does God even hint that this was what happened. Not one verse in the entire Bible alludes to evolution, natural selection or billions of years utilized in the creation of man. You would think that a truth so foundational, fundamental, and basic to God's involvement in mankind's origin would include this. Don't you think that something so important would warrant even just *one bit* of biblical evidence? *One* chapter? *One* verse? *One* explanation by the prophets or Jesus or Paul as to what Moses *really* meant way back in Genesis 1–2.

But there's nothing.

This is why, as a Christian, you face an intellectual and spiritual problem with believing in "theistic evolution." It's simply incompatible with Scripture and belief in Jesus. If theistic evolution is true, apparently God told Jesus to be quiet about this "Covert Creation Conspiracy." He was content to let Israel, the disciples, and 1,800 years of theologians, biblical scholars, and experts go on believing the fairy tale of a six-day creation.

I mean, come on, God. Couldn't You have just thrown us a bone (pun intended) somewhere amid those 31,173 verses You inspired?

Apparently not.

God had to wait for His humble servant, Charles Darwin, to break the good news of evolution to the world. The author of *The Origin of Species* would be the chosen truth-bearer to those ignorant, gullible, science-rejecting, backward believers of the Bible. Forget the Bible and its antiquated tale of man being formed miraculously from the dust of the ground. Moses must have hallucinated that due to the intense heat of the Sinai Desert. Poor guy. Of course, I'm being sarcastic, and for good reason.

Even the oft-cited 2 Peter 3:8 fails to leave an open door for this interpretation.

> But, beloved, be not ignorant of this one thing, that one day is with the Lord as a thousand years, and a thousand years as one day.

Turning to Psalm 90:4 we read a similar verse: "For a thousand years in thy sight are but as yesterday when it is past, and as a watch in the night." But in both 2 Peter and Psalm 90 the whole context is that God is neither limited by natural processes nor by time. To the contrary, God is "outside" time, for He also "created" time. Neither verse refers to the days of creation in Genesis, for they are specifically addressing the fact that God is not bound by time. In 2 Peter 3, the context is in relation to Christ's Second Coming, pointing out the fact that with God a day is just like a thousand years or a thousand years is just like one day. He is outside of time. This has nothing to do with the days of creation in Genesis.

Further, in 2 Peter 3:8 the word "day" is contrasted with "a thousand years." The word "day" thus has a literal meaning which enables it to be contrasted with "a thousand years." It could not be contrasted with "a thousand years" if it didn't have a literal meaning. Thus, the thrust of the Apostle's message is that God can do in a very short time what men or "nature" would require a very long time to accomplish, if they could accomplish it at all. It is interesting to note that evolutionists try to make out that the chance, random processes of "nature" required millions of years to produce man. Many Christians have accepted these millions of years, adding them to the Bible and then claiming God took millions of years to make everything.[26]

So the context is clear here. Peter is speaking about the principle of God's infinitude and timelessness. In other words, God is *beyond* time and is not measured by it. Secondly, to apply this faulty logic and interpretation directly to the Genesis creation account would mean that God made the world in six *thousand* years and not six *days*. By this same reasoning and interpretation, it would also mean that God took one thousand years to make man. But even an evolutionist will tell you that this time frame is woefully insufficient to create and evolve humanity from literally nothing to becoming an upright primate.

Besides, apart from the fact that there isn't viable, believable evidence for the billions of years required in the evolutionary concept, is it really so hard to believe in the scriptural account? If you believe in an eternal, all-powerful, infinite God who can do whatever He pleases, could He not just as easily create the world and mankind in six *seconds* instead of six days? (Psalm 115:3). Could He not have merely spoken everything into existence immediately, as He did when He said, "Let there be light: *and there was light*" (Genesis 1:3, emphasis added). You see, the actual *time* it took God to create man and the universe is technically irrelevant. However, assuming we believe in God and His creation of man and the universe, we must ask ourselves three questions: (1) What does the Bible say and what did Scripture's original writer's and hearer's understand it to mean? (2) What did Jesus teach about creation and Adam? and (3) What intelligent evidence supports which theory of origins?

One additional reason I believe God chose six literal days to create the world and mankind is because we, as the highest of all His creations, were designed to live our lives based on 24-hour days (based on the earth's rotation cycle). Again, Jesus affirmed God's literal creation of humanity in Mark 10:6 and 13:19, among other places. Jesus believed in Moses writings (John 5:45–47), as did all the rest of believing Jews, accepting them as the inerrant and inspired Word of God. Jesus also believed in a *literal* Adam and Eve (Matthew 19:3–6). As we've seen, Moses claimed God made the world in six literal days (Genesis 1–2; Exodus 20:11). Our God is intelligent enough and fully able to reveal the truth about origins thousands of years ago so that when sinful man made up his own theory, we would have a reliable source to consult for the truth. Again, all this stems from an intelligent belief that God inspired the Bible as truth. And as of yet, no scientific discovery by man has come close to disproving or invalidating God's Word.

I have staked my approach to science on the fact that God is Creator. I do this, not just because the Bible says it's true, but because it *is* true. Science and logic also scream *creation*. My firm belief in creation doesn't merely play a part in my philosophy of science; it plays the *lead* role. Though I have been honored for my scientific achievements, again, my greatest discovery was not a machine or physical principle. Rather, my highest honor is to serve the will of God for my life; exploring and applying the laws of nature and of nature's God for the benefit of mankind.

Since Gutenberg's printing of the Bible in A.D. 1455 (figure 2), God's truth has been the cornerstone of Western civilization. Chip away the mortar of Scripture's morals from the foundation of our miraculous nation and it is only a matter of time before the entire edifice collapses in on itself. When the infrastructure of our civilization is eroded away by the denying of God and His creative role in mankind and rejecting His standards and values, then we become a house built on sand. And according to Jesus, any number of forces can bring down such a house (Matthew 7:24–27). So how can the United States return to the godly principles on which this country was built? How does one rebuild a civilization?

I believe it begins with giving people more exposure to the truth. Granted, we live in a free country with access to libraries and the Internet containing a world of information. However, our "official" educational philosophy is to indoctrinate our young people with classroom brainwashing regarding evolution. If children are taught that they are the products of random mutation and chance with no personal God attached to their identity, they will be forced to conclude they are nothing more than a glorified animal. Just a smarter ape with primal urges. And we wonder why many go off to college and act like they do. Or why teenagers today are nine times more likely to engage in sex outside of marriage than their parents were.[27] Evolution teaches them that nothing is really "right or wrong." All events are "chance" occurrences. It's "what's right for you" that really matters. This relativistic approach to life and morality directly stems from the cesspool of evolutionary philosophy. No God = no absolute morals. No absolute morals means you can do whatever you want, provided you don't get caught. We have now successfully produced a generation of young people who are enslaved to popular thought and culture. And popular culture can be like an immature child — easily entertained and occupied, but not able to generate independent, rational thought.

Eventually, what you end up with is a nation filled with moral chaos, crumbling slowly from within. So that's one reason why we must fight for scientific creationism to be taught in schools alongside the official, prescribed teaching of the State. Someone is going to influence the thinking and understanding of our nation's children. Nature abhors a vacuum. They will be taught and influenced by someone — be it some pagan philosopher, clueless teacher, morally bankrupt culture, or by someone with the truth.

I realize there are enormous obstacles to overcome in bringing "creation science" back to the classroom. It will be a state-by-state battle, and it will not be easy. We will have to overcome the obstacle of creation science being viewed as religion, revisiting the age-old debate of separation of church and state. We will have to dispel the rumors that creation science is just a disguise for "Bible indoctrination." We will have to elect Christian politicians and those who are sympathetic to giving a fair and balanced treatment of the teaching regarding science and origins.

Also, creationism offers a more accurate and prosperous alternative. A creationist is a person who, for many credible and convincing reasons, rejects the theory of evolution. Instead of Darwin's faulty naturalism, we confidently and scientifically assert instead that everything on earth was created by God, effectively putting Him at the center of the human and universal equation. Those who buy into evolution's ideology believe that including God in the origins debate automatically makes it a religious issue. That's because evolutionists act on the presumption that they alone have access to the scientific *evidence*, when no such *evidence* exists. When asked to produce the evidence, the evolutionist often changes the subject and resorts to attacking creationism. The evolutionist insists he has established "evolutionary change" as the sole source of origins. This, despite the total lack of intermediate life forms ("transitional links" as Darwin characterizes them) necessary to prove it. Simply put, because of its epic failure to produce the required evidence for verifiable intermediate life forms ("transitional links"), evolution is officially more *science fiction* than actual science. Even so, it remains the accepted template through which we read the story of man. And those who question it are as ridiculed, mistreated, and misunderstood as Daniel refusing to bow in ancient Babylon or a first-century Christian claiming Jesus as Lord (*kurios*) in place of Caesar. Our young people today are programmed by the public education system to swallow the fairy tale falsehood of evolution. At the same time, they are denied classroom access to genuine scientific truth regarding the origin of man.

Think of it — if evolution were actually true, creationists would have no case. None. Evolutionists perform scientific experiments they believe to be the source and conclusion of all truth including all of history. But sadly for them, their experiments only address *currently existing phenomena* for which they seek (often *presuming*) an answer. History itself cannot be addressed directly by experiment because the history itself has ceased to exist. The actual experiment is only an experiment in the doable present. I can't do any *experiment* to definitively prove the origin of the solar system because that event is unrepeatable. The experimental scientist is therefore limited by the present-day procedures he generates. Using current-day experiments in order to make assertions on the historical origins of the sun, moon, and stars is devoid of the *experimental evidence* necessary to uphold such conclusions. In short, such assertions are purely untenable.

Evolution is a lie, instigated no doubt by the father of lies himself. The resulting outcome is the slow destruction of our civilization. Rejecting God as Creator means neither He nor His laws have any contemporary role or authority in governing or influencing man's behavior. This suppression of truth has opened a cellar door leading to cultural chaos (Romans 1:18–32).I have seen speakers portray the debate of creation vs. evolution as an argument of *religion* vs. *science*. I believe that's a mischaracterization and an insult to both religion and science alike. I would argue instead that it is a debate of genuine science vs. science fiction.

But the reason I still remain hopeful is because I believe truth eventually wins over ignorance and falsehood. As Launcelot Gobbo in

Shakespeare's *The Merchant of Venice* put it, "But in the end *the truth will out*." Notwithstanding evolutionary indoctrination, this generation also has free access to the work of Henry Morris, Ken Ham, and John Morris, whose published works provide convincing truths regarding creation while clearly demonstrating the absence of any scientific evidence supporting evolution. When researching, reading, and learning are replaced by iPhones, video games, and social media, that's when alarm bells need to sound. We have to work to reverse this trend. We have to become more productive at generating quality, truth-based media for them, by publishing and promoting books, materials, and videos by creation scientists.

In helping people know the truth about origins and the scientific details that support godly creation, we're making progress, but we still have a ways to go. We cannot stop until the general public knows the facts about origins — the credible, scientific proof for creation and the truth concerning *evolution's absence of scientific evidence*.

For parents whose children are being taught evolution in school, we have to make sure they have the information necessary to deconstruct the falsity of evolution and its harmful consequences. We must provide valuable resources for them to give a reasonable defense of their faith. The reality is that the vast majority of American parents are consumed by their day-to-day lives, too busy to transform their own thinking into a biblically oriented ideology. Therefore, we must reach them as well so they understand enough to teach their children.

Obviously, our Christian ideological foundations seem irrelevant to those in the secular world. They are focused on short-term goals and the tyranny of the immediate and urgent objectives (such as careers, how much money can they make, or whether they will even have a job). That's why we have to be both creative and shrewd about how we bring truth back into the public debate.

By contrast, those with a creationist mindset should be more focused on long-term goals and consequences. We're concerned about what ultimate impact creation truths will have on society and on our children. The question remains: how do we persuade them to switch to a big-picture perspective for the sake of their children?

I am grateful for authors and theologians like Henry Morris, whose teachings are *relevant* to this generation. Before I read Morris, I thought evolution was the truth. In my academic schooling I had been unknowingly "programmed" with the unsubstantiated doctrine of evolution.

Although I was raised in a church-going family and even was chosen as vice president of our church youth group, I was nevertheless duped by evolution. I was never taught about the inconsistency between evolution and my Bible, and why one was a religious fairy tale and the other God's established fact.

My hope is that this book, written by a scientist grounded in both science and technology, will help every reader recognize the science fiction of evolution. It's a lot easier to dismiss a lie when presented with clear evidence for the truth. Again, I highly recommend answersingenesis.org where you will find hundreds of articles and practical resources that elaborate the contradictions of evolution and the absence of scientific evidence to support it.

Morris has produced colossal amounts of convincing data in support of creation, enlightening others to the destructive consequences of evolution's folly. Sadly, from my observation, the average person has yet to read Henry Morris. We have to reintroduce him and the truth he championed to a new generation.

One arena where we must continue to fight is in public schools, where equal time is needed to present the scientific proof for creation. In the one place our children are taught the exchange of ideas and to think for themselves, its crucial that we demonstrate that the scientific evidence for evolution is *non-existent*. We then need to show them the scientific evidence for creation and let the students make up their own minds. This is a huge battle that we seem to be losing at the moment. However, this battle is nothing new.

This ongoing war between evolution (or naturalism) and creationism started well before Charles Darwin published *The Origin of Species* in 1859. Naturalism — the scientific philosophy of all existing phenomena being the sole product of natural events, to the exclusion of any supernatural participation — became vigorous following Swedish physician Carl Linnaeus' finding in A.D. 1758 of a pre-existing "order of nature." This was the product of his conviction that the study of nature would reveal the divine order of God's creation. This idea enabled the elaboration of his binomial (two name) system for classifying biological organisms as genus and species. Many years later, following Darwin's famous publication, the 1925 Scopes Monkey Trial featured Clarence Darrow's classic battle with three-time presidential candidate William Jennings Bryan. The issue was the enforcement of a Tennessee statute prohibiting teaching the theory of evolution alongside creation in public school classrooms. The evolutionist, Clarence Darrow, demanded equal time to present his evidence. Back then they argued that it was "bigotry" to only teach one theory of origins in the classroom. Today, some 90 years later, bigotry hasn't changed, only the "bigots"! Creation science, because of its foundational importance to modern science and technology, needs to receive the same equal time.

Evolution gained a huge victory in 1968 when the U.S. Supreme Court ruling in *Epperson vs. Arkansas* banned the Establishment Clause because their primary purpose was deemed to be religious. More than 20 years later the court used the same rationale in *Edwards vs. Aguillard*, striking down a Louisiana law that required biology teachers who taught the theory of evolution to also discuss evidence supporting the theory called "creation science," a clear violation of the Establishment Clause since the Louisiana law required both perspectives, evolution and creation, to be equally addressed. In so doing, the court arbitrarily *mis*labeled "creation science" (which is *genuine* science) as a "religious" idea. Hence, it failed to acknowledge the genuine scientific discipline that it is, the overwhelming scientific evidence that supports it, and the total absence of scientific evidence supporting evolution.

But beyond the classroom, it appears we have also lost many pulpits as well. Many pastors feel pressure to steer clear of the controversial topic of creation vs. evolution for fear of dividing a congregation indoctrinated in conventional worldly thinking. This, even though the biblical *and* scientific evidence *for* creation and *against* Darwinian evolution is overwhelming. Amazingly, some pastors (men whose task is to give a defense for the truth) ignore the evidence presented in their own Bibles. Those who have been appointed by God to protect their sheep, from among other things, lofty speculations and false doctrine, are neglecting the sheepfold, and instead allowing ravenous wolves to devour the minds of God's people. This is a tragedy of the worst kind.

Many churchgoers also blindly accept evolution as fact, effectively carrying Darwin in one hand and a Bible in another. They must be shown why these two books are mutually exclusive and cannot coexist on the same mental bookshelf or carry equal weight. The law of non-contradiction states that something cannot both be true and non-true at the same time. Either the Bible is true or it is not. Either Darwin is true or he is not. While it is theoretically possible for them both to be *wrong*, they both cannot be *true* because they clearly make claims that contradict one another. Someone is lying here.

Which one is it?

So the war over beginnings is not solely fought on the battlefields of science and academia. If America is to be rescued, she must also be rescued from the pulpit.

In a study done by the Pew Research Center, six in ten Americans believe humans and other living things "have evolved over time."[28] Thirty-three percent reject evolution and believe humans and other living beings have existed in their current state "since the beginning of time."

London-based YouGov also conducted a survey on the topic in 2013. That study found 37 percent believe God created mankind in its present state. Also, that 37 percent believe humans were created within the last ten thousand years.[29] That notion certainly will anger the scientific community.

In yet another poll taken in 2013, this one by *The Blaze* with 3,988 respondents, an astonishingly high 96 percent believes God created the world.[30]

One would think that with such high numbers, there might be more of an outrage over the teaching of evolution in our schools without the opportunity to present the truth as well.

I believe the spirit of the age is working overtime, denying school children access to the truth, while at the same time exposing them to immorality and ungodly values. While in school, you are forbidden to talk about God's role in creating them, but you can give them counseling on how to end the life of their unborn child. This is beyond madness, and is characteristic of a nation that has lost its way. This double standard is part of what is propagating ignorance while promoting the downgrading of humanity.

And it is precisely what we must work to change.

Endnotes

1. Bernard Ramm, *Protestant Christian Evidences* (Chicago, IL: Moody Press, 1953).
2. http://www.universetoday.com/109551/keplers-universe-more-planets-in-our-galaxy-than-stars.
3. http://www.nwcreation.net/evolutionfraud.html.
4. Charles Darwin, *The Origin of Species* (New York: Barnes & Noble Classics, 2004), p. 226–227): *"In the sixth chapter I enumerated the chief objections*

which might be justly urged against the views maintained in this volume. One, namely the distinctness of specific forms and their not being blended together by INNUMERABLE TRANSITIONAL LINKS IS A VERY OBVIOUS DIF-FICULTY. . . . *Why then is not every geologic formation and every stratum full of such intermediate links? . . . Geology assuredly does not reveal any such finely graduated organic chain; and this perhaps is the most obvious and gravest objection which can be urged against my theory"* (emphasis added).

5. Darwin, *The Origin of Species*, p. 146.
6. Ibid., p. 227.
7. Ibid., p. 226–227.
8. Ibid., p. 146.
9. Darwin, *The Origin of Species*, p. 226–227.
10. Ibid., p. 227.
11. Ibid., p. 146, 226–227.
12. Henry Morris, *The Biblical Basis of Modern Science* (Green Forest, AR: Master Books, Inc., 2002), p. 365–376.
13. Ibid., p. 368–369.
14. Ibid., p. 371, 398.
15. Ibid., p. 371, 398.
16. Ibid., p. 371.
17. Darwin, *The Origin of Species*, p. 227, emphasis added.
18. Ibid., p. 156, 227, emphasis added.
19. Ibid., p. 156, "To suppose that the eye . . . could have been formed by natural selection, seems I freely *confess* ABSURD in the highest possible degree" (emphasis added).
20. https://en.wikipedia.org/wiki/Human_genome.
21. Darwin, *The Origin of Species*, p. 380.
22. Ibid.
23. Ibid., p. 380, emphasis added.
24. Ibid., p. 226.
25. *Wall Street Journal* (WSJ), Dec. 25/26, 2014.
26. https://answersingenesis.org/days-of-creation/why-did-god-take-six-days/.
27. The Barna Group, "Young Adults and Liberals Struggle with Morality," www.barna.org (8-25-08).
28. http://www.pewforum.org/2013/12/30/publics-views-on-human-evolution/.
29. http://www.medicaldaily.com/62-americans-believe-god-guided-evolution-life-earth-247982.
30. http://www.theblaze.com/stories/2013/09/20/did-mankind-evolve-or-were-humans-created-by-god-in-their-current-form-blaze-readers-weigh-in/.

CHAPTER
10

A BRIGHT HORIZON

Helen Keller is one of the most iconic figures of the last 125 years. Her unbelievable accomplishments in spite of her many disabilities make her one of our country's most amazing historic figures. But what most people don't know about Helen Keller is that at her birth in 1880 she possessed both the ability to hear *and* see. It wasn't until the age of 19 months, when Helen was stricken with a childhood illness, that she was left deaf and blind. That illness would change everything for the young girl. As a result, she was unable to effectively speak or communicate during her formative years. Then, following a series of strategic contacts and arranged meetings, including one with inventor Alexander Graham Bell, Helen ended up under the instruction of 20-year-old Anne Sullivan, who herself was visually impaired due to a childhood eye infection. Begun when Helen was 7, theirs would grow into a 49-year-long friendship. Sullivan, whose work with Helen was later portrayed on stage and in the movie *The Miracle Worker*, became Keller's live-in teacher from childhood into her adult life. Helen went on to graduate from Radcliffe College, and became the first deaf and blind person to do so. She also was an outspoken advocate for the blind, and devoted much of her life to improving the quality of life for those with vision loss.

Keller eventually did learn to speak, becoming world famous as a speaker and author, traveling to some 40 countries. Helen even learned to "hear" by placing her hands over peoples' lips. Though controversial in some of her political views, no one can ever deny that she was one of history's most inspiring people.

One of Helen Keller's many memorable quotes is,

Life is either a daring adventure or nothing at all.

And of course, she would know.

I believe God places us on this earth so we can know Him and to enjoy the great adventure of life He alone provides (John 10:10). For those who believe on Jesus Christ, we are not only called to be different, but also to *make a difference* as well (Matthew 28:18–20; Galatians 6:10; Ephesians 4:28). Gratefully, He granted me the thinking that originated the idea of scanning the human body by NMR (MRI)(Colossians 2:3) and the *discovery* of the signals that achieved it. As a Christian, I can testify to the spirit of that "daring adventure" Helen Keller spoke of. There have been times when that adventure has felt like more of a roller coaster ride, while at other times I managed to wander off course into the desert, spiritually speaking. But in every season and chapter of my life, I can say with confidence that the journey was anything but boring.

As a result, part of this adventure has afforded me the privilege of receiving many awards and accolades for my research and work. In addition to those previously mentioned, in 1999 the Alumni Association of the Downstate Medical Center College of Medicine made me an Honorary Alumnus (figure 75). Many other awards and honors would follow.

It was naturally heartwarming in 2007 when I was awarded the "National Inventor of the Year Award" for the development of the UPRIGHT® Multi-Position™ MRI by the Intellectual Properties Owners Association Education Foundation. We were also instrumental in helping to develop an MRI-compatible pacemaker. However, all this began in obscurity, alone at my desk or purposefully tinkering in my laboratory, seeking answers to questions that few were even asking at the time.

I am still amazed that God's divine providence allowed me to be the first to recognize the difference of relaxation times between healthy and cancerous cells. I express a prayer of gratitude every time I remember that we were also the first to build a human-sized MRI scanner, producing the world's first-ever MRI image of the human body. We also created the first commercial scanner in the world. Of course, since that time, we have attracted a lot of attention *and* competition. Today, we compete with the country's medical industry giants, and though I know we're all working toward similar goals, economically and commercially, we're still fighting in a "David vs. Goliath" scenario.

Looking back over my professional life, I can say without hesitation that MRI imaging was not a single moment of discovery, but rather the result of an important subsequent sequence of contributions, added by men like Lauterbur and Mansfield, that followed my origination of the idea to turn a test tube NMR spectrometer into a scanner of the live human body (figures 21, 22, and 24) and my discovery of the disease-detecting tissue NMR *signal* (figures 79, 80, and 81) that makes the MRI image. Lauterbur's contribution was, for example, a key contribution without which there might well be no MRI images today.[1] Lauterbur realized that the NMR *signal differences* in diseased and normal tissues I discovered could be used to construct a picture (image) and originated the use of the magnetic field gradient to do so.

Figure 75

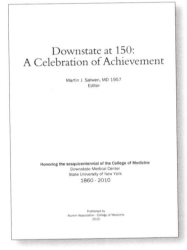

Figure 76

Figure 77

Figure 75–78 (here and on the following page). The 150-year Celebration of Achievement award to Dr. Damadian for the Invention of the MRI by the Downstate Medical Center

Raymond V. Damadian, MD, 1999H
Inventor of magnetic resonance imaging

Paul Dreizen, MD, 2001H

As a faculty member in the Department of Medicine and Biophysics Graduate Program at Downstate from 1967 to 1978, Raymond Damadian made fundamental contributions to the discovery and development of magnetic resonance imaging. These contributions include the original conception of magnetic resonance imaging for whole-body scanning of living humans; the discovery of differences of proton T1 and T2 relaxations among normal tissues and between normal and cancerous tissues that provides the biological basis for MRI; and devising a scanning method used in construction of the first full-body human MRI machine in his laboratory at Downstate.

The first MRI scanner, The Indomitable, has been on permanent display in the Hall of Medical Sciences at the Smithsonian Institution since 1986. The National Medal of Technology was awarded jointly to Raymond Damadian and Paul Lauterbur by President Reagan in 1988 with the citation, "For their independent contributions in conceiving and developing the application of magnetic resonance technology to medical uses including whole body scanning and diagnostic imaging."

Damadian was inducted into the National Inventors Hall of Fame in 1989. His 1972 patent for magnetic resonance imaging based upon T1 and T2 proton relaxations was affirmed by the U.S. Supreme Court in 1997. Among other honors, he has received honorary doctorates from the University of Wisconsin, Albert Einstein College of Medicine, and Downstate.

Early Scientific Career (1960 to 1969)

Damadian was born and grew up in New York City and attended the Juilliard School of Music. Forsaking a promising career as a concert violinist, he became a Ford Foundation Scholar at University of Wisconsin, received his MD degree at Albert Einstein College of Medicine, and entered residency training in medicine at Kings County Hospital in 1960. With strong encouragement from Ludwig Eichna, the recently appointed chairman of medicine at Downstate [See Eichna monograph. Ed.], Damadian began postdoctoral research in renal physiology with Neil Bricker at Washington University School of Medicine (1962), followed by a fellowship (1963-1965) in Arthur Solomon's biophysical laboratory at Harvard Medical School, a main center for biophysical studies of membrane transport. While there, Damadian identified and isolated an *E. coli* mutant deficient in the active transport of potassium ions (Damadian and Solomon, *Science* 1964). This project was continued during military service at the U.S. Air Force School of Aerospace Medicine (1965-67).

Damadian returned to Downstate as assistant professor of medicine and biophysics in 1967. In research supported by grants from the NIH and the Health Research Council of New York City, the relation between intracellular ionic composition and transmembrane potential of *E. coli* was studied in native and mutant forms (Damadian, *J. Bacteriology.* 1968; *Science* 1969). This work led to the first measurements, in collaboration with Freeman Cope, of potassium (K^{39}) NMR relaxations in bacteria, intended to provide information about the physical states of intracellular K^+. Using *Halobacter halobium*, a microbe from the Dead Sea with high intracellular K^+ concentration, and

Figure 78

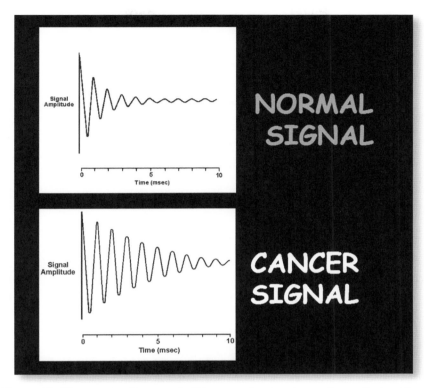

Figure 79. The newly *discovered* differences in the decay times ("relaxation times") of the tissue NMR (MRI) signals of cancerous and normal tissue and between the normal tissues themselves. The amplitudes of the tissue NMR signals acquired during the MRI scan are used to set the brightness of the picture elements (pixels) that make up the image. The signals with the longer relaxation times (e.g., cancers) have a higher computed signal amplitude that increases the brightness of the picture elements (pixels). The larger relaxation-generated signal amplitudes provide the visualization of diseased tissues on the MRI image.

I originated the idea of transforming a 24-year-old analyzer of test tubes (the NMR spectrometer) into a scanner of the live human body (figures 21 and 24) and discovered the *NMR signals that make the image*, without which there would be no MRI today. I discovered the pronounced *differences in the NMR signals* from diseased and normal tissues (figures 22 and 79) and the pronounced *differences in the NMR signals* among the normal tissues themselves (figure 22): *the signals that make the image*.

Rat No.	Weight (g)	Rectus muscle T_1	Rectus muscle T_2	Liver T_1	Liver T_2	Stomach T_1	Small intestine T_1	Kidney T_1	Brain T_1
1	156	0.493	0.050	0.286	0.050	0.272	0.280	0.444	0.573
2	150	.548	.050	.322	.060	.214	.225	.503	.573
3	495	.541	.050	.241	.050	.260	.316	.423	.596
4	233	.576 (0.600)*	.070	.306 (0.287)*	.048	.247 (0.159)*	.316 (0.280)*	.541 (0.530)*	.620 (0.614)*
5	255	.531			.300	.360	.150	.489	.612
Mean and standard error		0.538 ± 0.015	0.055 ± 0.005	0.293 ± 0.010	0.052 ± 0.003	0.270 ± 0.016	0.257 ± 0.030	0.480 ± 0.026	0.595 ± 0.007

Table 1. Spin-lattice (T_1) and spin-spin (T_2) relaxation times (in seconds) of normal tissues.

* Spin-lattice relaxation time after the specimen stood overnight at room temperature.

Table 2. Spin-lattice (T_1) and spin-spin (T_2) relaxation times (in seconds) in tumors.

Rat No.	Weight (g)	T_1	T_2
		Walker sarcoma	
6	156	0.700	0.100
7	150	.750	.100
8	495	.794 (0.794)*	.100
9	233	.688	
10	255	.750	
Mean and S.E.		0.736 ± 0.022	.100
P		< .01†	
		Novikoff hepatoma	
11	155	0.798	0.120
12	160	.852	.120
13	231	.827	.115
Mean and S.E.		0.826 ± 0.013	0.118 ±
P		< .01†	0.002
		Fibroadenoma (benign)	
14		0.448	
15		.537	
Mean		.492	
		Distilled water	
		2.691	
		2.690	
		2.640	
Mean and S.E.		2.677 ± 0.021	

* Spin-lattice relaxation time after the specimen stood overnight at room temperature. † The P values are the probability estimates of the significance of the difference in the means of T_1 for the malignant tumor and for brain.

Tables 1 & 2.

R. Damadian, Tumor Detection by Nuclear Magnetic Resonance. Science, 19 March 1971, Vol.171, Tables 1 & 2, pp. 1151-1153

Figure 80. Dr. Damadian's 1971 publication in *Science* of the elevated NMR relaxation times (T_1 and T_2) of cancer tissues as compared to normal that initiated the MRI.

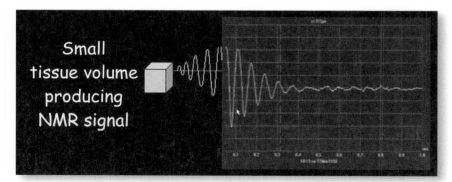

Figure 81. Photo of a live NMR signal such as that generated by a small tissue volume connected to an oscilloscope; an NMR signal that generates the MRI image.

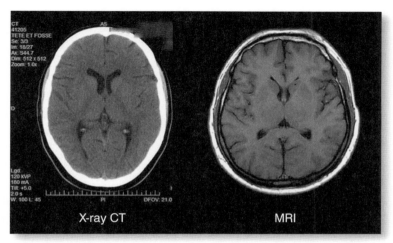

Figure 82. X-ray CT/MRI comparison showing MRI's visualization of the brain grey matter/white matter discrimination not seen on the CT.

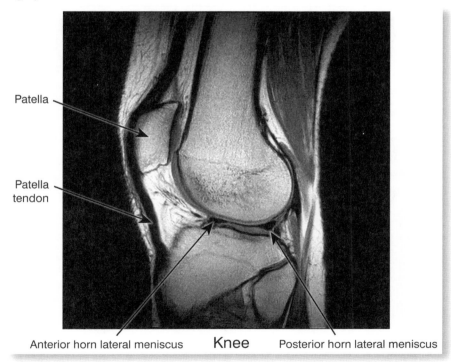

Figure 83. Figures 83 through 94 exhibit the exceptional anatomic detail visualized by MRI imaging for the first time in medical history that was made possible by the discovery of Dr. Damadian of the pronounced NMR relaxation differences of the body's healthy tissues.

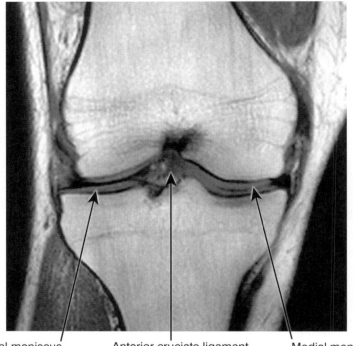

Lateral meniscus   Anterior cruciate ligament   Medial meniscus
Figure 84.   Knee

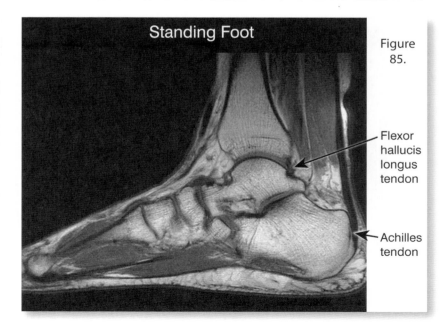

Standing Foot

Figure
85.

Flexor
hallucis
longus
tendon

Achilles
tendon

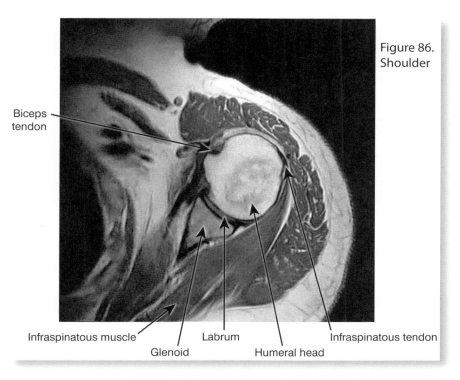

Figure 86. Shoulder

Biceps tendon

Infraspinatous muscle

Glenoid

Labrum

Humeral head

Infraspinatous tendon

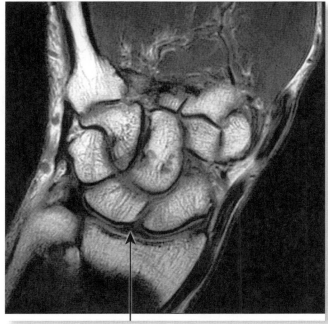

Figure 87. Wrist. The triangular fibrocartilage complex (TFCC)

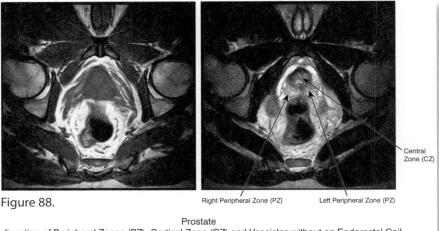

Figure 88.

Right Peripheral Zone (PZ)   Left Peripheral Zone (PZ)

Central Zone (CZ)

Prostate
Delineation of Peripheral Zones (PZ), Cortical Zone (CZ) and Vescicles without an Endorectal Coil.

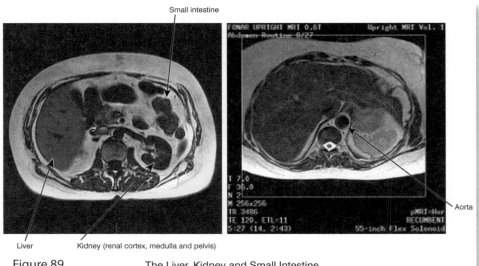

Small intestine

Aorta

Liver   Kidney (renal cortex, medulla and pelvis)

Figure 89.   The Liver, Kidney and Small Intestine

The discovery of these disease-detecting *signals* set in motion my original idea: that perhaps this 24-year-old chemical analyzer, known as the NMR spectrometer (figures 17 and 19), with its 2¼" magnet gap for 10mm test tube samples (figure 18), which prior to my discovery had been in use for 24 years by thousands of chemists worldwide for obtaining chemical spectra from test tube samples, might ultimately be transformable into a scanner for detecting disease within the live human body.

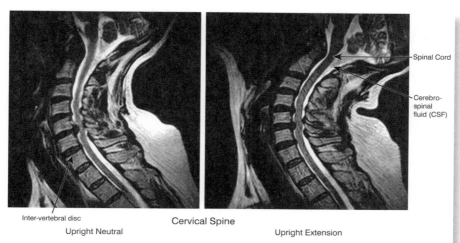

Inter-vertebral disc

Spinal Cord

Cerebro-spinal fluid (CSF)

Cervical Spine

Upright Neutral

Upright Extension

Figure 90.   Unsuspected Disc Herniation in Extension

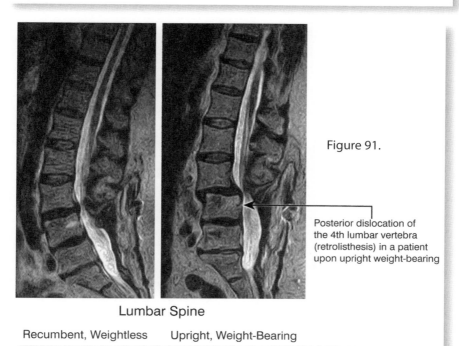

Figure 91.

Posterior dislocation of the 4th lumbar vertebra (retrolisthesis) in a patient upon upright weight-bearing

Lumbar Spine

Recumbent, Weightless   Upright, Weight-Bearing

The observation that followed, namely my discovery of the marked *NMR[2] signal differences* (figures 21 and 22) that existed between diseased tissues (e.g., cancer) and normal tissues, and also between the normal tissues themselves, (figure 22) opened the way for a new technology for

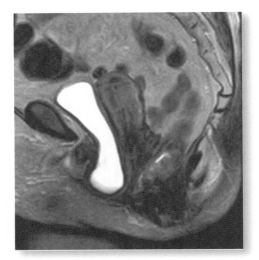

Figure 92. The FONAR UPRIGHT MRI provides a comprehensive *non-invasive* fully weight-loaded visualization of the pelvic floor for the evaluation of pelvic floor disorders (PFD's), such as rectoceles, paradoxical puborectalis syndrome, levator syndrome, coccygodynia, pudendal neuralgia, and proctalgia fugax.

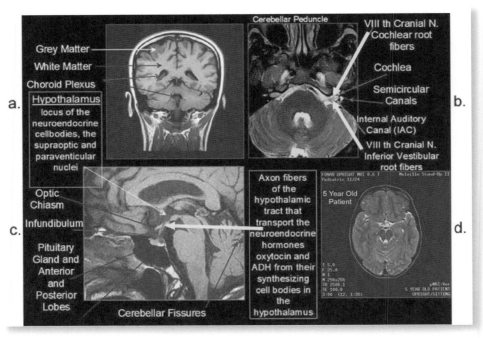

Figure 93. The extraordinary detail of the medical MRI image of the vital organs of the human body (e.g., visualization of the grey matter/white matter discrimination within the cerebral cortex of the human brain, the hypothalamic tract within the pituitary inlundibulum, the IAC (interal auditory canal), and the cochlear and vestibular nerve root fibers within the auditory nerve) made possible by Dr. Damadian's discovery.

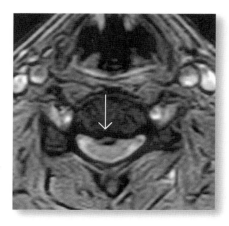

Figure 94. Axial image of the spine showing a herniation of the intervertebral disc (arrow) impinging on the spinal cord (grey elliptical structure).

non-invasively visualizing anatomy at an unprecedented level of detail within the live human body (figures 82–93), i.e., detailed visualization for the first time of the body's vital organs (e.g., brain [figure 93], heart, liver, kidney, spleen, pancreas [figures 89, 93], etc.). Prior to my discovery, these vital soft tissues were being poorly and inadequately visualized in clinical medicine by x-ray technology. My discovery likewise enabled the visualization and detection of diseased tissue within the live human body at an unprecedented level of detail and sensitivity (figures 95–97).

Origin of the NMR Scanning Idea

A fundamental curiosity I have puzzled over for many years has been —

> How did the NMR scanning idea happen to me? What caused it to arise suddenly from out of nowhere? Why would someone looking at a 24-year-old ¼" test tube analyzer of lifeless chemical samples, with a magnet opening of 2¼" suddenly say to himself (or anyone else), "Let's use it to scan the human body"?

A bizarre thought, *at the time*, to say the least! and, with few exceptions, everyone who heard about it reacted to it the same way. It was branded "Visionary Nonsense," and in my own confoundment I wondered, "How indeed did it happen?" With no other answer for an idea "out of the blue," I can only conclude that "He put it there!" As Johannes Kepler (A.D. 1596) characterized it regarding his own discoveries of planetary orbits, "I am devoting my effort . . . for the Glory of God who wants

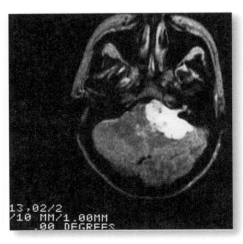

Figure 95. An MRI image of a tumor of the brain, an acoustic neuroma of the auditory nerve. The striking differences in pixel brightness that separate the tumor from surrounding normal tissue so that it can be detected on the T_2 MRI image are created by the marked differences in T_2 relaxation between tumors and normal tissue discovered by Damadian (R. Damadian, "Tumor Detection by Nuclear Magnetic Resonance," *Science*, 1971, 171, p. 1151–1152).

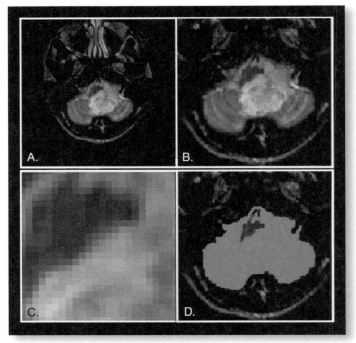

Figure 96. The increased pixel brightness of the MRI pixels of a cerebellum tumor of the brain generated by the newly discovered increased decay times (B) of diseased tissue (cancerous and non-cancerous) that enables unprecedented visualization by MRI of diseased tissue within the body's vital organs. D is an image where all the MR signal differences discovered by Damadian have been removed and all the image pixels consequently have the same brightness and the image is a blank.

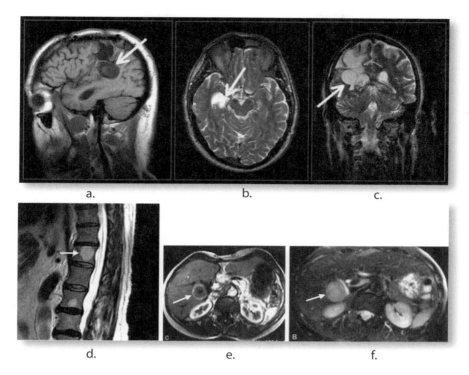

a. b. c.

d. e. f.

Figure 97. T_1 images of the brain (52a) and T_2 images of the brain (52b, c) spine vertebra (52d) and liver (52e, f).

a. A sagittal T_1 image of the brain showing the tumor as reduced pixel brightness on the T_1 image.
b. An axial T_2 image of the brain showing enhanced pixel intensity generated by the elevated T_2 relaxations of tumor tissue.
c. A coronal T_2 image of the brain visualizing the enhanced tumor pixel brightness generated by the increased T_2 relaxations of cancerous tissue.
d. e, and f. T_2 images of the vertebra and liver, showing a tumor mestastasis to bone (d) as well as their visualization within the livers of patients because of their elevated T_2 relaxation times.

to be recognized from the Book of Nature."[3] My ultimate conclusion regarding the origin of the NMR scanning idea acknowledges the same originator identified by the legends of scientific history — as the author of their ideas (figure 2) and as John elaborates (John 16:13–15), "When he, the Spirit of truth, is come he will guide you into *all truth* . . . and he will shew you things to come. . . . he *shall take of mine, and shall shew it unto you*" (emphasis added).

It is hard for me to attribute the origin of this bold *idea*, which I proposed for the first time to Dr. Cope during our K^{39} NMR experiments at NMR Specialties in New Kensington (see chapter 3), to any straightforward scientific deduction. It simply arose *de novo*. I don't know who to attribute it to, but the Apostle Paul answers the question without ambiguity: *"In [Christ] are hid all the treasures of wisdom and knowledge"* (Colossians 2:3, emphasis added). In fact, for any research scientist, young or old, keen on making a valuable discovery from his experiments, the Apostle has supplied the formula. It's Colossians 2:3. Invoke it!

The discovery of the tissue NMR signal differences that make the image provided for the first time the ability to visualize the body's *critical* soft tissue vital organs (figures 89 and 93) at an unprecedented level of detail. The discovered differences in the decay times (relaxation times) of the diseased and normal tissues generated the differences in signal strength (signal amplitude) needed to provide the brightness differences (contrast) in the picture elements (pixels) that make up the image. They provided the pixel brightness differences within the image (pixel contrast) needed to distinguish the diseased tissues within the image from the surrounding normal tissue in the image. In the absence of such discovered NMR signal differences that set the pixel brightness differences that create the MRI image, the pixels that compose the MRI image would all have the same brightness and the MRI image would be a blank (figure 96d).

The discovery of these NMR signal differences between diseased and normal tissues and within the normal tissues themselves (figure 22) overcame a serious deficiency in medical imaging that existed prior to the MRI, namely, the absence of sufficient pixel brightness differences (contrast) within x-ray images of the body's soft tissue *vital organs* that limited x-ray's (and therefore CT's) ability to picture the anatomic detail that was critical for achieving satisfactory assessment and treatment of the health of these vital life-sustaining organs (e.g., brain [figure 93], heart, liver, kidney, spleen, pancreas, etc. [figures 89 and 94]). These differences were essential for providing the necessary pixel contrast needed to visualize detail in these critical vital organs. My discovery of these pronounced tissue NMR relaxation differences among the body's vital organs overcame this long-standing deficiency that had prevailed in medical imaging for more than 100 years, since the time x-ray medical imaging was first introduced by Roentgen in 1895. Today's MRI images provide unprecedented power for non-invasively visualizing anatomic detail within the body's critical vital organs, thanks to *the good Lord*.

When you encounter one of our MRI machines today, it resembles a space-like creation like something out of a futuristic sci-fi movie, like *Star Trek*. Sleek, modern, and initially intimidating, its modern exterior hides the technology and "moving parts" contained within. Just a short walk down the hallway from my office, I pass through a door into the manufacturing wing of our company, FONAR. In that large warehouse, I can see the various stages of MRI machines in development, from the raw materials — giant steel magnets in the making, wire, electrical components — to the area where the exoskeleton is assembled, giving *Indomitable*'s offspring and descendants a softer, more gentle appearance.

And all those who are an integral part of the FONAR family, from machinists, manufacturers, and high-tech engineers to technicians, sales, customer support, and management, make a significant contribution toward our common goal and mission to help people through MRI.

I am thoroughly convinced I could never have reached this point and made such groundbreaking advancements in science and technology without my early co-workers, Mike Goldsmith and Larry Minkoff. Both geniuses in their own right, their tireless efforts to bring *Indomitable* into existence were not without great sacrifice. Their intellect, sweat, and sheer will power and perseverance helped pave the way for our success.

But since those early days, we've made great strides in the advancement of MRI technology. In 1984, a team of researchers in our company made an important development. They realized that conventional MRI images were confined to the three right-angle planes — called the *axial*, *sagittal*, and *coronal* planes. After much research, design, and testing, a new kind of imaging was born out of this — *oblique* MRI imaging. This method led to multi-angle oblique imaging, which essentially allows us to make accurate pictures of structures and organs within the human body that are positioned at arbitrary angles. This method has been particularly useful in showing herniation of vertebral discs.

Today, after years of further developments in the field of Magnetic Resonance Imaging by our FONAR Corporation and others, MRI scanners are being used all around the world. These remarkable machines are helping medical professionals detect all sorts of diseases and life-threatening illnesses. Most importantly, its *capability* of visualizing soft tissue detail in the body's vital organs and in cancers now makes it possible to *monitor* the success of cancer therapies while they are underway, wherein detailed daily MRI imaging of the patient's lesion (in principle) can *quickly* assess the success of the therapy in use so that the dose being utilized can be adjusted early on during treatment as needed, or the therapeutic agent being used can be changed early on to another agent as soon as the MRI images show the absence of an effective MRI tissue response to the therapy being utilized. Additionally, MRI diagnoses bone and ligament injuries with greater resolution than other technologies, and this is done without exposing the human body to any of the damaging radiation of x-rays.

The passion that drove me all those years ago — learning classical violin, playing competitive tennis, and pursuing research — still motivates me today. This drive for excellence has helped keep FONAR as a leader in MRI technology. Our newest UPRIGHT® MRI's have enabled us to essentially reinvent the MRI machine.

This new technology allows physicians a first-ever look at the human body in its natural upright fully weight-bearing state. People live in motion and experience pain in motion. In other words, human physiology is greatly impacted by position and gravity. This is especially true of the weight-loaded spine. Since approximately half of all the MRI scans done on the planet today are of the spine, the UPRIGHT® MRI offers invaluable diagnostic advantages. Most importantly, the improved diagnoses lead to changes in surgical protocols and improved surgical outcomes. Of course, the UPRIGHT® also scans people in the usual recumbent position. That's one reason why this innovation is a marked improvement on traditional approaches to MR imaging.[4]

One of our surgeons once told us, "If you can't see it, you can't fix it. The most important image is the one that enables you to see the patient's problem." Therefore, our UPRIGHT® MRI units allow for imaging the body in its fully *weight-loaded natural physiological positions.* Our new high-field *open* (0.6T) MRI scanners give doctors the freedom to position the patient in virtually *any* position. This enables the MRI technologist to ask the patient to position himself/herself in the exact position that generates his/her pain so that images of the patient in the position that explicitly generates the patient's pain enables the physician to explicitly visualize the anatomic changes directly associated with the patient's pain. We can now take multiple scans, evaluating the complete motion of neck, arms, or spine, and by doing so we can detect abnormalities missed by conventional non-weight-bearing recumbent-only scanners.

Our new upright scanner has the *greatly enhanced technology* that enables UPRIGHT MRI imaging. In fact, at the moment, because of all of its capabilities it is less expensive than the GE 3.0 Tesla scanner but a little bit more expensive than what they are selling their 1.5T scanners (currently their principal product) for.

MRI has also enabled significant advances in the visualization of breast disease. One reason this is so significant is that viewing greater detail in the body's soft tissues, made possible by our discovery of the pronounced NMR (MRI) signal differences that exist within the body's normal soft tissues (figure 22), enables conventional operations to be reduced to more "closed" techniques (like laparoscopy), which in turn increases the operations' precision. It helps surgeons narrow their field of focus during operation, facilitating a more accurate surgical procedure. And better surgery means there is a better chance of a cancer-free life.

Our most recent breakthrough has to do with the Cranio-Cervical Syndrome (CCS). While early researchers had noted the spinal fluid was moving, its quantitatively dynamic physiologic role where 32 quarts of cerebrospinal fluid (CSF) are flowing in and out of the brain through the acqueduct of Sylvius each day and down the spinal column to the mid-sacrum (tailbone) was not fully appreciated until the MRI and its latest technology enabled cardiac gating of the acquisition of in vivo real-time images of the cerebrospinal fluid and full-fledged in vivo CSF videography.

Every year, millions of neck injury patients (including approximately 1.2 million automobile whiplash injuries annually in the United States alone) continue to suffer due to inadequate diagnosis and effective treatment for those injuries and their resulting symptoms. In fact, most people have no idea just how vulnerable the human neck really is. Some of these symptoms include (but are not limited to) severe headaches (migraines), chronic neck pain, tinnitus, loss of vision, dementia, numbness and tingling in the hands and fingers, numbness in legs, loss of motor skills in lower extremities, tingling in the legs or feet, vertigo upon standing, or difficulty walking.

When there is some sort of neck injury or trauma to that area (sports-related, car accident, whiplash, etc.) the C1 and C2 vertebrae (located at the top of the neck / base of the skull) can be dislocated, effectively impeding the flow of the cerebrospinal fluid (CSF) in and out of the brain. With the CSF being generated within the ventricles of the brain at the net rate of 500cc per day, wherein its normal circulation proceeds from the cranium down the full length of the spinal column to the mid-sacrum (tailbone) and back up, obstruction in the neck to CSF outflow by dislocations of the cervical vertebrae that obstruct the spinal canal results in a back-up of the 500cc of CSF being generated daily by the brain. The result is an increase in intracranial pressure (ICP) that gives rise to the above enumerated symptoms. The increased intracranial pressure produces leakages of CSF from the ventricles within the brain where it is generated to the surrounding brain tissue, producing lesions within the brain that we believe gives rise to multiple sclerosis,[5] Alzheimer's, Parkinson's, childhood autism, amyotrophic lateral sclerosis (Lou Gehrig's disease), dementia, and incapacitating headaches. We have designated this syndrome the "Cranio-Cervical Syndrome" (CCS).

Thankfully, however, our MRI technology can now (1) *quantitatively* measure the flow of the cerebrospinal fluid in cc/sec., (2) precisely locate the lesions, and (3) pinpoint exactly which vertebrae are dislodged or malaligned and obstructing the flow of CSF in and out of the brain. With the breakthrough of IGAT (Image Guided Atlas Treatment) technology invented by Dr. Scott Rosa[6] (and not to be confused with the AO technology), we can effectively correct the identified vertebral malalignment, thereby eliminating its impedance of spinal fluid flow. In other words, we can "break the dam" impeding the flow of spinal fluid into and out of the brain, thereby restoring normal intracranial flow of the cerebrospinal fluid. In cases where this procedure has been used in partnership with MRI, those intracranial lesions have actually gone away in some instances! We are continuing to treat patients, scanning them and using this IGAT technology. We believe our successful results will enable a breakthrough in the diagnosis and treatment of the above-mentioned symptoms and diseases.

This new application of MRI technology also has near limitless benefits for thousands of current and former athletes within the "contact sports" community wherein neck trauma injuries are most common (e.g., football, soccer, hockey, rugby, etc.). We have already treated some high-profile former NFL football players, with amazing results. After only one treatment, we are seeing previous debilitating symptoms (like dementia) disappear. Truly, the reach and application of this new

MRI-related discovery and procedure carries great hope for millions of lives being impacted.

When I first started out in my early years of research, I had no guarantees that anything would ever come of my work. The only thing I was sure of was that I wanted my work to help people during my lifetime. But even beyond that, I wanted my work to continue doing the same thing long after I'm gone.

Everywhere I go, I am approached by people whose lives (or the lives of friends or loved ones) were saved or greatly enhanced by MRI. I always try to be gracious as I thank them for their kind comments. However, in my heart I know Who deserves the real credit. Raymond Damadian did not invent the natural phenomenon of magnetic fields or radio frequency waves. And he certainly did not think up the idea of the human cell and its microscopic atomic composition. All I did was use the mind and training He provided me to discover how those components could work in concert to help mankind. God provided the sheet music, the melody, and the lyrics. I simply strung up an instrument to play the song.

And thankfully, millions can now dance to that music!

Since the Fall of man and sin's introduction into the world, humanity has been getting sick and dying. In one sense, medical science exists to prevent and treat disease, and to prolong the lives of people. Hopefully, in the process we can give them a better quality of life as well. But the more we understand about truth, science, and the human body, the more apt we are to discover new ways to treat some of the illnesses and diseases that threaten the human race today. There is currently no cure for the Ebola virus. There is currently no cure for cancer. But that doesn't mean we should stop trying, with His help, to find these cures (Colossians 2:3). Fifty years ago, no one would have believed it if you had told them you could detect cancer inside the human body anywhere it was located without even touching it. Today, that MRI technology is being practiced all over the world. There are no words that can adequately describe how wonderful that makes me feel.

Because I am a Christian, I believe that one day God will wipe out all disease and suffering in a time of His own choosing. He will destroy disease and everything that causes it. In that day, there will be no sin, nor any effects of sin. And no cancer . . . of any kind.

Scripture is very clear that in heaven we will be given new "incorruptible" bodies (1 Corinthians 15:53–54). In that day, we are promised:

> And God shall wipe away all tears from their eyes; and there
> shall be no more death, neither sorrow, nor crying, neither shall
> there be any more pain. . . . And he that sat upon the throne
> said, Behold, I make all things new (Revelation 21:4–5).

Once there, we will be able to drink from the "water of life freely" (Revelation 21:6), a never-ending supply of eternal health and refreshment. I look forward to that day when disease and death will be no more, the day when all believers will be under the constant, healing care of the Great Physician.

I think any man's legacy boils down to the particular hope of knowing that his life has been lived for something more than just his own benefit and enjoyment. I like to think my life and work have made a significant and lasting contribution to humanity. I will let God and history be the final judge of that.

When I was a boy playing violin at Julliard or building skyscrapers with my erector sets at home, I gave no thought to what my future might hold. Even later, in medical school, it was impossible to know just how endless note-taking in class and studying chemistry and human anatomy would contribute toward my ultimate life's work and calling. I had no way of knowing if anything would ever come of any of my long months of research.

But God knew.

My part was to keep following the continual passion He had placed within me. My commitment was to try to help as many as possible in my short lifetime. Deep down inside, I hoped that because of my work, maybe I could find a way to relieve some of the same suffering I had experienced in my own childhood. And perhaps I could help some other little boys keep their grandmothers around for a few more years.

My Heavenly Father has allowed me to live long enough to see my research and inventions help save many lives, help preempt the spread of cancer, give hope, and help people better understand the nature of the enemy they are facing. I am deeply humbled that the Creator would take someone like me — an Armenian-French kid from Queens — and lead me on a journey that took me through violin classes, competitive tennis, a salvation experience at Madison Square Garden with Billy Graham, the challenging world of academia and medical school, and years in the laboratory — all to develop research that would help change the landscape of medicine. Because of this, I can give you the assurance that if you are focused and determined, there is almost nothing you cannot accomplish in this life under His will. With God by your side, your potential is *exponentially* multiplied! The question always is, "Is He in your heart and by your side?" But as He states without qualifiers: *"If ye shall ask any thing in my name, I will do it"* (John 14:14). As I tell my fellow scientist researchers, "See for yourself. Do the *experiment*. Ask 'in His name.' It works!!"

Today, I find myself approaching 80 years on this earth. Many people pity us older folks, and perhaps some deserve that pity. But not Raymond Damadian. From where I sit, life is still an *amazing* adventure! There is still so much to know, to discover, to do, and to experience. I'm not winding down in my old age. You might say I'm just getting started! There is so much more for me to learn from my Savior, Jesus Christ, "in whom are hid all the treasures of wisdom and knowledge" (Colossians 2:3).

Part of what motivates that pursuit of Him are the human treasures He has graciously given me. From where I sit each day, I see those treasures all along the wall in my Long Island office. My favorite section is the "Damadian Art Gallery." There I see the smiling faces of my three precious children and nine grandchildren.

I see my oldest son, Timothy, who spent some of his high school years working diligently helping me in the laboratory with construction and engineering tasks related to developing the MRI. After starting his own company with some UPRIGHT® MRI machines purchased from us, he eventually went on to be in charge of 24 scanning centers in New York and Florida. He then returned to our company a few years ago. Today, he lives not far from me in Long island and runs the FONAR Corporation.

On that same wall, I see my son Jevan, an electrical engineer who now works on the electronic design of scanners and magnets at FONAR. He also runs our scanning centers located in Manhattan.

In those photographs, I see my wonderful daughter Keira, who is married to computer engineer Markus Reinmund. They and their four children live in Connecticut, though we still, thankfully, get to see them almost every week. And I also see multiple portraits of our incredible grandchildren, whose radiant smiles and laughter bring indescribable joy to the hearts of Donna and me. I love being involved in my grandchildren's lives, attending their various school and extracurricular activities.

216 · Gifted Mind

Occasionally, they even ask their old granddad to speak at a high school science fair, which I am more than happy to do.

One of God's greatest gifts in this life is family. Work is fulfilling. A career is rewarding. But family touches a place in your soul that machines and money cannot. It goes deeper than economic achievements and public accolades. As such, that wall of photos represents the heart and soul of who I really am. And there is not a day that goes by that I do not thank the good Lord for my great family.

I have been told I have a gifted mind. If that's true, it's only because I have a great and gracious God who gifted it. But far beyond being given a gifted mind, I have been given a blessed *life*. And make no mistake about it, for anything good that has ever come as a result of me, *all of the glory and all of the honor are His and His alone!*

Endnotes

1. Unless Damadian, in his search for ways to present his previously discovered abnormal NMR signals of diseased tissue in his proposed body scan, ultimately generated an image presentation.
2. MRI is NMR (Nuclear Magnetic Resonance) renamed. Upon its initial introduction in medicine, physicians wanted the "nuclear" name removed because it implied radioactivity that the NMR did not possess, and the radiologists wanted the "I" added to identify it as an imaging technology.
3. James R. Voelkel, *Johannes Kepler and the New Astronomy* (Oxford, UK; New York: Oxford University, 1999), p. 32, Johannes Kepler letter to Maestlin, October 1595.
4. Comments excerpted from an interview; http://www.imagingeconomics.com/2008/02/article-16776/.
5. R.V. Damadian, D. Chu, "The Possible Role of Cranio-Cervical Trauma and Abnormal CSF Hydrodynamics in the Genesis of Multiple Sclerosis," *Physiol. Chem. Phys. & Med. NMR*, September 20, 2011, 41:1–17.
6. Dr. Scott Rosa's IGAT treatment is not to be confused with more generic AO therapy. It is specifically UPRIGHT® MRI Image Guided therapy, assuring that the correct cervical vertebra is treated and correctly repositioned (e.g., C-2 clockwise rotated and not counter-clockwise rotated when clockwise rotation is the required treatment) as the axial UPRIGHT® fully weight-loaded MRI images of C-1 and C-2 (not acquired by a conventional recumbent MRI cervical spine scan) indicates. Specifically, if C-1 is clockwise rotated 16°, adjustment of C-1 requires a 16° counter-clockwise treatment rotation of C-1 by adjustment of the correct C-1 transverse process. Rotation treatment of the wrong transverse process of C-1 could further magnify the malrotation of C-1 (e.g., to 30°), confounding the patient's problem. Accordingly, it is mandatory that any atlas reorientation treatment undertaken must

be simultaneously monitored by a fully weight-loaded UPRIGHT® MRI to assure that the correct repositioning of the maloriented cervical vertebra is achieved and maintained (hence the name of Dr. Rosa's treatment — Image Guided Atlas Treatment [IGAT]).

APPENDIX

1

JESUS: THE INCARNATION AND SANCTIFICATION OF THE TRUTH

The Birth of Science

You and I get one shot at this life. One opportunity to make a difference. That's why David prayed for God to teach him to "number his days" and realize how short and fragile this life really is. Having this perspective allowed David to live a life worthy of the one who had called him, so that he might "gain a heart of wisdom" (Psalm 90:12; NIV). "Behold, thou desirest *truth* in the inward [innermost] parts: and in the hidden part thou shalt make me to *know wisdom*" (Psalm 51:6, emphasis added). Thus, David is making clear that wisdom derives directly from truth, with the ultimate consequence that corruption of the truth obstructs access to wisdom, and wisdom governs the sanctity or folly of all the choices of life. If you are looking for the best life possible, it begins with surrendering your heart to Jesus Christ, your Creator and the One who bore your sin.

Coincident with Jesus' incarnation and His eternal gift of salvation for the rebirth of humanity, Jesus endowed mankind with a simultaneous blessing: *access to the truth*. As the late Dr. Henry Morris distinguished it, Jesus *was the incarnation of the truth*.[1]

Indeed, as Jesus reveals, "I am the way, the *truth*, and the life; no man cometh unto the Father, but by me" (John 14:6, emphasis added). He further reveals that His provision of man's access to the *truth* will liberate mankind to realize its God-ordained liberation destiny: "Ye shall know the *truth*, and the *truth* shall make you free (John 8:32, emphasis added). With Jesus' divine endowment granting His access to the *truth* through His portal of salvation, He granted to His believers an unprecedented new power: the power of the *truth*. Acceptance of Him, His incarnation of the *truth* itself, opened the previously inaccesible doorway to His *truth* and to its incomparable power — the power made available only by Him.

Liberation of the TRUTH and Its POWER: His Eternal Gift of Salvation for the Rebirth of Mankind

As Jesus specified (John 8:32) in the Greek text (*ginosko*), "Ye shall ['come to know,' 'recognize,' 'understand' (*ginosko*)] the *truth,* and the *truth* shall make you free" (emphasis added). That is, by Him, the *incarnation of TRUTH* — "*I am the way, the TRUTH, and the life*" (John 14:6, emphasis added), you *shall "come to know" (ginosko) NEW TRUTHS.*

By carrying out scientific experiments we "came to know" (discovered) the *new TRUTH* He incarnated — the diseased and normal tissue T_1 and T_2 differences that gave us the MRI. And as John 16:13 and 14 further verify, "*When he, the Spirit of TRUTH is come, he will guide you into all TRUTH . . . and he will shew you things to come. He shall glorify me: for he shall receive of mine, and shew it unto you*" (John 16:13–14, emphasis added): the MRI.

Thus, when His disciples (e.g., the Pilgrims and Puritans) founded the miracle of America, the newly created legacy of national POWER was ceded to the TRUTH for the first time in history. Instead of monarchy, America's first potential monarch, General George Washington, refused monarchy, and insisted on the rule of the TRUTH instead — democracy: the empowerment of the TRUTH.

The outcome — TRUTH, the new ruler — propagated unparalleled national prosperity and the financial luxury of its individual citizens on a scale unprecedented in human history. Coincident with this economic explosion, and also its engine, the product of HIS TRUTH was an unbounded succession of new technological innovations — the internal combustion engine, automobiles, aircraft, electric lighting, steam engines, household electricity, and the MRI, etc. — technology that virtually transformed humanity's existence and relegated its prior existence to the "pre-historic." Noteworthy is the fact that the scientific-technologic boom that HIS TRUTH generated and the economic explosion in Western civilization it gave rise to did not occur in China or India where there is no shortage of smart people. Western civilization was the immediate beneficiary of HIS TRUTH and its incomparable power, for as Paul reveals, "In [Christ] are hid ALL the *treasures* of wisdom and knowledge" (Colossians 2:3, emphasis added) and to be without Him is to be without access to His fountainhead of new wisdom and new knowledge. Its product: historically unprecedented human prosperity (figure 98).

Fueling this prosperity were the explosive 16th- to 20th-century triumphs of science and technology, products of HIS TRUTH, that is, the birth of the *scientific experiment*.

As Sir Francis Bacon described in *Novum Organum*, Book 1, written in 1620, his object was to uncover *new scientific* TRUTHS by his new method of *the scientific experiment*. His method of *the experiment* would enable the revelation of *new scientific* TRUTHS, which by the experiment generated *new truths* for the first time. These in turn propagated the explosive economic prosperity (figure 98) that was unprecedented in human history. This remarkably occurred only in those nations, Western civilization, where HIS TRUTH had been given first priority and where its *author* was revered without qualification, that is, "I am the way, the TRUTH, and the LIFE: *no one comes to the father but by me*" (John14:6,

Figure 98. The sanctification of the *truth*: unparalleled economic prosperity.

emphasis added), and "Ye shall know the TRUTH, and the TRUTH shall make you free" (John 8:32, emphasis added). The obvious corollary to this reality is that the ignorance or denial of Him has a frightful personal and societal downside, namely loss of access to the TRUTH and its power.

The scientific experiment is undertaken with the assumption that *new absolute* TRUTHS exist that are discoverable and that possess the *power* to generate new technologies that *enrich* the well-being of mankind.

In the case of MRI, the discovery of one of *His new* TRUTHS gave rise to the new MRI technology that He enabled for the benefit of mankind. If I may, permit me to elaborate first on the nature of the scientific experiment itself and its objective of uncovering *new incarnated* TRUTHS from the AUTHOR.

As the experiment proceeds, the experimentalist poses the question to the AUTHOR, designs the actual experiment that the experimenter perceives will answer his question — that is, he poses a question that, if successful, might reveal a *new* TRUTH. Performing the experiment, he awaits the answer, uncertain at first how to interpret the *new* TRUTH he has uncovered. Experiencing the outcome of the first experiment, he is confronted with deciding whether the outcome of his first experiment is a genuine *new* TRUTH or an experimental error — has he uncovered a *new* TRUTH, or is it a technological error? He repeats the experiment a second time to inquire if it was a mistake. If it concurs, he repeats it a third time to certify it represents a genuine *new* TRUTH.

Such was the discovery of the MRI.

The question regarding the NMR's (nuclear magnetic resonance) power to non-invasively generate antenna detectable radio signals from the atoms (i.e., the nuclei within the human body) was, "Could such signals non-invasively distinguish diseased tissue (e.g., cancer) from healthy tissue?" In other words, was there a *new* TRUTH available from the AUTHOR?

Separate test tube samples containing cancerous tissue and healthy tissue were prepared. In the first experiment, the signal decay time ("relaxation time") of the cancer sample and the healthy tissue sample was measured. The difference between the two, Walker sarcoma and healthy tissue, was marked (figure 22). The result was exhilarating. It inferred the prospect of a scanner that could non-invasively detect diseases wherever they might be located within the live human body. But was it the TRUTH, or was it an experimental error — had I uncovered a *new* TRUTH, or had I made a mistake? The outcome would verify the credibility of such a scanner or eradicate its possibility. I repeated it a second time. The signal decay time of the malignant tissue was again much longer than the decay time of the normal. I repeated it a third time to try to achieve confidence that the apparent TRUTH of the experiment was real, that it was indeed the TRUTH of the experiment? The aspired TRUTH would mean a new scanner of the human body, but was it TRUE? Had He genuinely granted me access to HIS *new* TRUTH?

I was concerned that this observed delay in the relaxation (decay rate) of this tumor's NMR signal might be a peculiarity of this particular rat tumor and not the case for tumors in general. I determined that if I found the same delayed NMR relaxation in another rat tumor I could be more confident that it might be true of tumors in general.

I returned to Brooklyn, my home base at the State University of New York (SUNY) Downstate Medical Center, and grew a second set of rats with a different tumor, the Novikoff hepatoma, a tumor of the liver. Returning to New Kensington, Pennsylvania, and the NMR Specialties Corp. where I measured the first NMR signal relaxations of the Walker sarcoma tumor, I repeated the same measurements on the Novikoff hepatomas. To my surprise (and elation) the delay of the NMR signal decay (its relaxation) of the Novikoff hepatoma was even more pronounced — .826 seconds as compared to the .293 decay time of normal liver (figure 22) and even longer than the decay times of the Walker sarcoma at .736 seconds.

Confident now that this was more generally true of tumors, I submitted these findings to *Science* in 1970 where they were published.[2] And in the pursuit of the HIS TRUTH, there was a further consideration. The Walker sarcomas and Novikoff hepatomas were rat tumors. What was the prospect, though I considered it unlikely, that the same relaxation time differences between tumor and normal tissues would not be reaffirmed in human tumors, the tissues to be examined by the envisioned MR body scanner? While I considered it unlikely that the tissue relaxation time differences we observed in the rat tumor samples would not also be manifest in human tumors, it was unequivocally necessary to experimentally verify the TRUTH of this reality before proceeding with the construction of a human scanner. Verification that the same

NMR signal differences that would be used to make the human scans also existed in human tumors was accomplished.[3]

With the signal necessary to accomplish a scan now fully granted by *His incarnate* TRUTH, the prospect of a scanner of the live human body *had suddenly become reality. His incarnate* TRUTH and its ultimate provision of the MRI scanner was now the greatest gift of all!

I would like to conclude my account with a further and final deduction from Him. In my research into the subject, I was astounded by another *discovery: no scientific evidence, whatever, exists to uphold evolution.*

The *cardinal evidence* needed to ratify the existence of an evolutionary process in the *"chance"* generation of increasingly sophisticated life from a primordial form (Darwin's *"primordial one"*) is evidence that demonstrates a "transition" from a lesser life form (a lesser kind) to a more sophisticated life form (a more sophisticated kind). This is the *"transitional link"*[4] that Darwin defines as the connecting "link" from one *kind* to the next evolutionary *kind*. This *"transitional link"* constitutes the "missing links" in the contemporary terminology of paleontology. "Missing" genuinely characterizes their lack of existence in the archeology searches for them, plus their disputed reality when the proposed "missing links" such as Neanderthal man, Piltdown man, etc. fail to be verified as the "missing links" needed to validate evolution Why are they even designated as "missing" by modern paleontology when Darwin himself (1859) conceded they are absent altogether and that they should have been present as *"innumerable"* (chapter 9) intermediate "transition" fossil remnants at the time of his writing. Moreover, after an additional 155 years of modern technological searching for them, they continue to be "missing." In the absence of any evidence of their existence today or throughout the 155 years searching for them, any ordinary scientific delineation of them would depict them as ABSENT.

For an ideology (evolution) that has *entrapped civilization* for more than a century and a half, and my own research wherein there is a *total absence of scientific evidence* for the critical *"transitional links"* necessary to sustain it, as well as Darwin's own concession of their non-existence, the outcome is *astounding!*

A world-renowned accepted universal theory with no evidence to support it.

In short, the scientific verity of evolution is non-existent! It would never have built an MRI machine!

Endnotes
1. http://www.icr.org/article/7423/.
2. R. Damadian, "Tumor Detection by Nuclear Magnetic Resonance," *Science,* 171:1151, 1971.
3. Raymond Damadian, Ken Zaner, Doris Hor, and Theresa DiMaio, "Human Tumors Detected by Nuclear Magnetic Resonance," *Proceedings of the National Academy of Sciences of the USA,* April 1974, vol. 71, no. 4, p. 1471–1473.
4. Charles Darwin, *The Origin of Species* (New York: Barnes & Noble Classics, 2004), p. 226–227.

PUBLISHER'S NOTE

There are a number of different pioneering and significant discoveries that have been made by Dr. Damadian. Following is a summarized list of them and their importance:

1. Dr. Damadian *originated* the bold idea of taking a well-established test tube analyzer of 24 years duration and transforming it into a scanner of the live human body, as evidenced by the 1969 grant request to the Health Research Council of the City of New York, George S. Mirick, MD, Scientific Director (figure 24).

2. He discovered the *signals* that made it happen — that is, discovery of the abnormal T_1 and T_2 values of the NMR *signals* generated by diseased tissue within the human body (figures 22 and 80), as well as the discovery of the marked variations of T_1 in the NMR *signals* of the body's normal tissues (figure 22 and 80) that brought the vision for such a scanner to reality.[1] These important T_1 and T_2 abnormalities of diseased tissues which he discovered, together with the discovery of the marked variations of the T_1 values of the body's healthy tissues themselves (figures 22 and 80), gave rise to the "T_1 weighted" and "T_2 weighted" scans obtained by all MRI scanners. The "T_1 weighted" and "T_2 weighted" scans acquired by today's MRI scanners constitute more than 95 percent of all MRI scans obtained throughout the world today. Therefore, with approximately 30 million MRI scans being conducted annually worldwide, approximately 27 million "T_1 weighted" or "T_2 weighted" MRI scans are being acquired each year worldwide. Prior to discovery of the pronounced T_1 and T_2 differences of normal and diseased tissue and the pronounced T_1 differences among the normal tissues themselves, "T_1 weighted" and "T_2 weighted" MRI scans did not exist anywhere in the practice of medicine.

Reduction to Practice

3. Dr. Damadian, together with his graduate students Larry Minkoff and Michael Goldsmith, built the first-ever MRI scanner, *Indomitable*,

that proved that such a scanner could be built and that it could achieve invaluable disease-detecting scans of the live human body.[2]

If you ask today's MRI image-reading radiolgist, "Where would you be today in MRI without the tissue T_1 and T_2 differences discovered by Damadian?" the answer would be, "Nowhere, since more than 95 percent of the MRI images you read today, the T_1 and T_2 weighted images generated by these newly discovered T_1 and T_2 tissue relaxation differences, would not exist!"

T_1 and T_2 Imaging

4. T_1 and T_2 existed nowhere in the practice of medicine prior to his discovery of their power for detecting disease.

In NMR, two ways exist to characterize the nuclear signal response of the resonating atomic nucleus. You can analyze either the frequency dependence of the nuclear signal (NMR spectroscopy) or its time dependence, that is, its rate of decay (relaxation time). Both characterizations are manifestly informative, but until Dr. Damadian's discovery of the key sensitivity of the decay time of the nuclear resonance signal to the existence of disease within medical tissues, the overwhelming majority of the uses of NMR technology (prior to his medical application of the technology) were its chemical applications (NMR spectroscopy) for determining, non-destructively, the molecular composition of organic molecules.

Thus, the nuclear resonance signal has two properties — its frequency response to excitation (its spectrum) and the time dependence of the nuclear signal's response to excitation (its "relaxation time") — that are very informative regarding the chemical composition of molecules and their surroundings.

Regarding the time dependencies of the nuclear resonance signal, there are two time decay (relaxation) parameters, one of which is eminently visible in the oscilloscopic display of the signal as a function of time (T_2) (figure 81), and a second, usually not visible, that is a measure of the time required by the stimulated nucleus to return to its equilibrium state after its excitation (T_1) (figures 22 and 80) The times of these two time-dependent nuclear signal responses, T_1 and T_2, commonly differ markedly in tissue (figures 22 and 80), e.g., $T_1 = 538$ msecs in muscle, $T_2 = 55$ msecs in muscle (Tables 1, 2; figure 80).

The Time-Dependent Decay (Relaxation)
of the Nuclear Resonance Signal

In the time-dependence characterization of the nuclear resonance signal, two time-dependent phenomena are experimentally encountered — the rate of dissipation (T_1) of the stimulating energy (the r.f. pulse) after it has been applied and generated the NMR signal, and the rate at which the individual signals generated by each resonating nucleus within the sample dephase and destructively cancel the composite resonant signal of the individual nuclear resonance signals (T_2).

The T_1 Relaxation

The T_1 decay rate (its T_1 relaxation time) is the time of dissipation, e.g., muscle T_1 = 538msecs. (Table 1) to the surroundings (the "lattice"), of the r.f. pulse energy used to stimulate the NMR signal; i.e., the "spin-lattice relaxation time": the "thermal relaxation time."

The T_2 Relaxation

The T_2 decay rate (its T_2 relaxation time) is the time rate of decay of the live NMR signal actually observed on the oscilloscope (figure 81), e.g., muscle T_2 = 55msecs. (Table 1; figure 80). It is the time for the destructive interferences of the phase incoherencies of all of the NMR signals generated by the individual atoms within the sample to reduce the magnitude of the observed composite signal to zero.

Noteworthy is the fact that the great majority of all MRI images acquired today are either T_1 or T_2 weighted images (more than 95 percent). The use of such T_1 and T_2 relaxation dependent images explicitly exploit the benefit of Dr. Damadian's discovery[3] (figures 21 and 80) that the T_1 and T_2 signal relaxations exhibit the most pronounced and most discriminating visualization of anatomic detail in the body's normal and diseased tissues (figures 22, 82, 95–97, 99) as compared to their differences in hydrogen content (proton density images). Of all patient MRI scans performed today, therefore, more than 95 percent utilize either T_1 (T_1 weighted) or T_2 (T_2 weighted) imaging protocols. With approximately 15 million patient MRI scans being performed each year in the United States, and an equal number being performed each year in the rest of the world, 30 million T_1 (or T_2) MRI scans are being performed worldwide each year using the original T_1 and T_2 tissue MR (NMR) signal differences which he discovered.

These MR signal T_1 and T_2 differences of diseased tissue (*excluded* by the Nobel Prize [NP]) as well as the T_1 and T_2 differences of the MR signals of normal tissues (figure 22) (*excluded* by the NP), are *the signals that make the MRI image* (figures 22, 79, 99, 81–97, 99), the signals used by the MR scanner to construct the MRI images. Without these tissue MR signal differences that Dr. Damadian discovered, the brightness differences in the 65,000 picture elements (pixels) that make up the MRI image would not exist, the MRI image would be a blank (figure 96d), and there would be no MRI today.

With each T_1 or T_2 scan consisting of approximately 15 image slices (15 images/scan) per patient scan, 30 image slices are being acquired from each patient for both scan types (T_1 and T_2). Thus, 450,000,000 x .95 T_1 or T_2 images (427,500,000 T_1 or T_2 images) are being acquired worldwide each year (or approximately 4.27 billion in the past ten years) for the benefit of humanity, thanks to the T_1/T_2 NMR signal tissue relaxation differences he discovered.

Indeed, the MR signal T_1 and T_2 differences of the MR signals of diseased and normal tissues Dr. Damadian discovered (and *excluded* by the NP [figures 21 and 22]) make all the T_1 (T_1 weighted) and the T_2 (T_2 weighted) images of MRI that represent more than 95 percent of all the MRI images produced around the world today.

While the original imaging techniques awarded the NP have long been significantly upgraded (e.g., phase contrast imaging) or replaced, the T_1 and T_2 images based on his discovery (and *excluded* [figure 56] by the NP) continue to produce every MRI patient examination in the world that is acquired today. Indeed, it is difficult to imagine, for example, how the T_2 MRI scan originated by his discovery (and *excluded* by the NP) that visualizes all diseased tissues (figure 99) wherever they might occur within the human body can ever be replaced. It is, in fact, hard to envision how it will not persist as the forever component of the patient MRI examination while the initial techniques[4] to make use of the tissue MR (NMR) signal differences Dr. Damadian discovered to make the image have long been replaced.[5]

But the discovery of the *signal differences* themselves arose from the *originating question*, which can only be attributed to the Lord's providence (Colossians 2:3). Looking at the existing 10mm test tube NMR

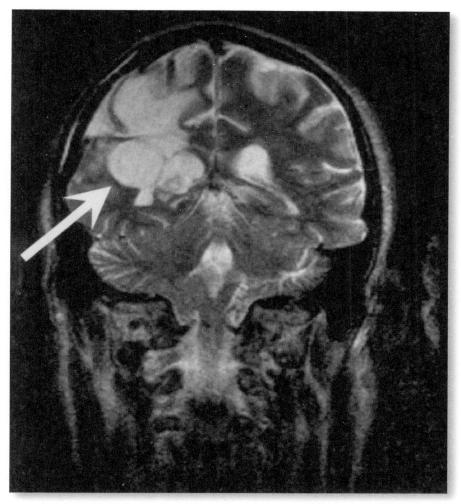

Figure 99. T$_2$ MRI visualization of a tumor of the brain made possible by the discovery of Damadian of the abnormal T$_2$ (and T$_1$) MR (NMR) relaxations of cancerous tissue.

technology, Dr. Damadian asked the question, "Could this highly informative non-invasive technology possibly be transformed from an analyzer of 10mm test tubes to a scanner of the live human body — that is, could it provide the early detection of a fatal disease like cancer?"

An example of the revolution in medical imaging generated by MRI and its achievement, for the first time in medical history, of the

2nd MAJOR DISCOVERY
(EXCLUDED BY THE N.P.) (figures 55 and 57)
BEST MEDICAL IMAGE QUALITY
IN MEDICAL HISTORY!
The SIGNAL MAKES THE IMAGE!
The NMR Signal Differences of the Body's Vital Organs
Discovered by Damadian (figure 22)
Overcame a Historical Major Deficiency in Medical Imaging:
Unsatisfactory Visualization of the Body's Critical Vital Organs
(Brain, Heart, Kidney, Liver, Intestine . . .)
The PRONOUNCED NMR signal
differences discovered by Damadian
of the body's
CRITICAL **NORMAL** TISSUES,
(Tables 1 & 2 — figures 22 and 80),
the body's life-sustaining soft tissue vital organs
(brain [figures 89 and 93], heart, liver,
kidney, spinal cord, intestines, etc.)
can be visualized in
unprecedented detail (figures 89 and 93)
on a medical image because of Damadian's discovery.
for the
FIRST TIME IN MEDICAL HISTORY!!!

The NMR signal differences of the body's vital organs,
discovered by Dr. Damadian (figures 22 and 80), supply the
missing anatomic detail that had been lacking in medical images
for more than a century.
(Roentgen, 1895)

extraordinary level of detail of the body's vital organs (brain, heart, liver, kidney, spleen, intestines, pancreas, etc.) made possible by Dr. Damadian's discovery of the pronounced NMR (MRI) relaxation differences among these tissues (figure 22), is exemplified in figure 93.

Note, for example, the pronounced grey matter/white matter delineation (figures 82 and 93) visualized in the MRI image of the brain because of the T_1 differences in the soft tissue vital organs of the body which Dr. Damadian discovered, and its absence from the x-ray images (CT) (figure 82) of the brain.

As a result of his discovery of the tissue NMR relaxation differences that existed among the body's vital organ tissues, a 131 percent signal difference (brain vs. small intestine, figure 22) replaced the maximum 4 percent discrimination in the body's soft tissue vital organs provided by x-ray.

Exemplary also in figure 93 is the visualization of the cochlear and vestibular nerve root fibers within the auditory canals, and the neuroendocrine hypothalamic tract in the pituitary infundibulum never visualized before in a medical image.

Likewise is the example of figure 93c, a T_1 image of the base of the brain visualizing the optic nerve, the pituitary gland with its anterior and posterior lobes, the pituitary infundibulum and its hypothalamic tract. The delineation and visualization of the hypothalamic tract *within* the pituitary infundibulum is exemplary of the anatomic detail achieved by the MRI within the body's vital organs that is accomplished by the tissue NMR relaxation differences of the T_1 brain image of figure 93c *"discovered"* by Dr. Damadian, the *"discovery"* that originated MRI, and which *"discovery"* specifically complies with Alfred Nobel's restriction of the Nobel Prize in Physiology or Medicine to *"discovery"* only (figure 55) which the awards for the *"methods"* provided by Lauterbur and Mansfield do not (figure 56).

The visualized detail in the T_1 and T_2 images of the brain shown in figure 93 is generated by the tissue T_1 and T_2 NMR relaxation differences he *"discovered"* (figures 22 and 80) in 1970.[6] Those tissue relaxation differences supply the image pixel contrast that provides the exceptional anatomic detail characteristic of the MRI image and which are not available from any other imaging modality.

In conclusion: As initially asserted, the absence of the intermediate life forms, ("transitional links" in Darwin's nomenclature),[7] that is, the critical evidence necessary to sustain the concept of evolution from an elementary life form through a successive chain of increasingly complex "KINDS" to a human being, compelled the conclusion that evolution was "science fiction."

As a result of the probability calculations in chapter 9, however, Dr. Damadian concluded that he was wrong.

Evolution by "CHANCE" is not scientific fiction
it is
SCIENTIFIC NONSENSE!
YOU CAN'T GET THERE WITHOUT HIM!!

Endnotes

1. Raymond Damadian, "Tumor Detection by Nuclear Magnetic Resonance," *Science*, 1971, p. 1151–1153.
2. R. Damadian, M. Goldsmith, and L. Minkoff, "NMR in Cancer: XVI. FONAR Image of the Live Human Body, Physiol. Chem. and Phys (9), 1977; Raymond Damadian, Larence Minkoff, Michael Goldsmith, and Jason A. Koutchev, "Field-Focusing Nuclear Magnetic Resonace (FONAR) Formation of Chemical Scans in Man," Naturwissenschaften 65, 220–252 (1978).
3. Damadian, "Tumor Detection by Nuclear Magnetic Resonance," p. 1151–1153.
4. By phase contrast frequency scanning.
5. P.C. Lauterbur, *Nature* (1973) 242:190–191 (NP 2003) (PhD. 1962); A.N. Garroway, P.K. Grannell, and P. Mansfield (1974) (PhD. 1962) *J. Phys. C: Solid State Phys.*, 7:L457-L462, (NP 2003).
6. Regarding Paul Lauterbur and Peter Mansfield, recipients of the NP, both had been working in the field of NMR for nine years prior to Dr. Damadian's discovery. Neither conceived of the idea of scanning the human body by NMR nor provided the means to bring it about by discovering the tissue NMR *signal* differences that made it happen. Neither did anything in the field of NMR scanning for nine years until *after* Dr. Damadian first conceived of the NMR body scanner concept (1969) and published the means (the *signals*) to accomplish it (1971) (figures 21, 22, and 80).
7. See chapter 9 of this book; also Darwin, *The Origin of Species*, p. 1146.

INDEX